Spellbinders

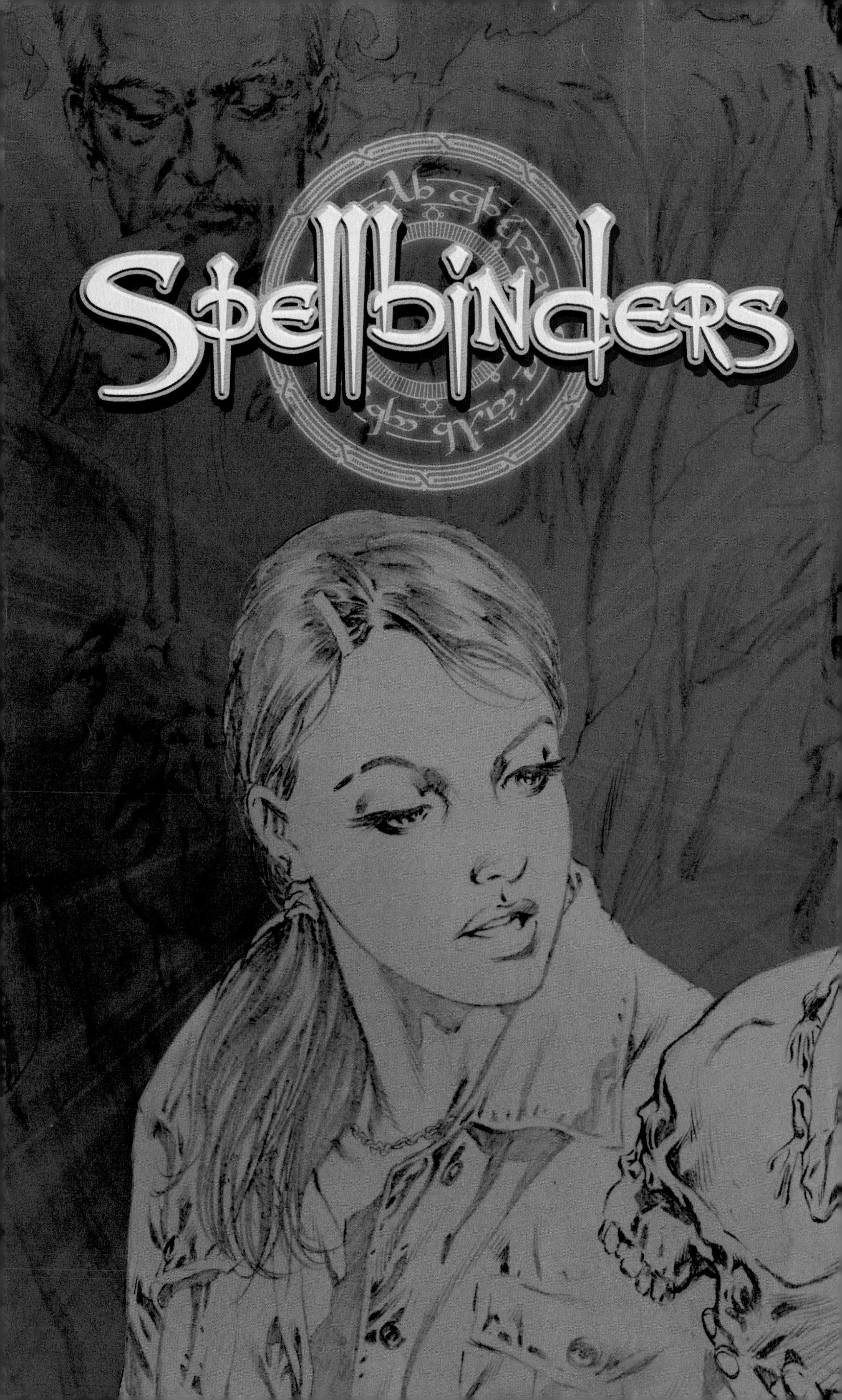
Spellbinders

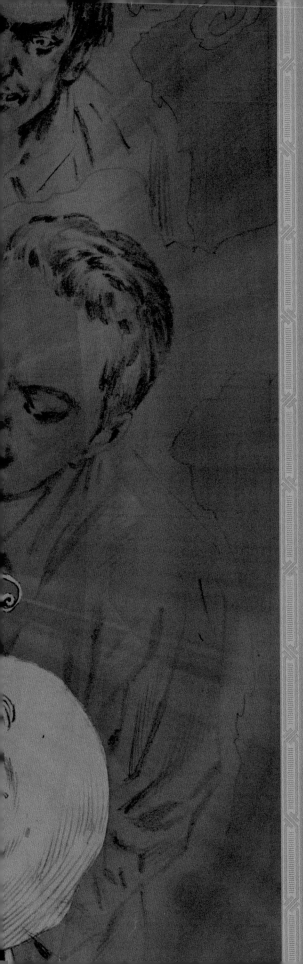

SIGNS & WONDERS

WRITER
MIKE CAREY

PENCILS
MIKE PERKINS

INKS
DREW HENNESSY

COLORS
GURU-eFX

LETTERS
VC'S RANDY GENTILE

EDITOR
MACKENZIE CADENHEAD

CONSULTING EDITOR
MARK PANICCIA

COLLECTION EDITOR
JENNIFER GRÜNWALD

ASSISTANT EDITORS
ALEX STARBUCK & NELSON RIBEIRO

EDITOR, SPECIAL PROJECTS
MARK D. BEAZLEY

SENIOR EDITOR, SPECIAL PROJECTS
JEFF YOUNGQUIST

SENIOR VICE PRESIDET OF SALES
DAVID GABRIEL

SVP OF BRAND PLANNING
& COMMUNICATIONS
MICHAEL PASCIULLO

BOOK DESIGN
JEFF POWELL

EDITOR IN CHIEF
AXEL ALONSO

CHIEF CREATIVE OFFICER
JOE QUESADA

PUBLISHER
DAN BUCKLEY

EXECUTIVE PRODUCER
ALAN FINE

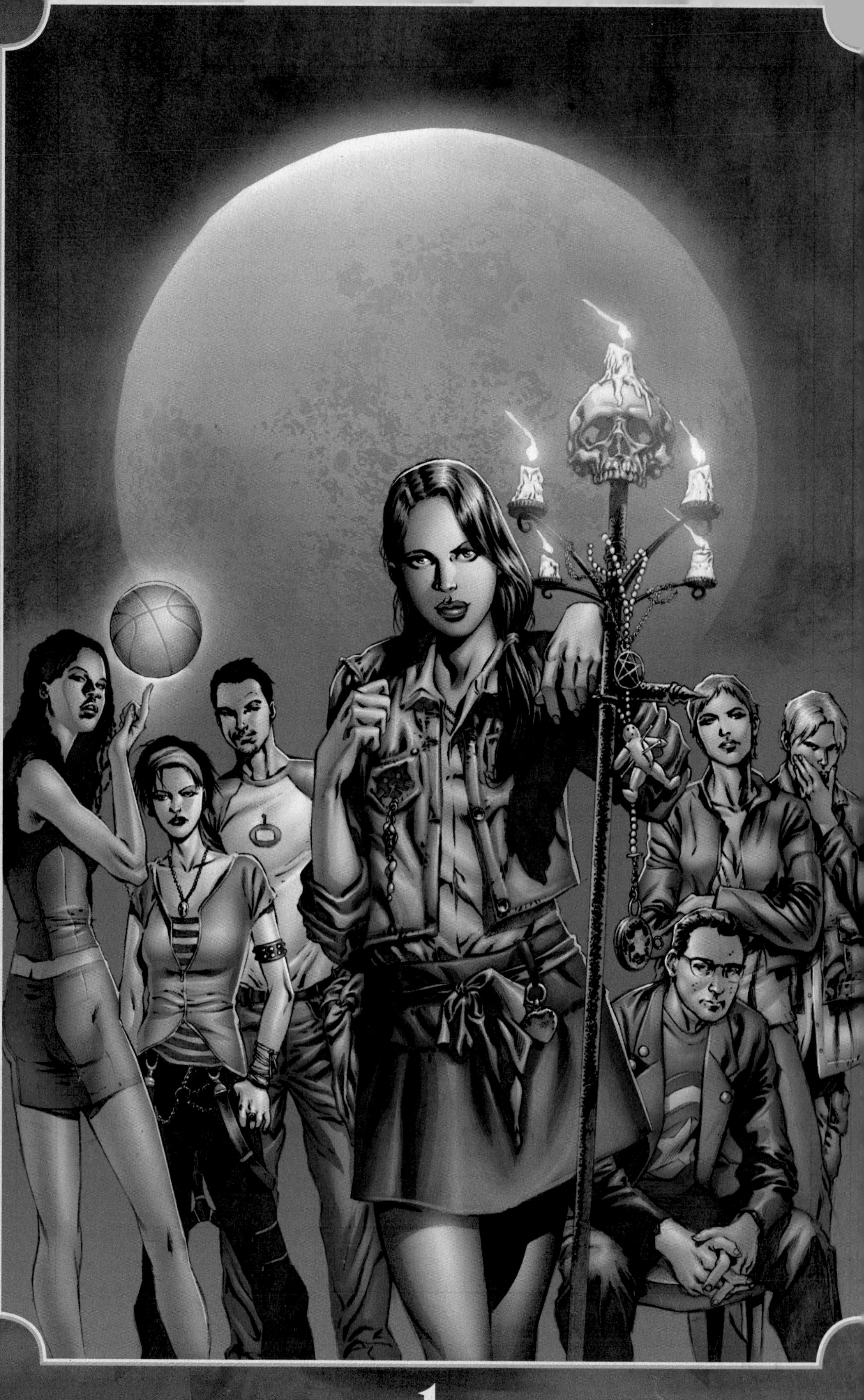

1

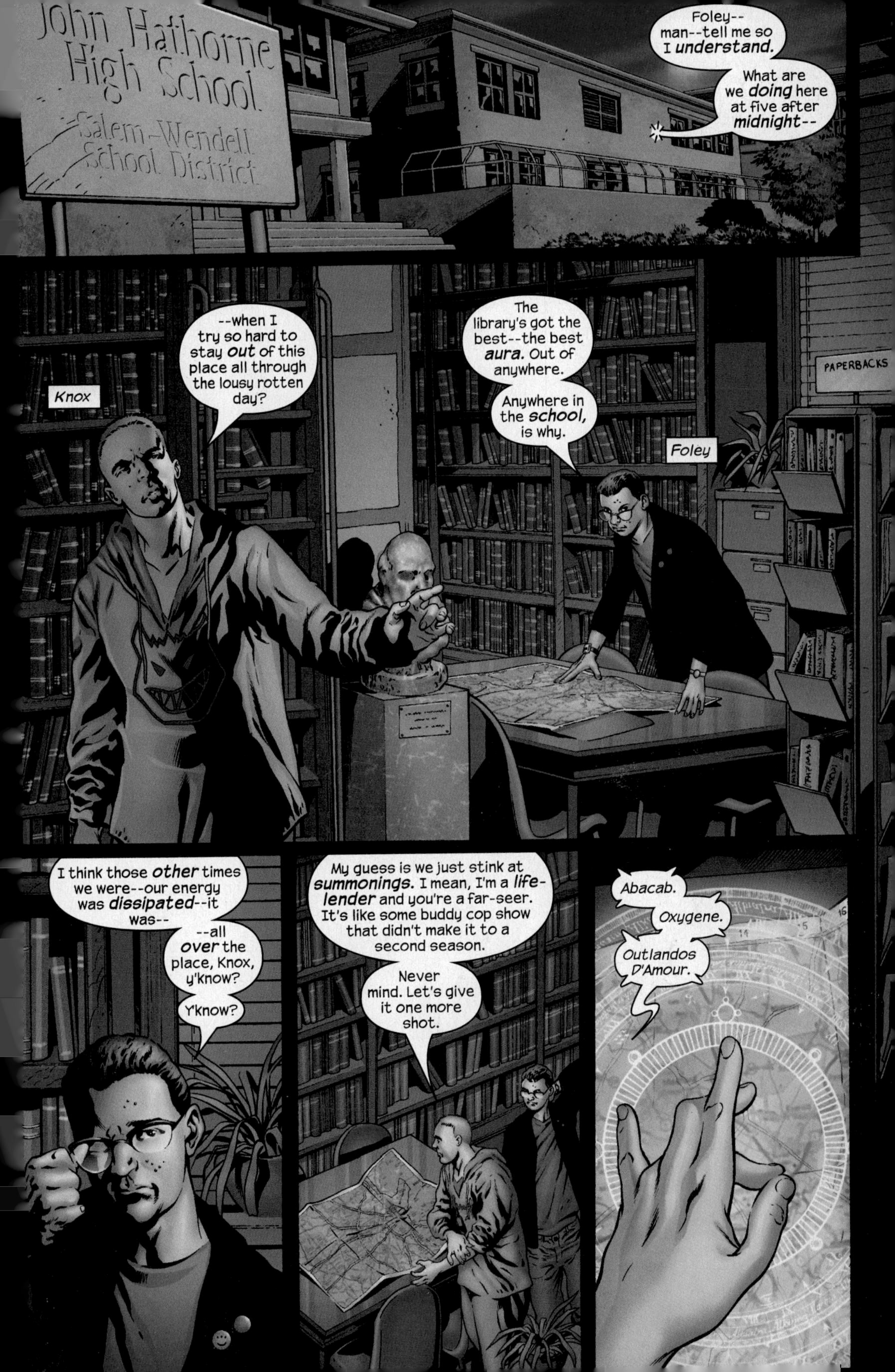
John Hathorne High School
Salem-Wendell School District
Foley--man--tell me so I understand.
What are we doing here at five after midnight--
Knox
--when I try so hard to stay out of this place all through the lousy rotten day?
The library's got the best--the best aura. Out of anywhere.
Anywhere in the school, is why.
Foley
PAPERBACKS
I think those other times we were--our energy was dissipated--it was--
--all over the place, Knox, y'know?
Y'know?
My guess is we just stink at summonings. I mean, I'm a life-lender and you're a far-seer. It's like some buddy cop show that didn't make it to a second season.
Never mind. Let's give it one more shot.
Abacab.
Oxygene.
Outlandos D'Amour.

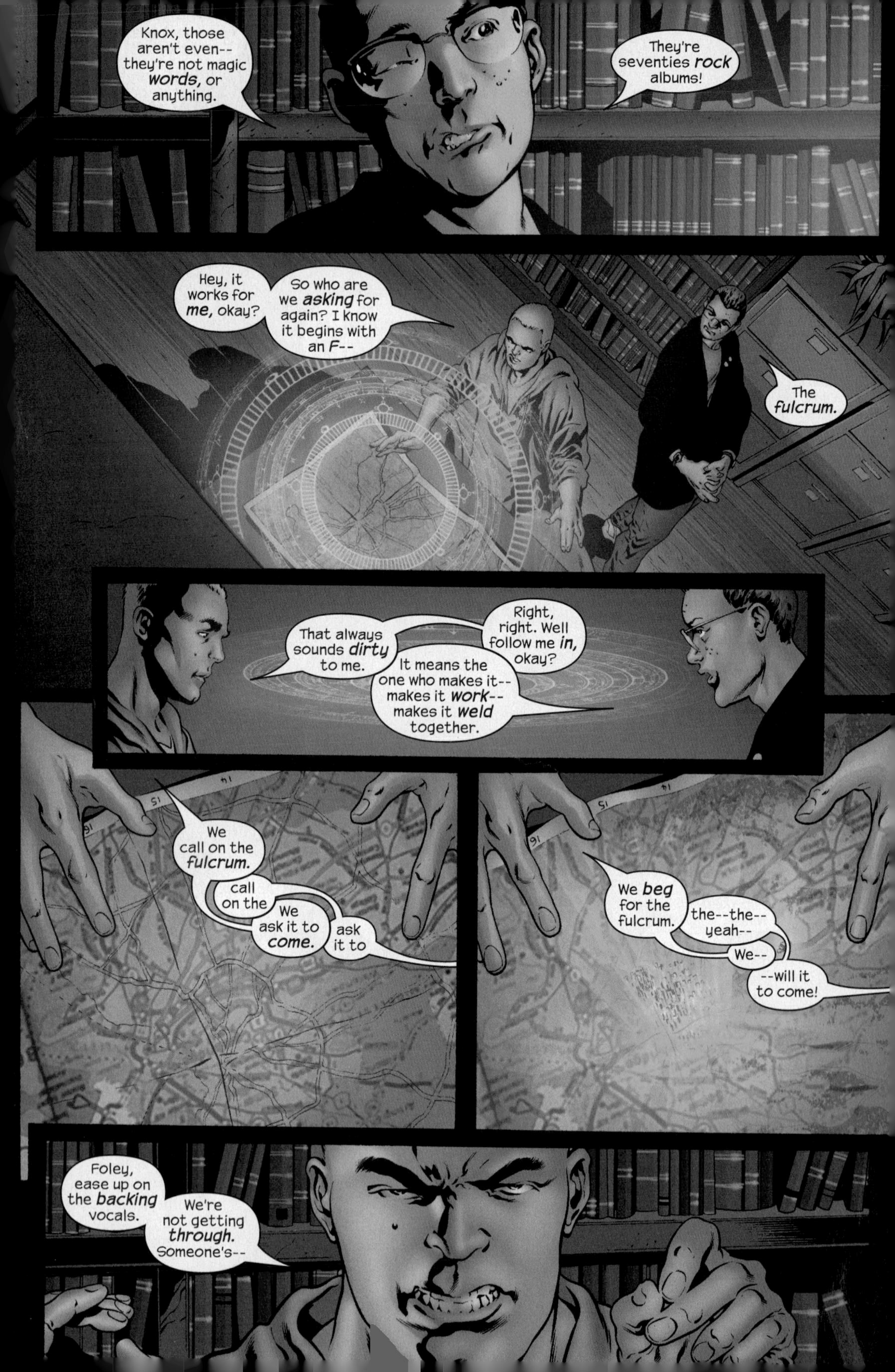
Knox, those aren't even-- they're not magic words, or anything.
They're seventies rock albums!
Hey, it works for me, okay?
So who are we asking for again? I know it begins with an F--
The fulcrum.
That always sounds dirty to me.
Right, right. Well follow me in, okay?
It means the one who makes it-- makes it work-- makes it weld together.
We call on the fulcrum.
call on the
We ask it to come.
ask it to
We beg for the fulcrum.
the--the-- yeah--
We--
--will it to come!
Foley, ease up on the backing vocals.
We're not getting through. Someone's--

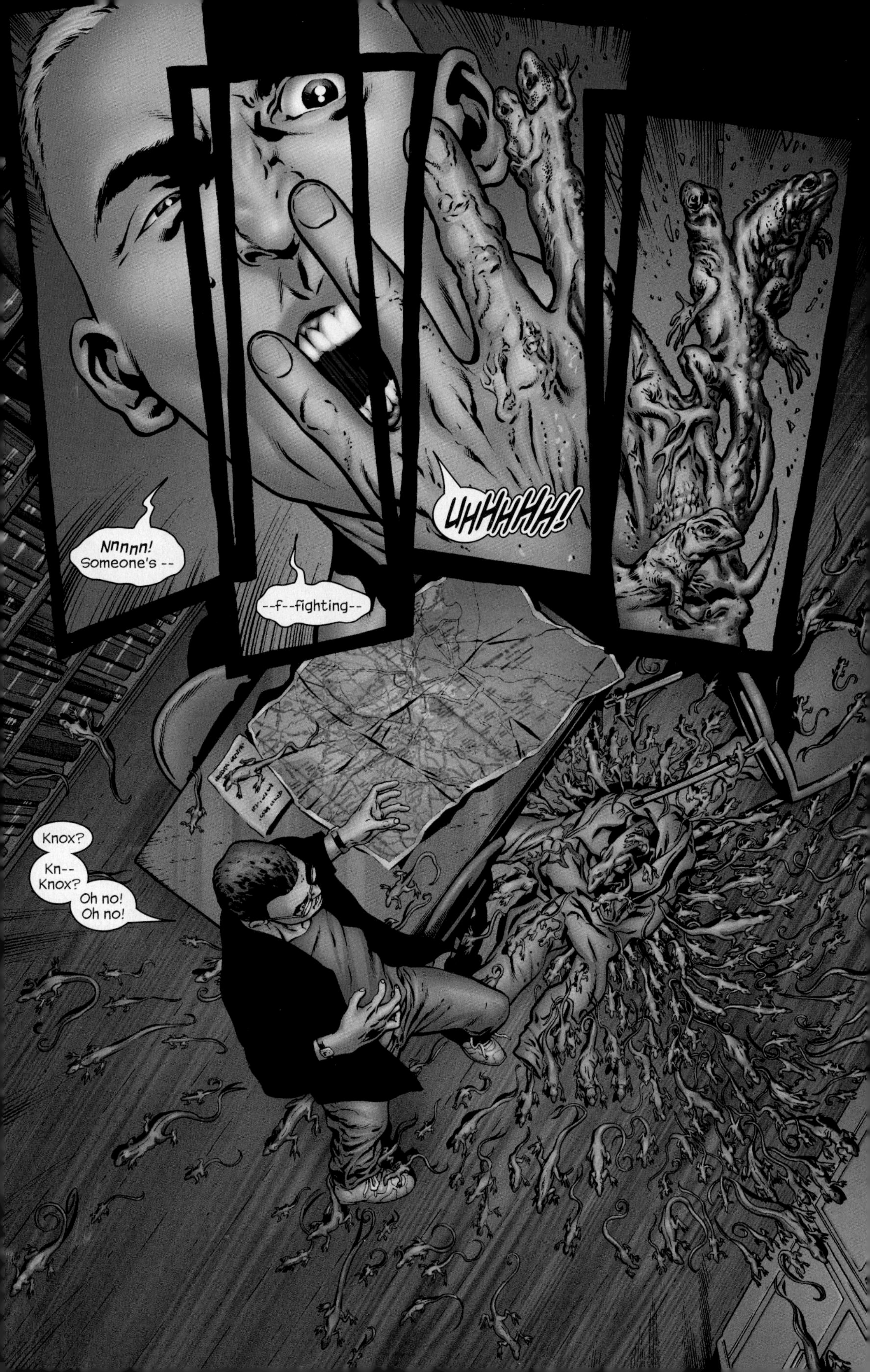

Nnnnn! Someone's --
--f--fighting--
UHHHHH!
Knox?
Kn-- Knox?
Oh no! Oh no!

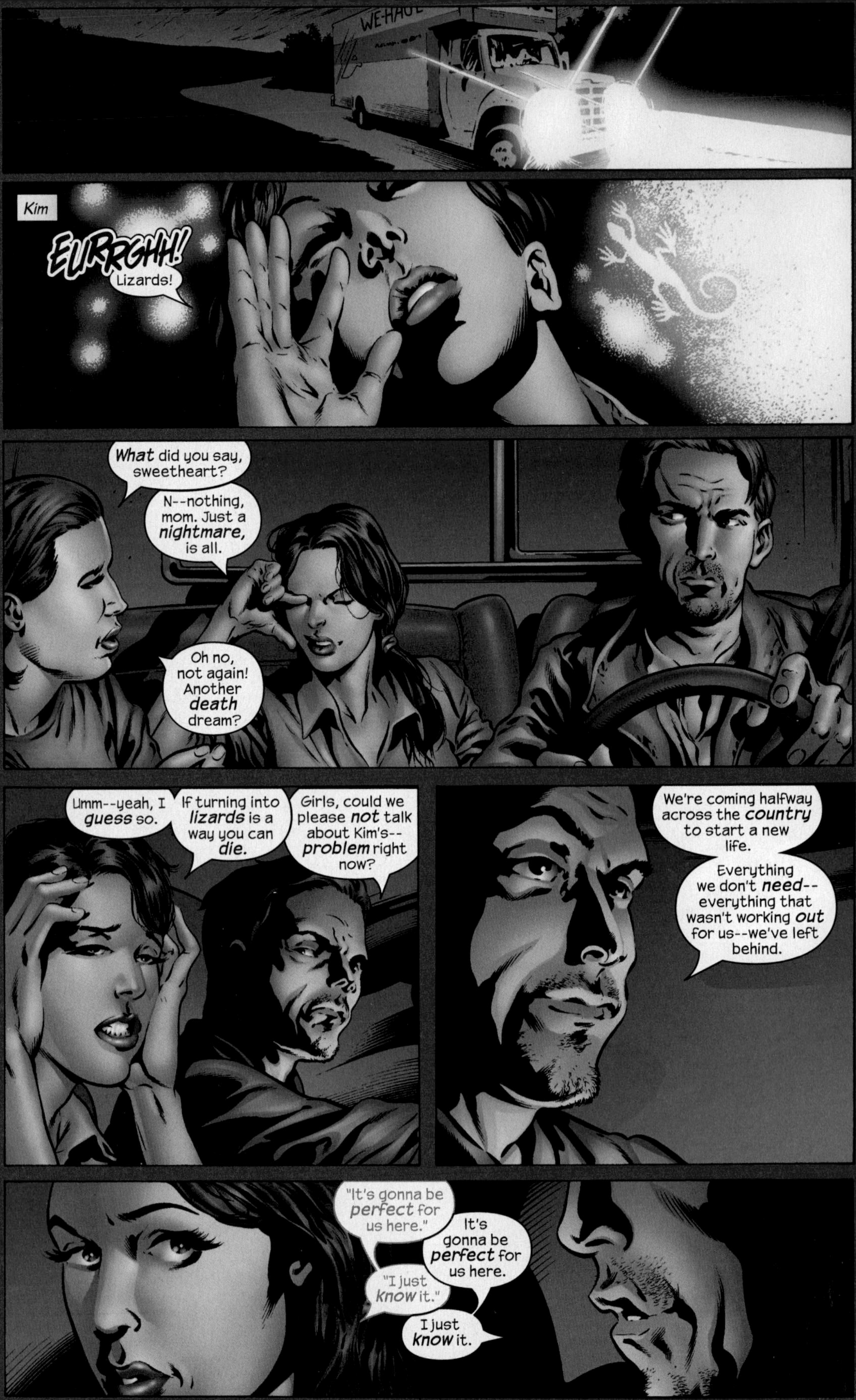
WE-HAUL
Kim
EURRGHH!
Lizards!
What did you say, sweetheart?
N--nothing, mom. Just a nightmare, is all.
Oh no, not again! Another death dream?
Umm--yeah, I guess so.
If turning into lizards is a way you can die.
Girls, could we please not talk about Kim's--problem right now?
We're coming halfway across the country to start a new life.
Everything we don't need--everything that wasn't working out for us--we've left behind.
"It's gonna be perfect for us here."
It's gonna be perfect for us here.
"I just know it."
I just know it.

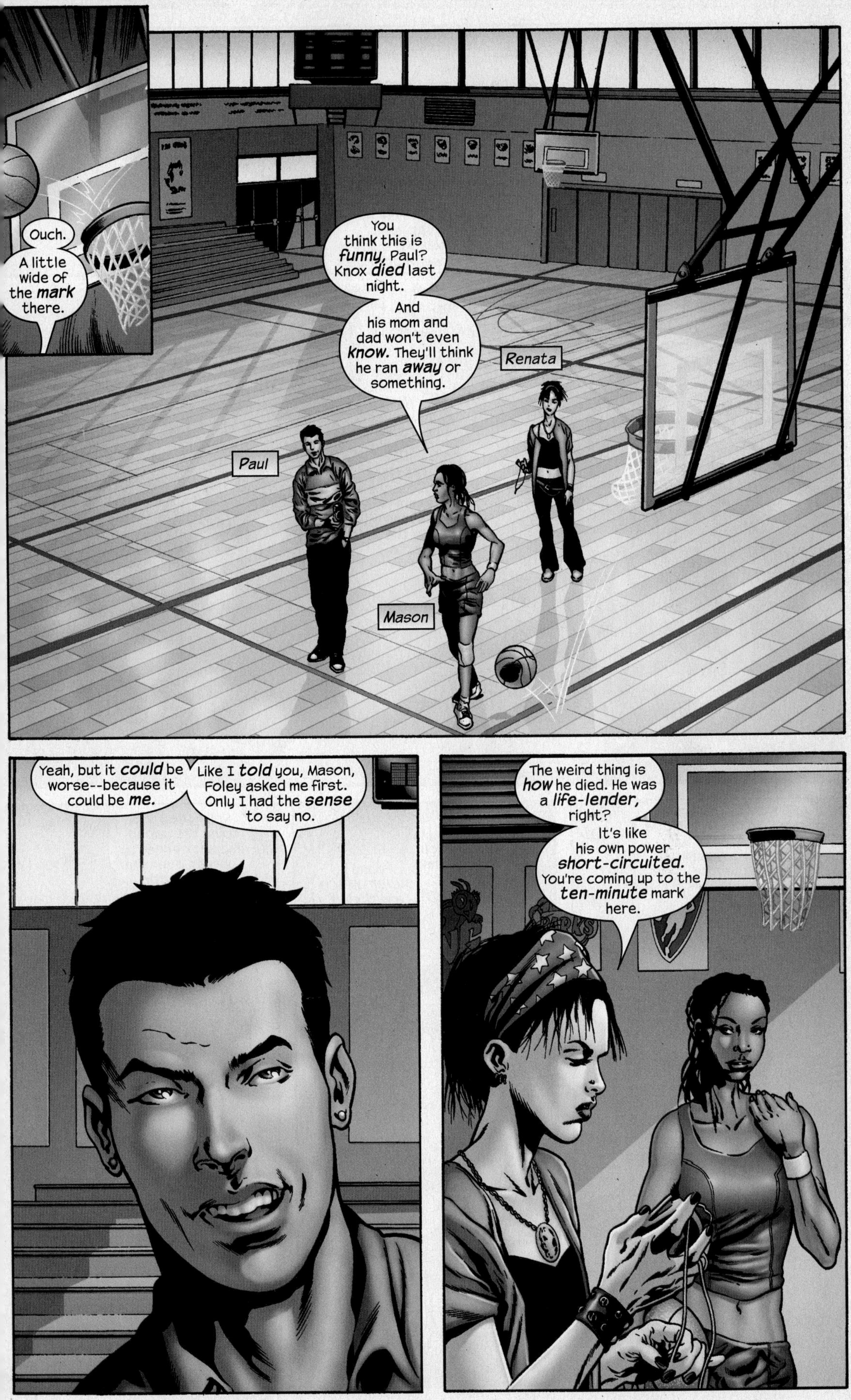

Ouch.
A little wide of the *mark* there.
You think this is *funny,* Paul? Knox *died* last night.
And his mom and dad won't even *know.* They'll think he ran *away* or something.
Renata
Paul
Mason
Yeah, but it *could* be worse--because it could be *me.*
Like I *told* you, Mason, Foley asked me first. Only I had the *sense* to say no.
The weird thing is *how* he died. He was a *life-lender,* right?
It's like his own power *short-circuited.* You're coming up to the *ten-minute* mark here.

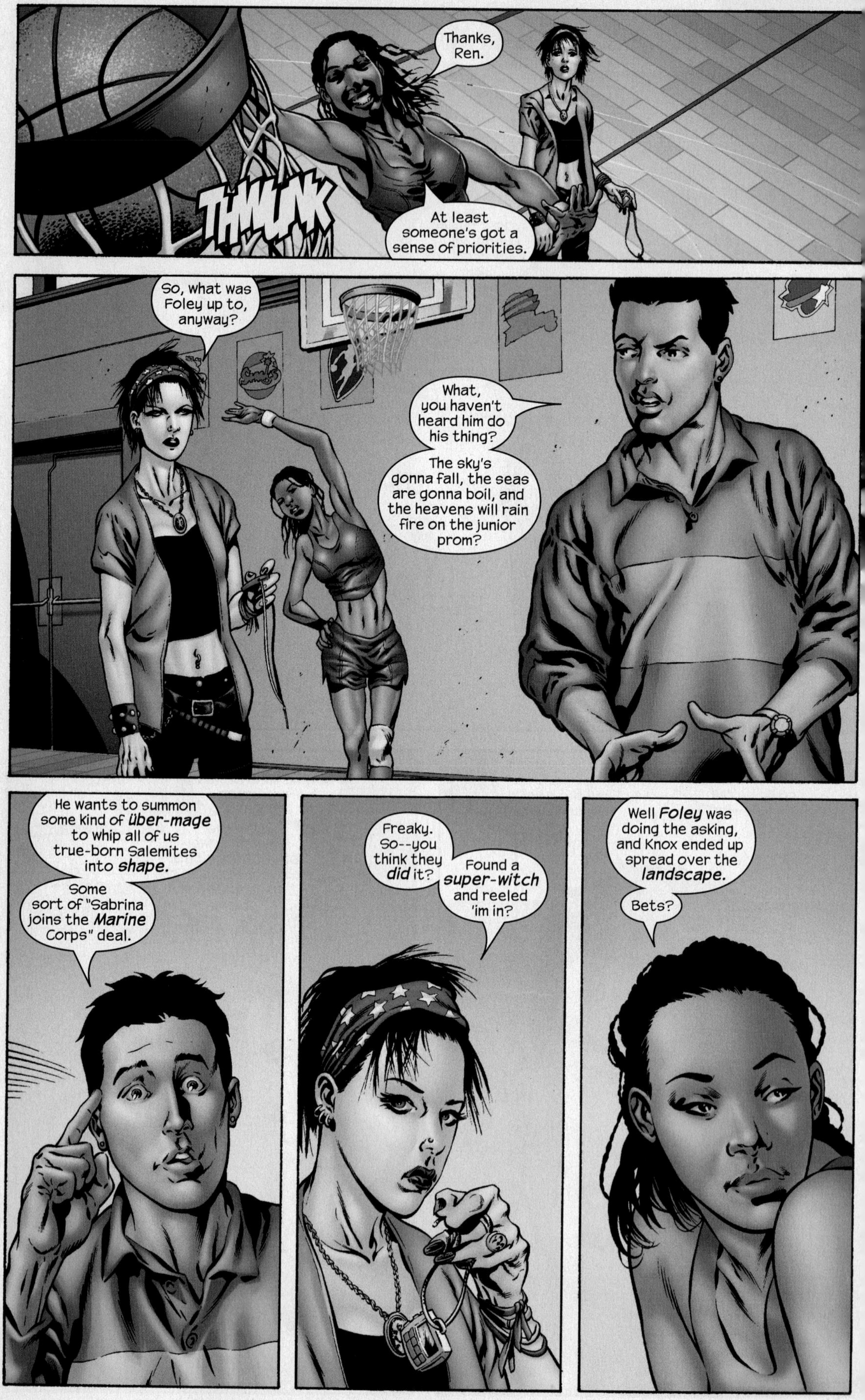
Thanks, Ren.
THWUNK
At least someone's got a sense of priorities.
So, what was Foley up to, anyway?
What, you haven't heard him do his thing?
The sky's gonna fall, the seas are gonna boil, and the heavens will rain fire on the junior prom?
He wants to summon some kind of *über-mage* to whip all of us true-born Salemites into *shape.*
Some sort of "Sabrina joins the *Marine* Corps" deal.
Freaky. So--you think they *did* it?
Found a *super-witch* and reeled 'im in?
Well *Foley* was doing the asking, and Knox ended up spread over the *landscape.*
Bets?

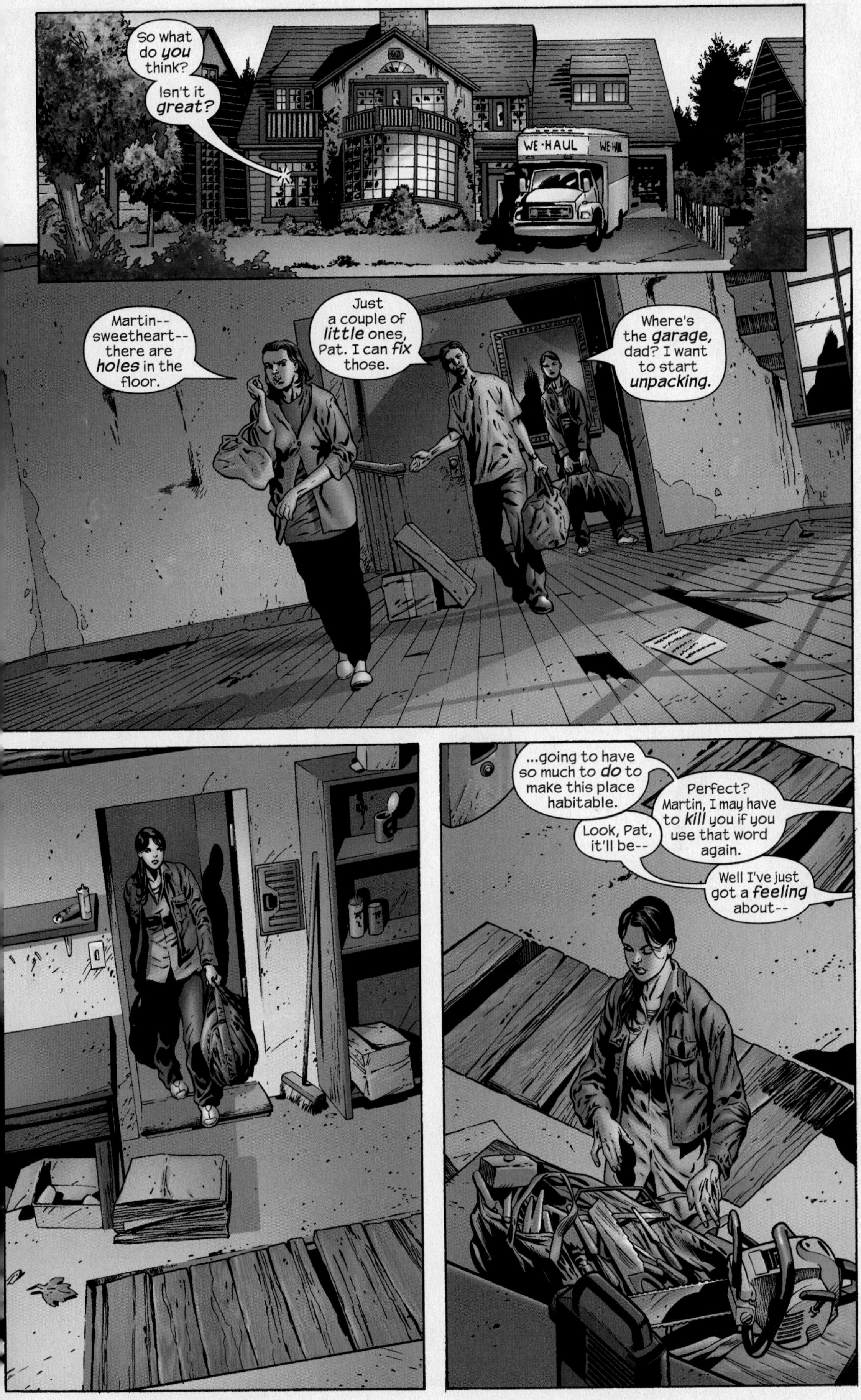
So what do you think?
Isn't it great?
Martin-- sweetheart-- there are holes in the floor.
Just a couple of little ones, Pat. I can fix those.
Where's the garage, dad? I want to start unpacking.
...going to have so much to do to make this place habitable.
Look, Pat, it'll be--
Perfect? Martin, I may have to kill you if you use that word again.
Well I've just got a feeling about--

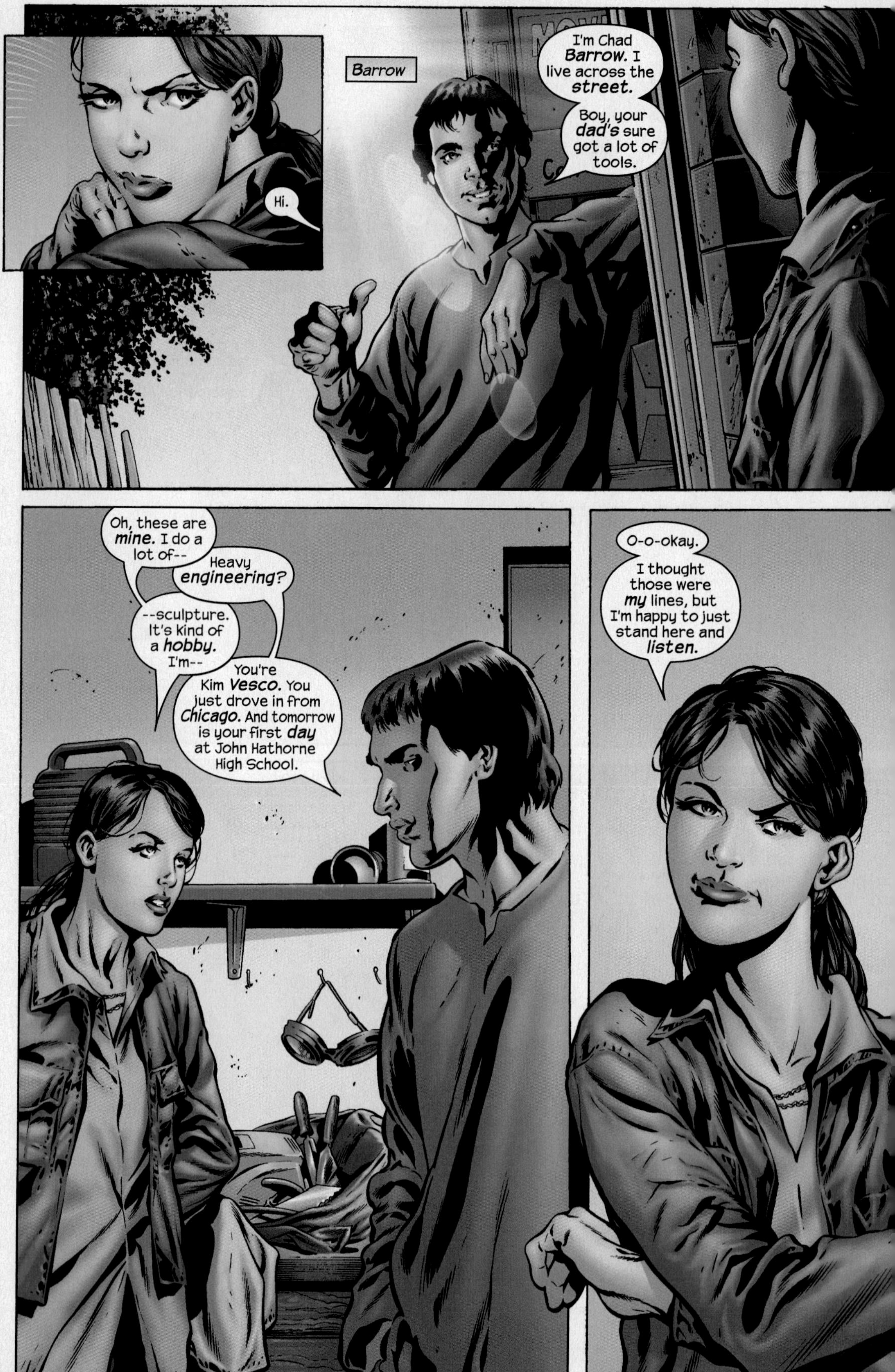

Hi.
Barrow
I'm Chad Barrow. I live across the street.
Boy, your dad's sure got a lot of tools.
Oh, these are mine. I do a lot of--
Heavy engineering?
--sculpture. It's kind of a hobby. I'm--
You're Kim Vesco. You just drove in from Chicago. And tomorrow is your first day at John Hathorne High School.
O-o-okay.
I thought those were my lines, but I'm happy to just stand here and listen.

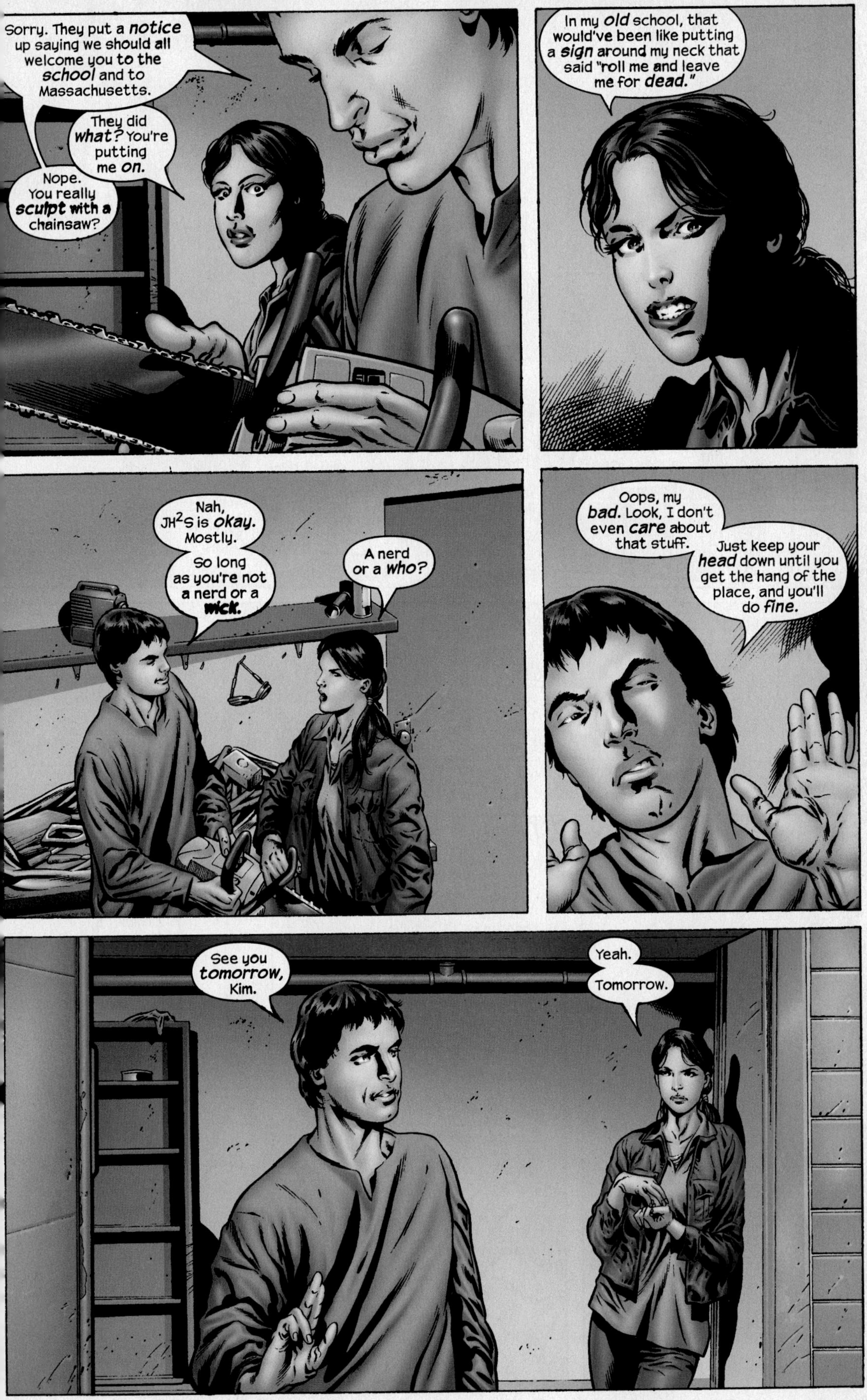

Sorry. They put a notice up saying we should all welcome you to the school and to Massachusetts.
They did what? You're putting me on.
Nope. You really sculpt with a chainsaw?
In my old school, that would've been like putting a sign around my neck that said "roll me and leave me for dead."
Nah, JH2S is okay. Mostly.
So long as you're not a nerd or a wick.
A nerd or a who?
Oops, my bad. Look, I don't even care about that stuff.
Just keep your head down until you get the hang of the place, and you'll do fine.
See you tomorrow, Kim.
Yeah.
Tomorrow.

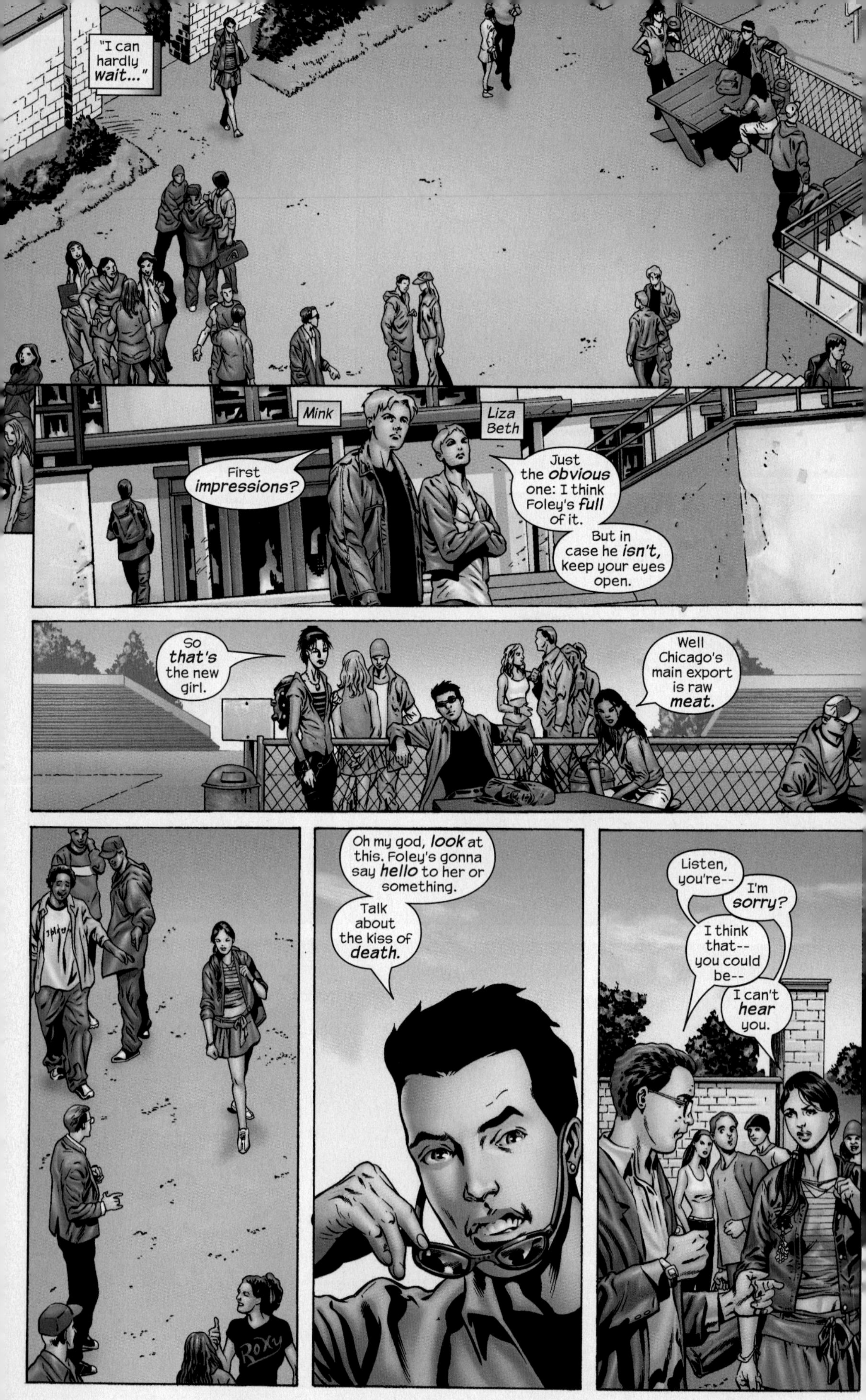
"I can hardly wait..."
Mink
Liza Beth
First impressions?
Just the obvious one: I think Foley's full of it.
But in case he isn't, keep your eyes open.
So that's the new girl.
Well Chicago's main export is raw meat.
Oh my god, look at this. Foley's gonna say hello to her or something.
Talk about the kiss of death.
Listen, you're--
I'm sorry?
I think that-- you could be--
I can't hear you.

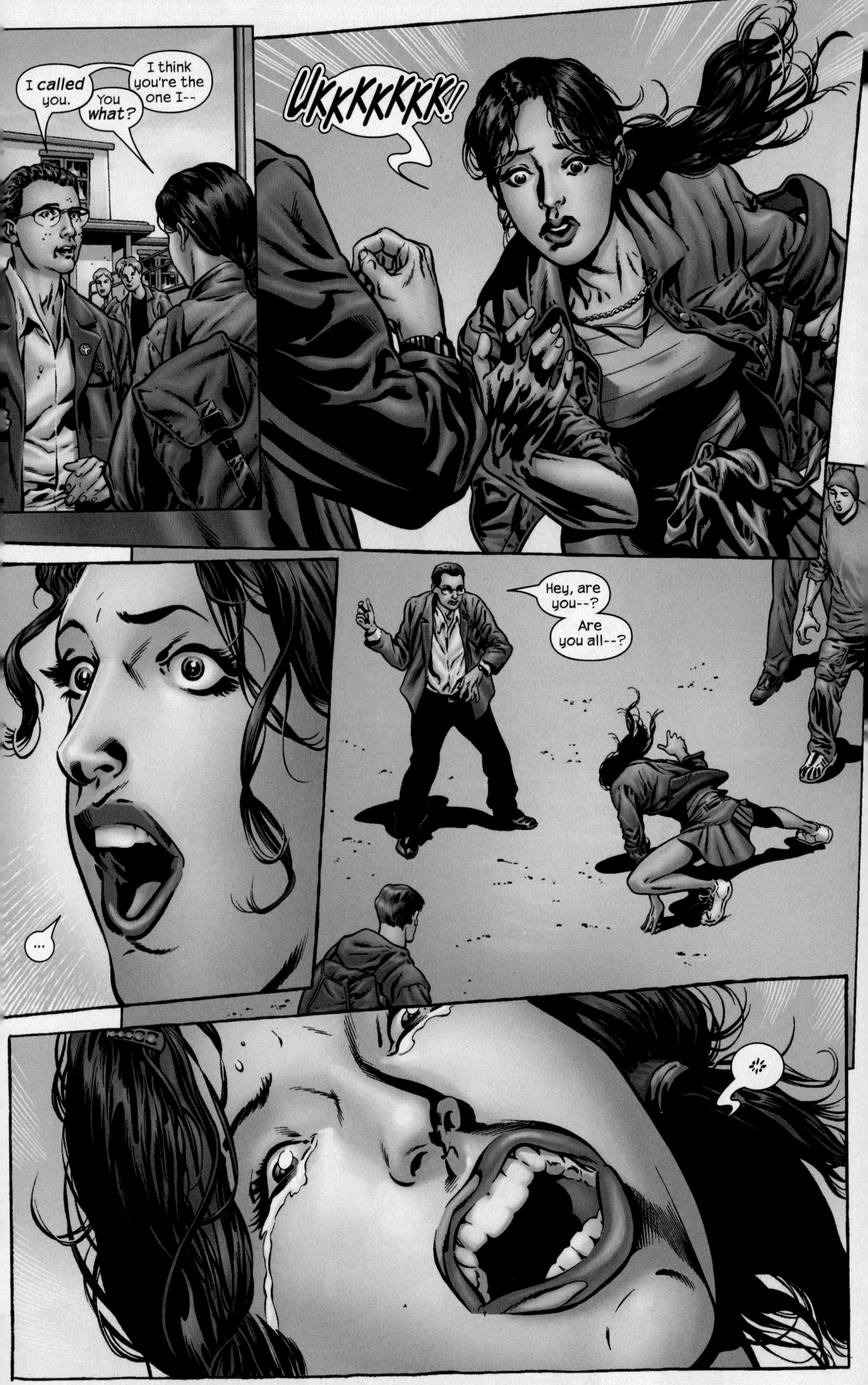

I called you.
You what?
I think you're the one I--
UKKKKKKK!
Hey, are you--?
Are you all--?
...

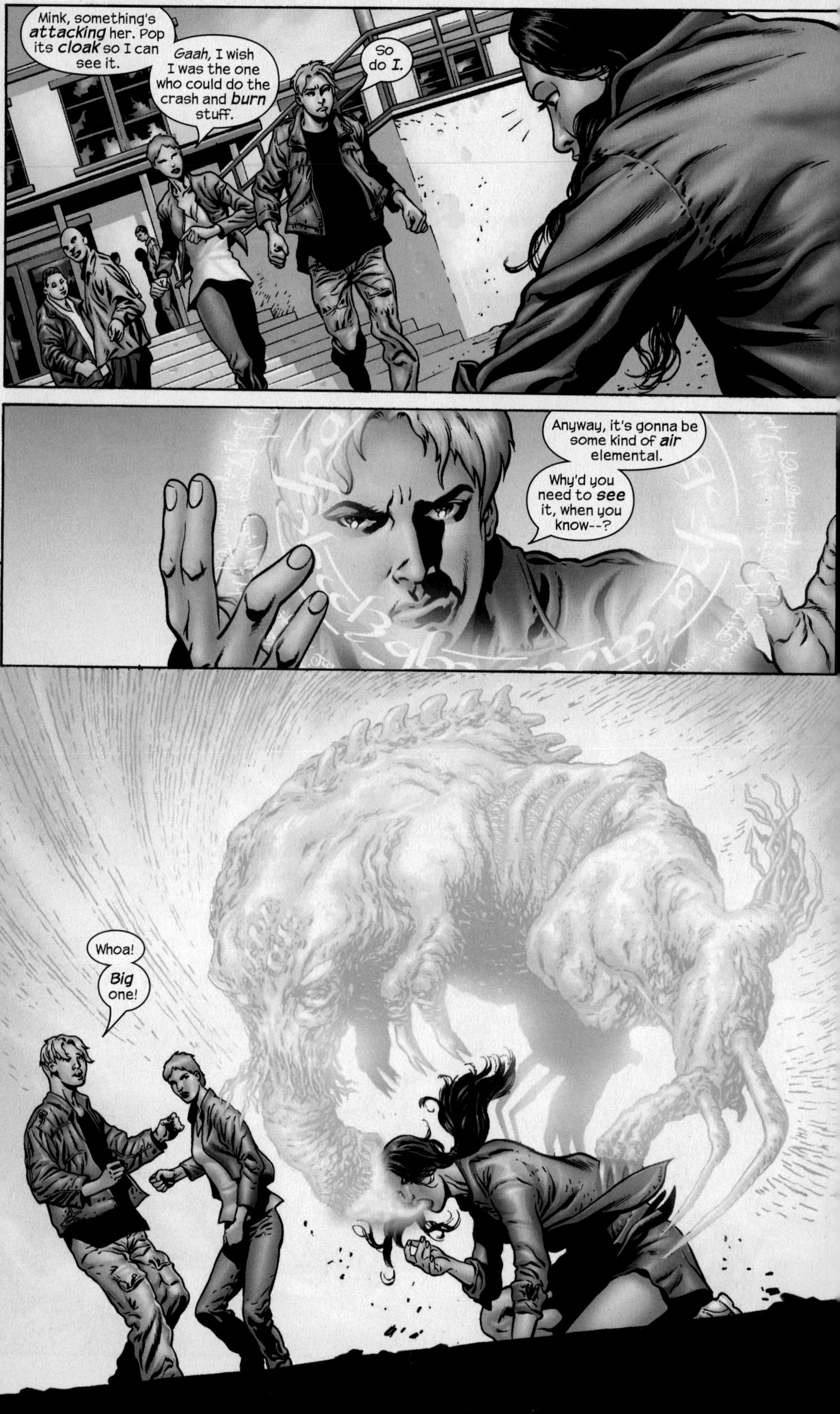

Mink, something's *attacking* her. Pop its *cloak* so I can see it.
Gaah, I wish I was the one who could do the crash and *burn* stuff.
So do *I.*
Anyway, it's gonna be some kind of *air* elemental.
Why'd you need to *see* it, when you know--?
Whoa! *Big* one!

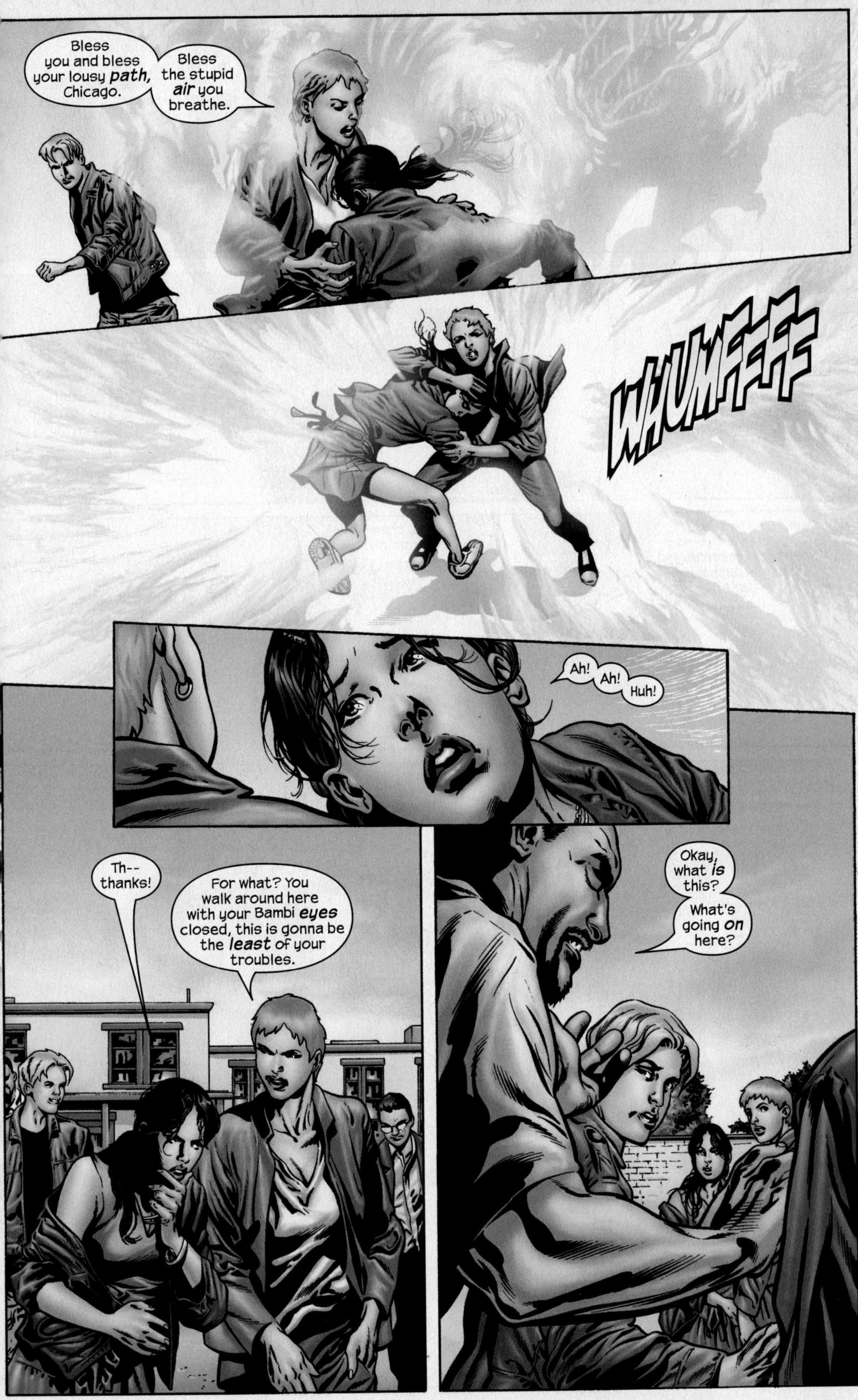
Bless you and bless your lousy *path,* Chicago.
Bless the stupid *air* you breathe.
WHUMFFF
Ah!
Ah!
Huh!
Th-- thanks!
For what? You walk around here with your Bambi *eyes* closed, this is gonna be the *least* of your troubles.
Okay, what *is* this?
What's going *on* here?

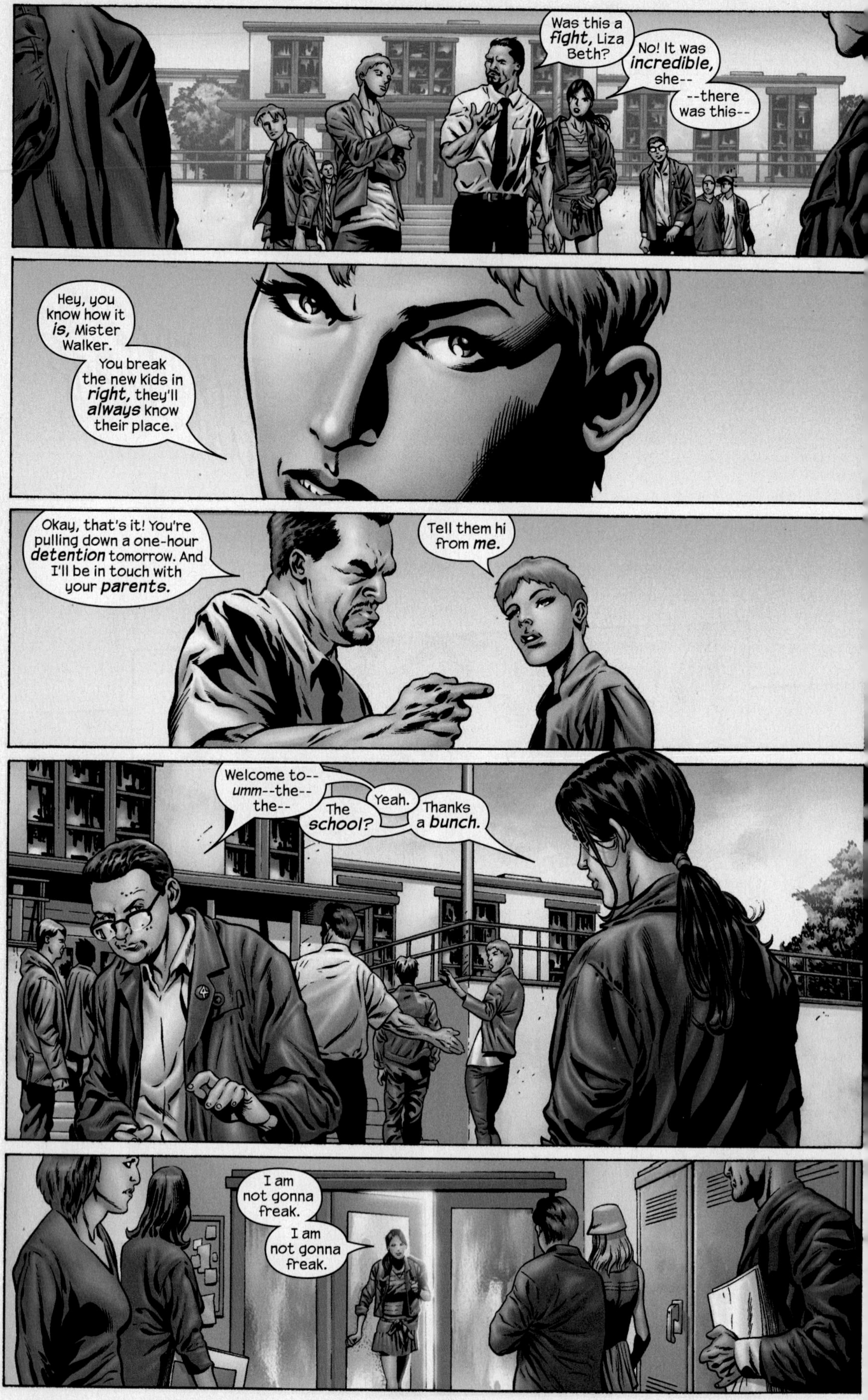
Was this a fight, Liza Beth?
No! It was incredible, she--
--there was this--
Hey, you know how it is, Mister Walker.
You break the new kids in right, they'll always know their place.
Okay, that's it! You're pulling down a one-hour detention tomorrow. And I'll be in touch with your parents.
Tell them hi from me.
Welcome to-- umm--the-- the--
The school?
Yeah.
Thanks a bunch.
I am not gonna freak.
I am not gonna freak.

Well, I suppose I'll *overlook* the late arrival of Miss Vesco.

Provided she can tell us why Prague's *Hunger* Wall is so called.

Totally got *pounded* by an air elemental.

Bummer!

Is she a *wick* or something? 'Cause I heard--

Claro que le daremos a Kim un gran bienvenido *bilingüe* de John Hathorne High School.

Todos juntos.

BIENVENIDA KIM

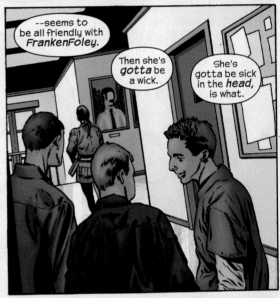

--seems to be all friendly with *FrankenFoley.*

Then she's *gotta* be a wick.

She's gotta be sick in the *head,* is what.

No, no! Try to *feel* it. Try to feel the *tragedy* of it.

"The heavens *themselves* blaze *forth* the *death* of princes!"

She got *chomped* on by a suckbag?

Yeah, her!

Man, what do they *teach* them in Chicago?

SCIENCE

LANGUAGES

CAFETARIA

LIBRARY

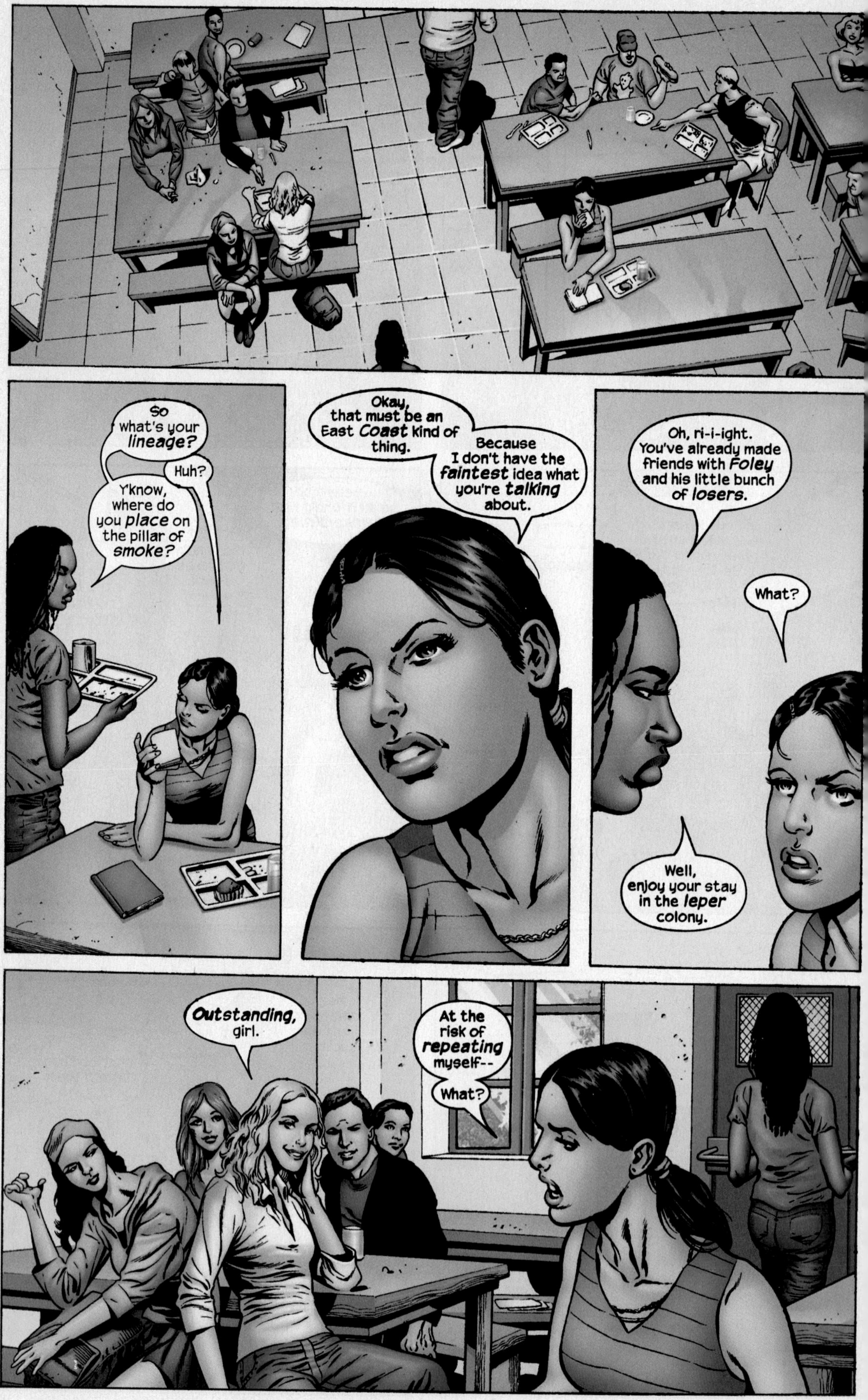
So what's your lineage?
Huh?
Y'know, where do you place on the pillar of smoke?
Okay, that must be an East Coast kind of thing.
Because I don't have the faintest idea what you're talking about.
Oh, ri-i-ight. You've already made friends with Foley and his little bunch of losers.
What?
Well, enjoy your stay in the leper colony.
Outstanding, girl.
At the risk of repeating myself--
What?

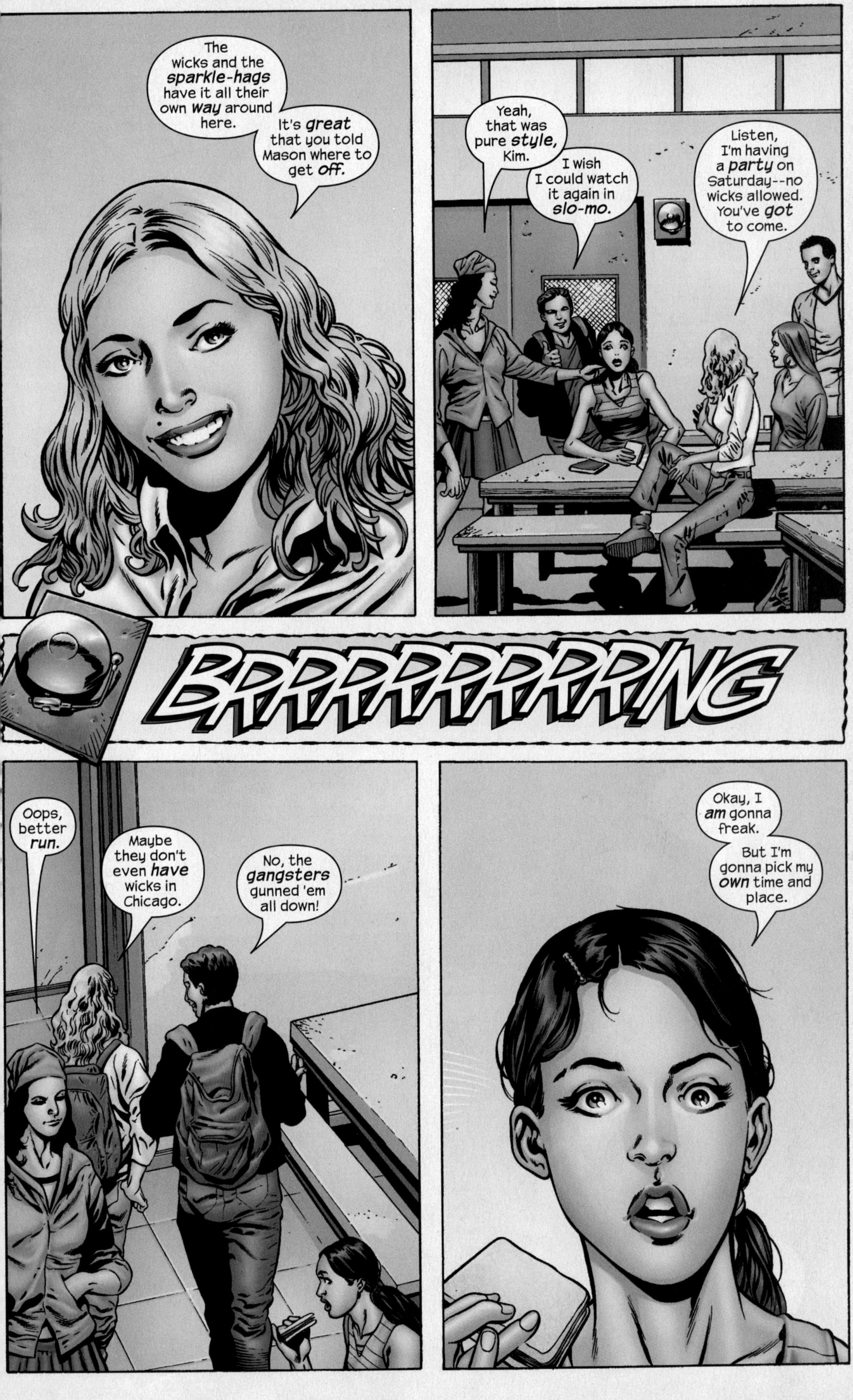
The wicks and the sparkle-hags have it all their own way around here.
It's great that you told Mason where to get off.
Yeah, that was pure style, Kim.
I wish I could watch it again in slo-mo.
Listen, I'm having a party on Saturday--no wicks allowed. You've got to come.
BRRRRRRRRRING
Oops, better run.
Maybe they don't even have wicks in Chicago.
No, the gangsters gunned 'em all down!
Okay, I am gonna freak.
But I'm gonna pick my own time and place.

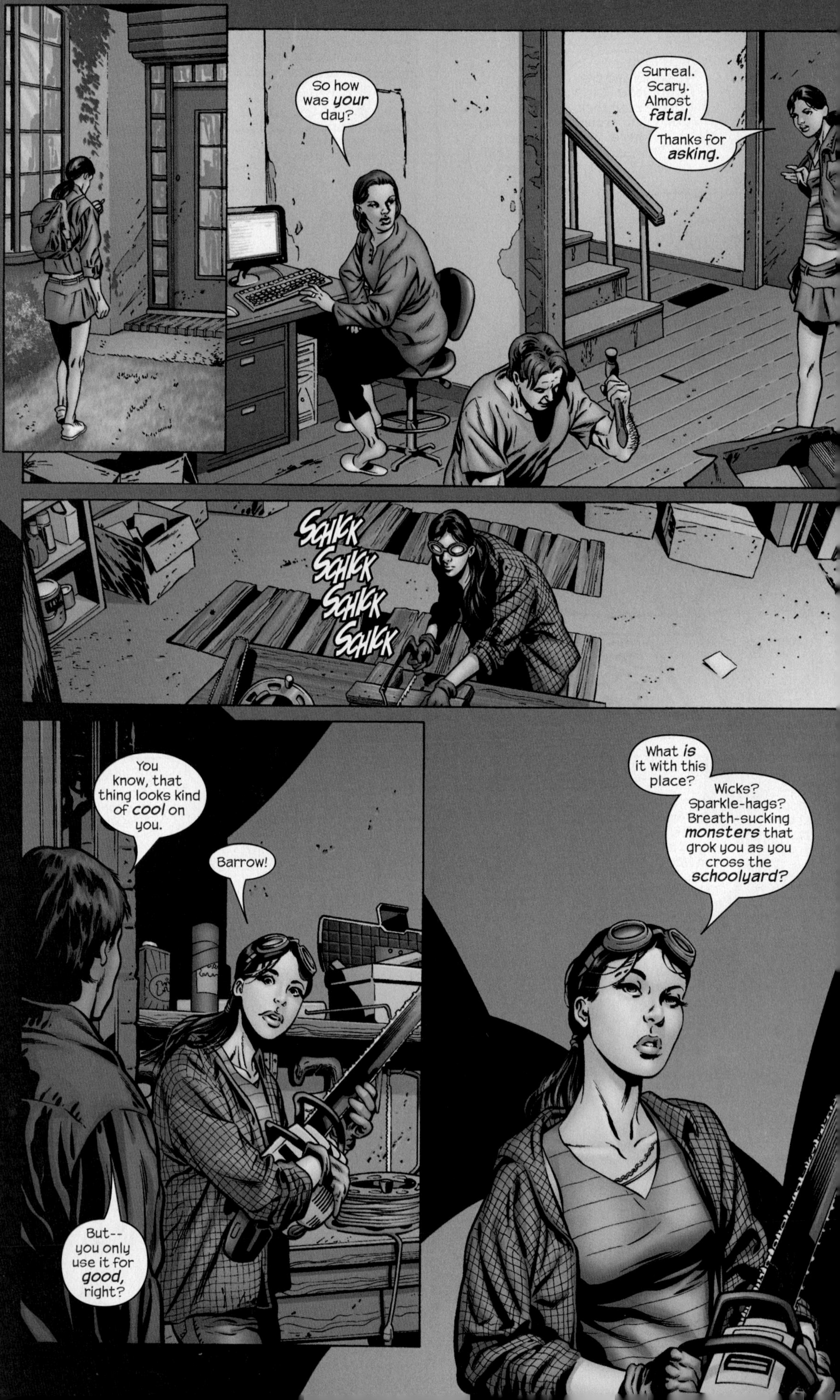
So how was your day?
Surreal. Scary. Almost fatal.
Thanks for asking.
SCHICK SCHICK SCHICK SCHICK
You know, that thing looks kind of cool on you.
Barrow!
But-- you only use it for good, right?
What is it with this place?
Wicks? Sparkle-hags? Breath-sucking monsters that grok you as you cross the schoolyard?

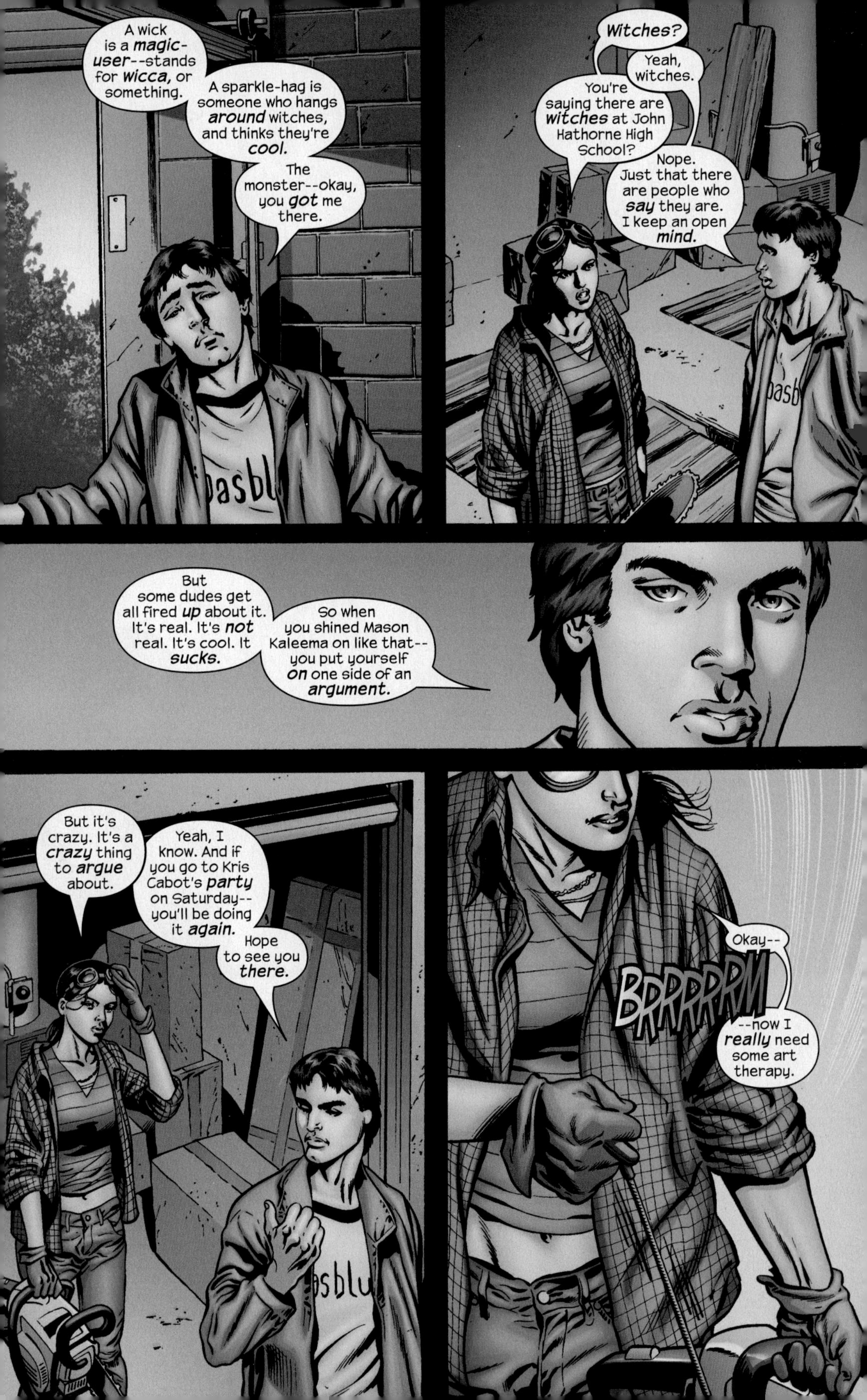
A wick is a magic-user--stands for wicca, or something.
A sparkle-hag is someone who hangs around witches, and thinks they're cool.
The monster--okay, you got me there.
Witches?
You're saying there are witches at John Hathorne High School?
Yeah, witches.
Nope. Just that there are people who say they are. I keep an open mind.
But some dudes get all fired up about it. It's real. It's not real. It's cool. It sucks.
So when you shined Mason Kaleema on like that--you put yourself on one side of an argument.
But it's crazy. It's a crazy thing to argue about.
Yeah, I know. And if you go to Kris Cabot's party on Saturday--you'll be doing it again.
Hope to see you there.
Okay--
BRRRRRM
--now I really need some art therapy.

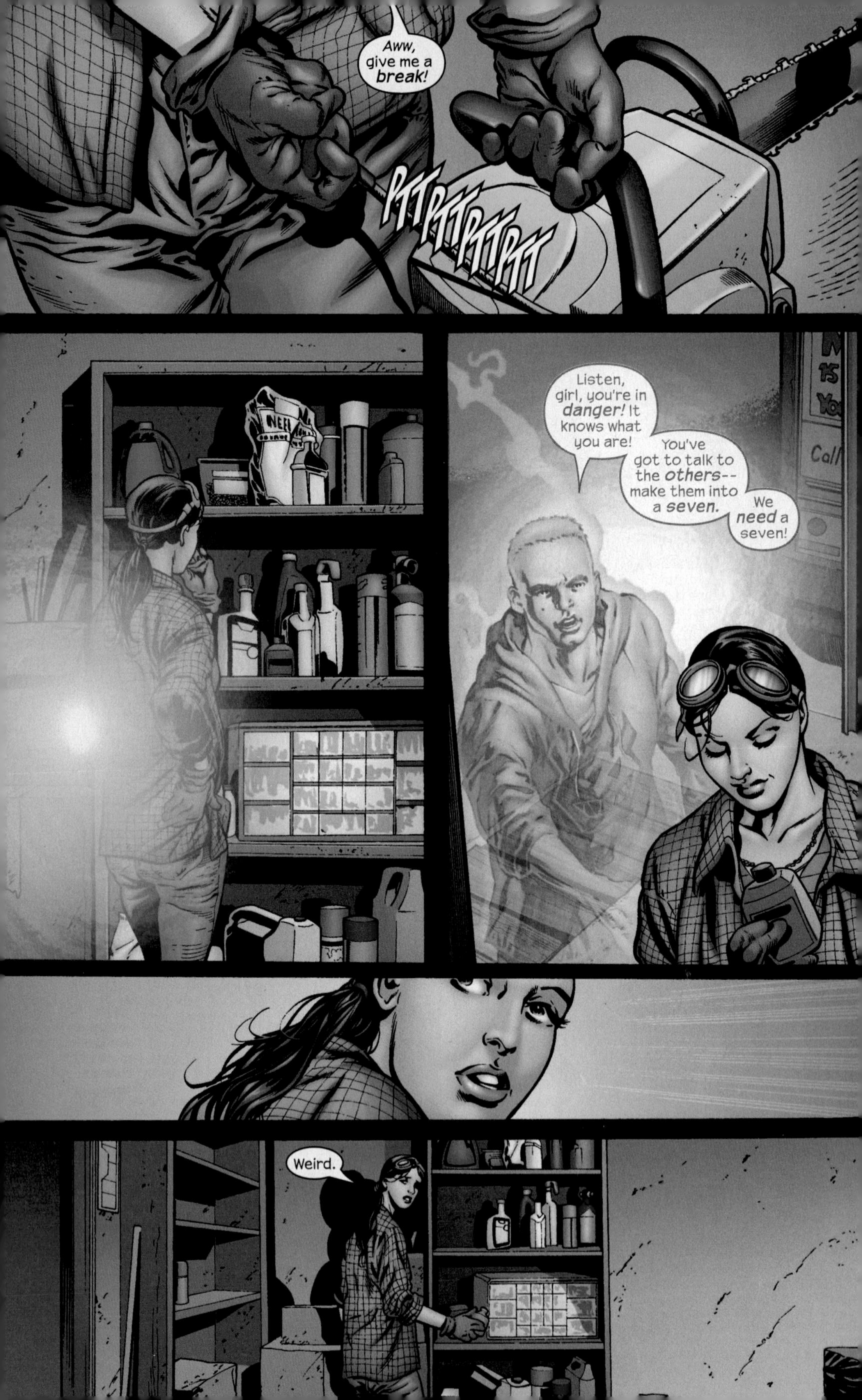
Aww, give me a break!
PTTTPTTTPTTTPTT
Listen, girl, you're in danger! It knows what you are!
You've got to talk to the others-- make them into a seven.
We need a seven!
Weird.

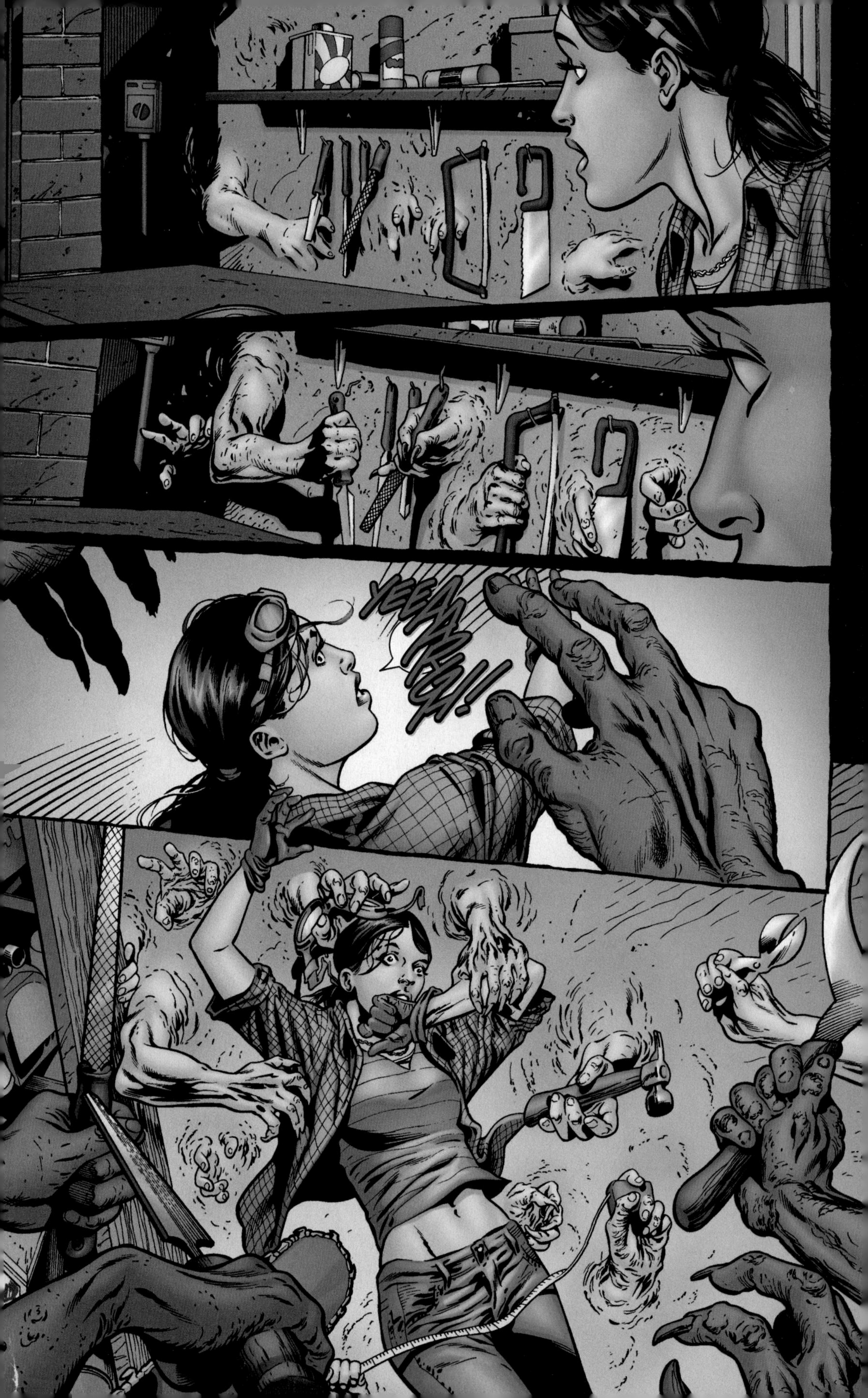
YEEAAAKKGH!!

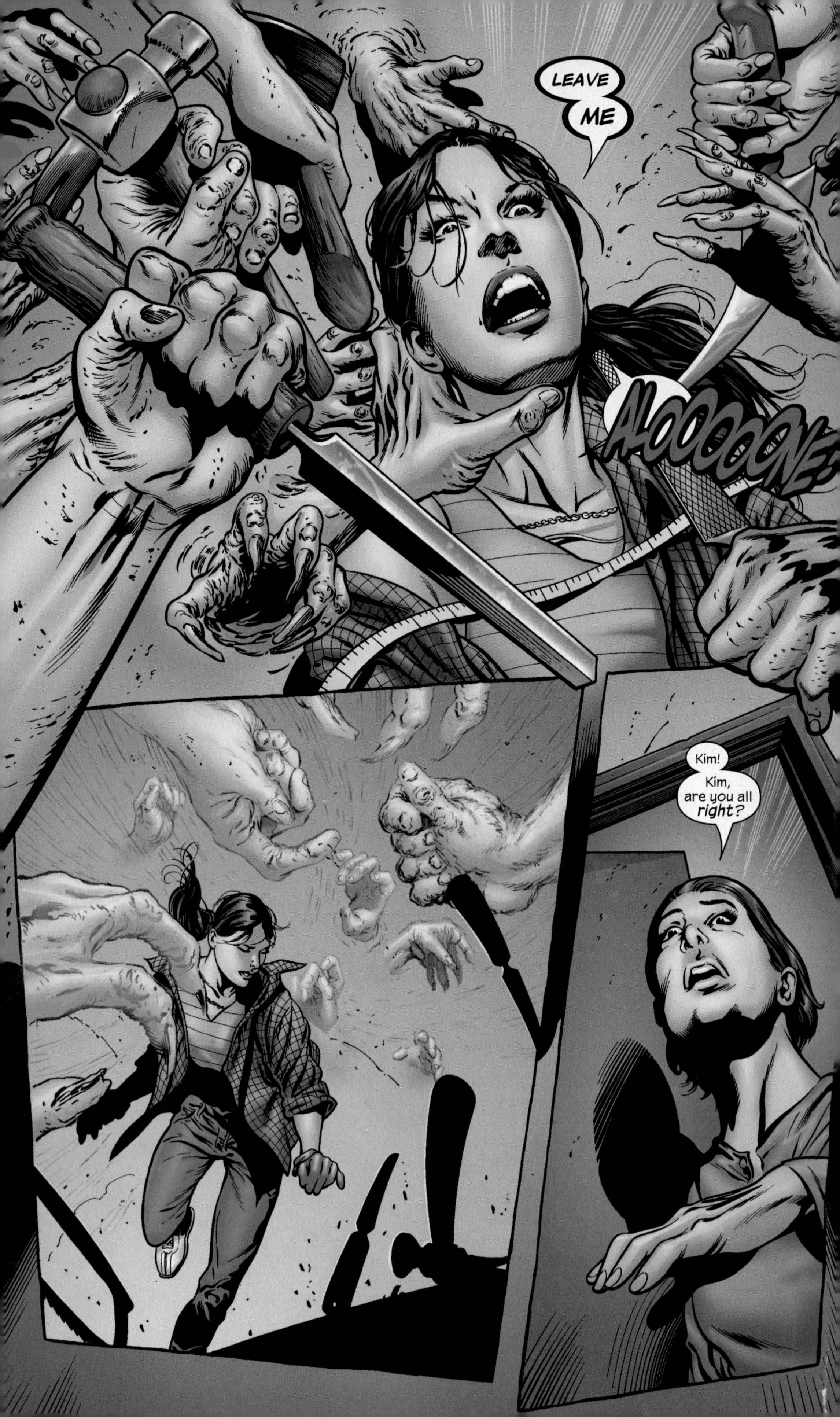
LEAVE ME
ALOOOOONE!
Kim!
Kim, are you all right?

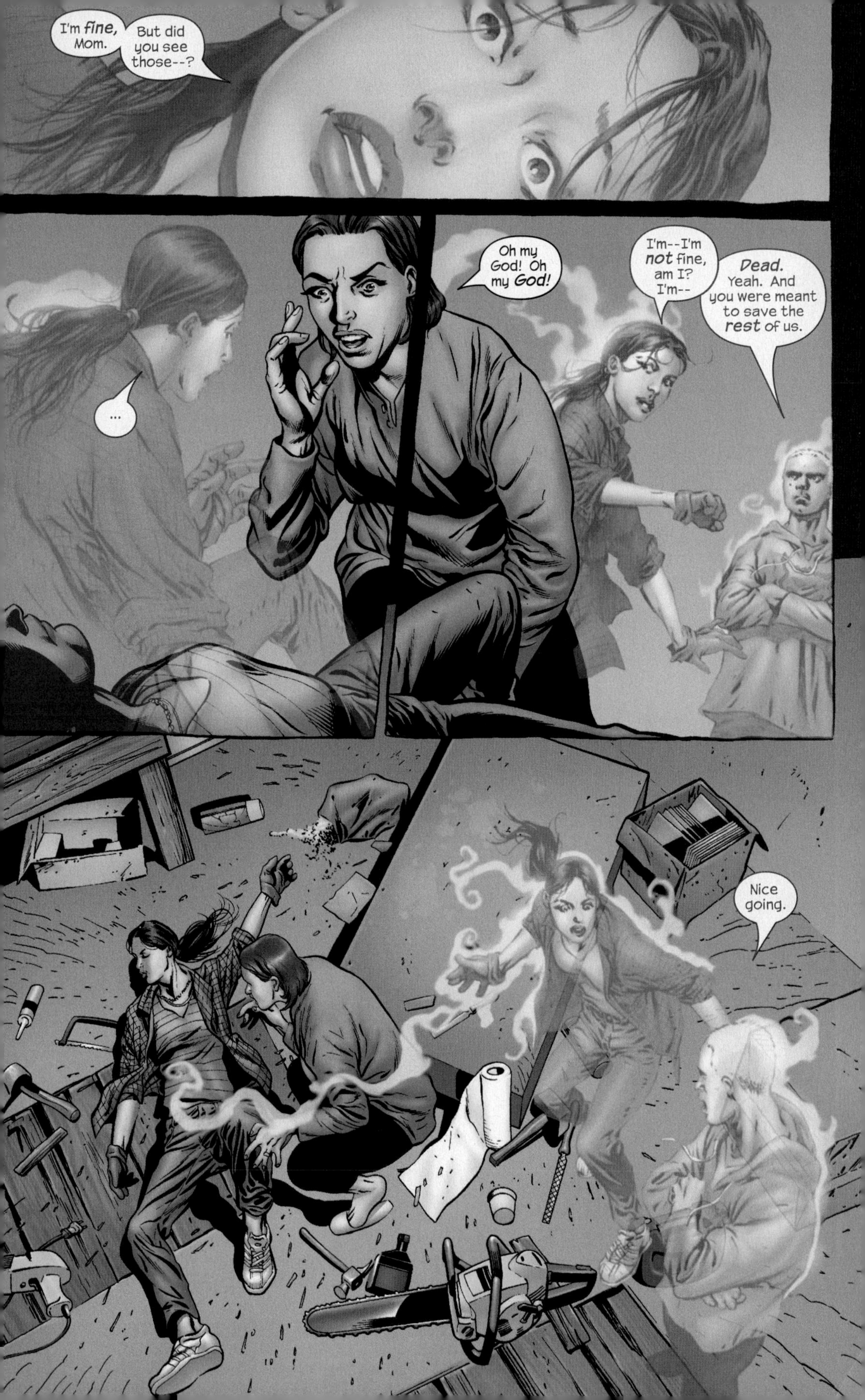
I'm fine, Mom.
But did you see those--?
...
Oh my God! Oh my God!
I'm--I'm not fine, am I? I'm--
Dead. Yeah. And you were meant to save the rest of us.
Nice going.

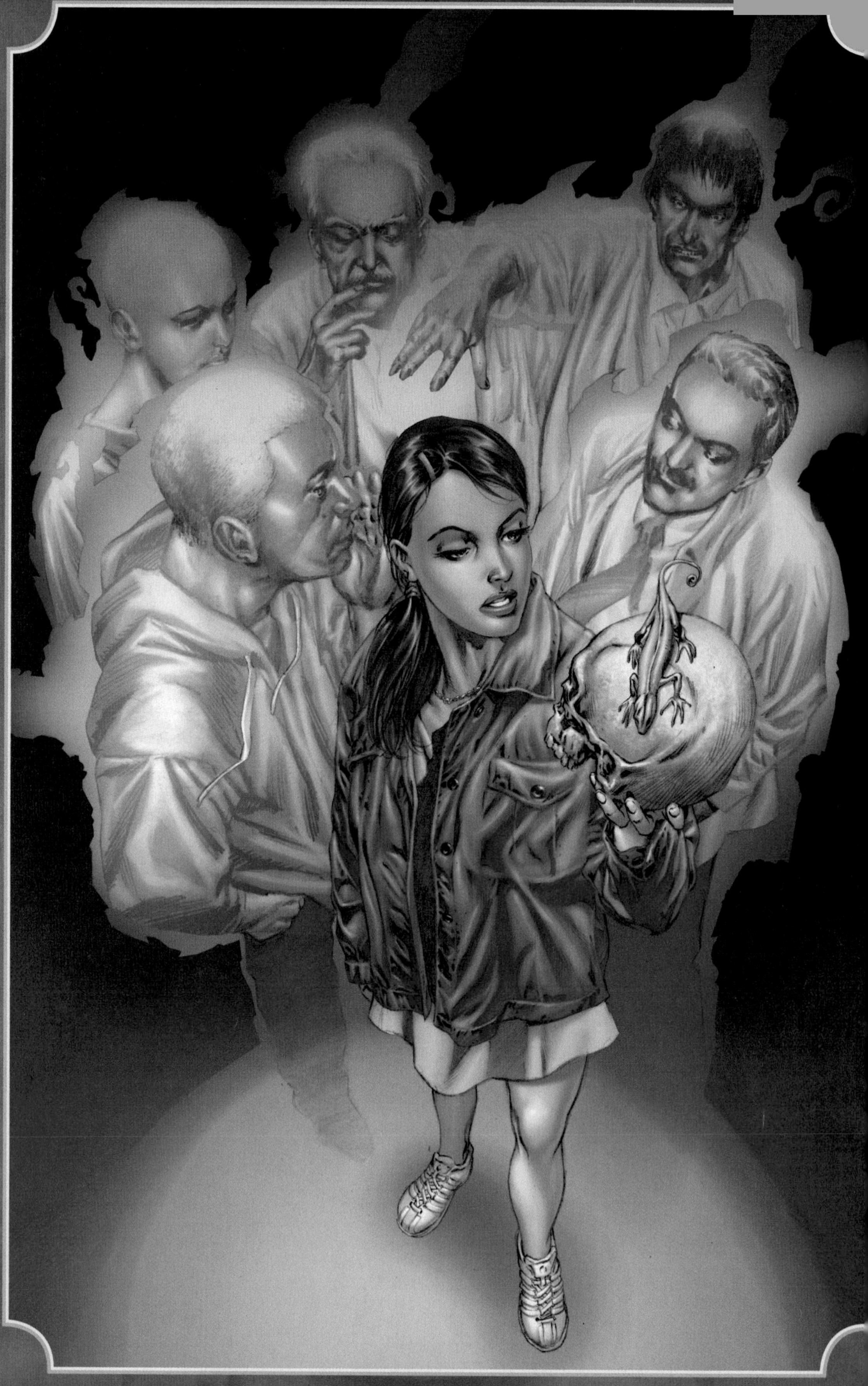

2

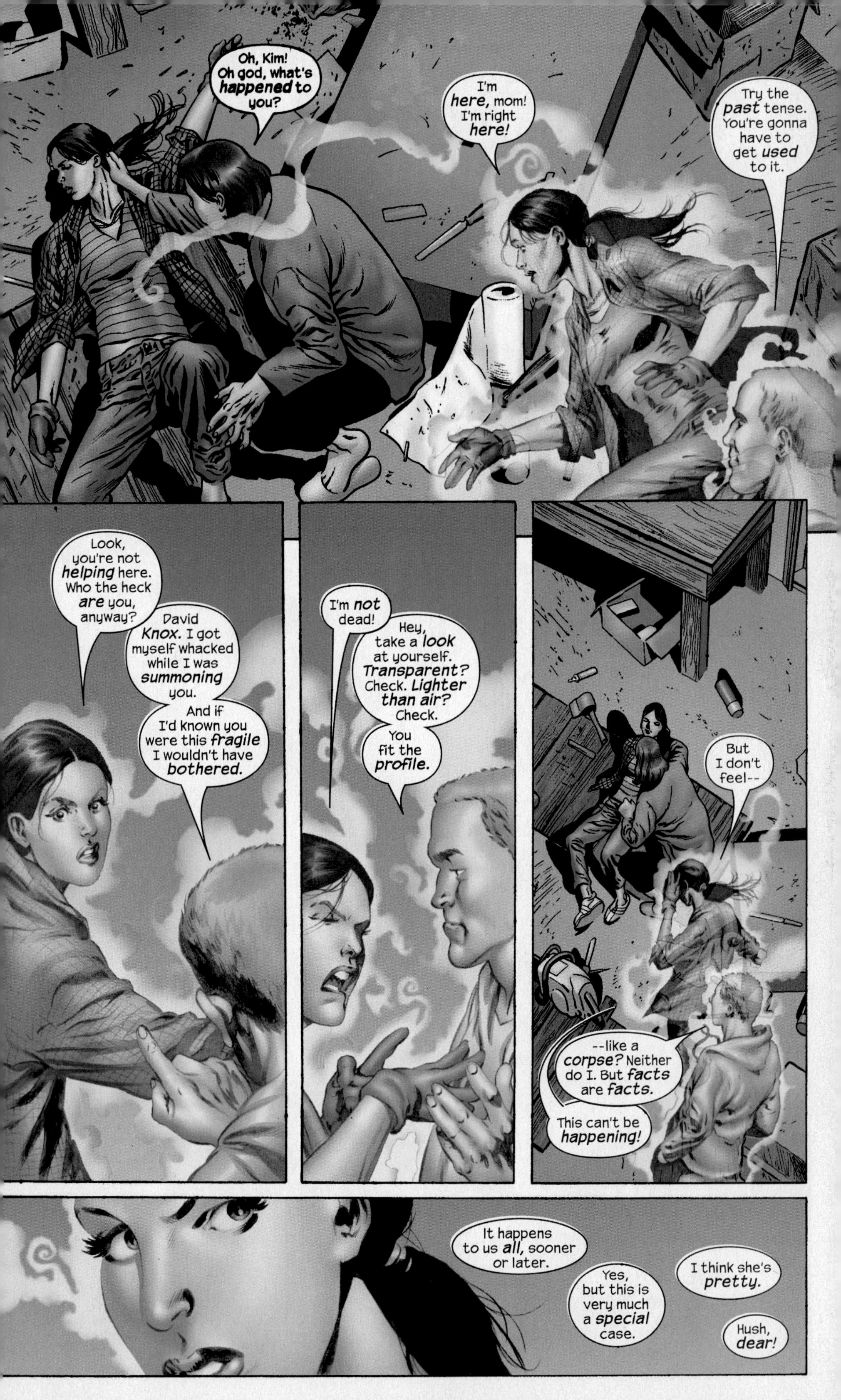

Oh, Kim! Oh god, what's happened to you?
I'm here, mom! I'm right here!
Try the past tense. You're gonna have to get used to it.
Look, you're not helping here. Who the heck are you, anyway?
David Knox. I got myself whacked while I was summoning you.
And if I'd known you were this fragile I wouldn't have bothered.
I'm not dead!
Hey, take a look at yourself. Transparent? Check. Lighter than air? Check.
You fit the profile.
But I don't feel--
--like a corpse? Neither do I. But facts are facts.
This can't be happening!
It happens to us all, sooner or later.
Yes, but this is very much a special case.
I think she's pretty.
Hush, dear!

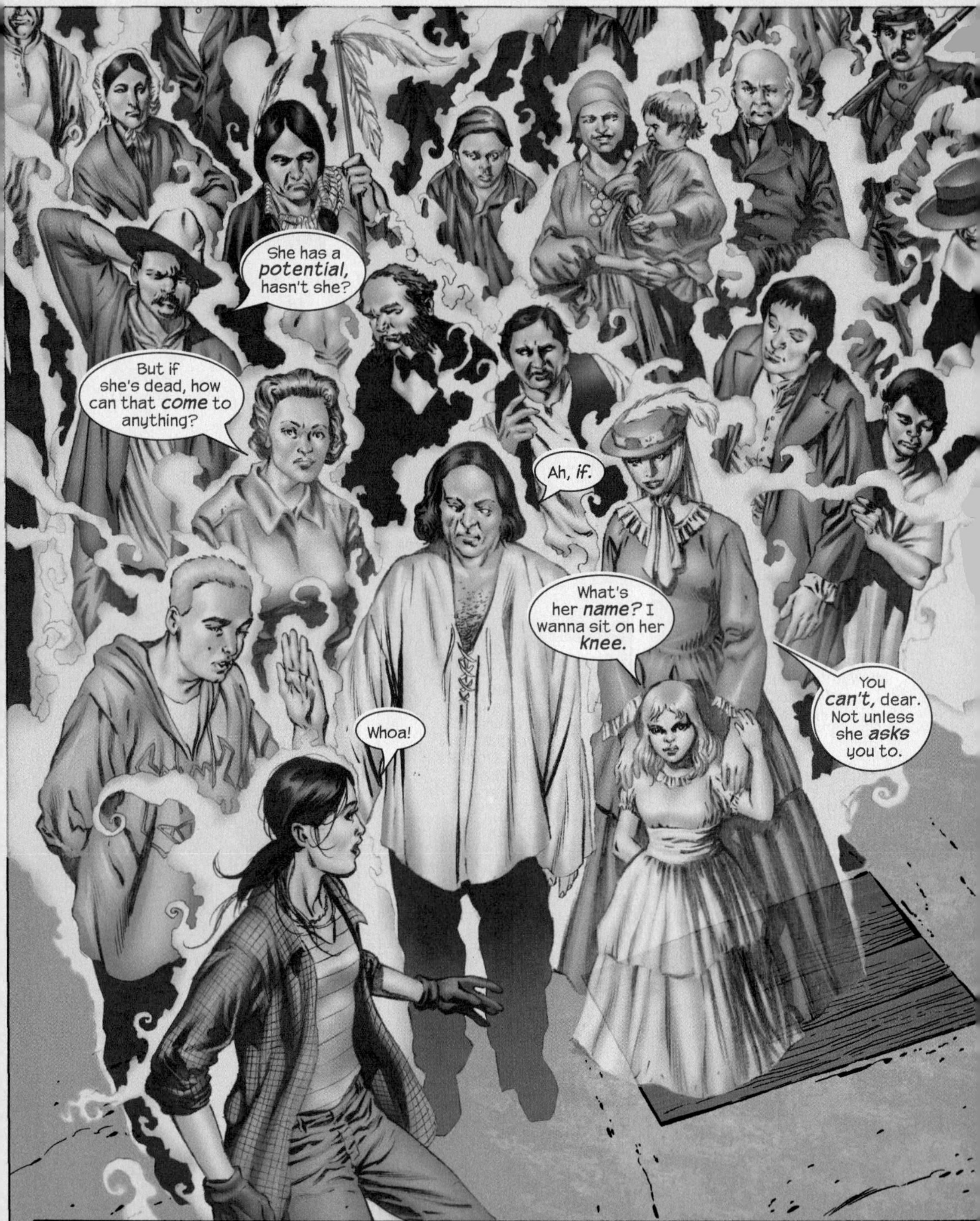
She has a potential, hasn't she?
But if she's dead, how can that come to anything?
Ah, if.
What's her name? I wanna sit on her knee.
You can't, dear. Not unless she asks you to.
Whoa!

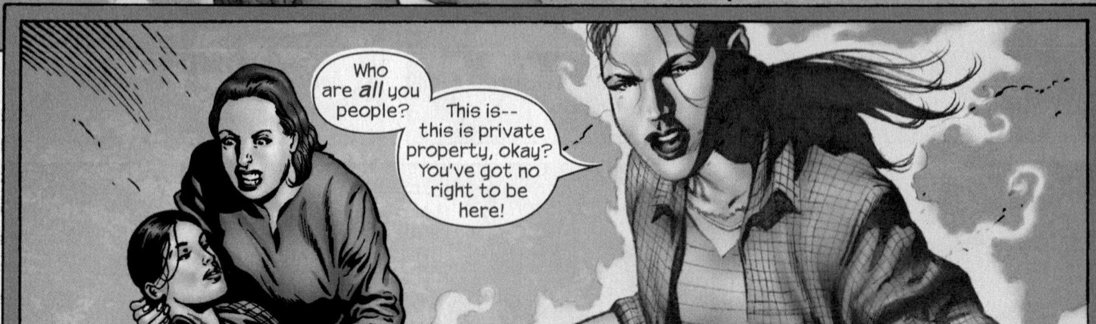
Who are all you people?
This is-- this is private property, okay? You've got no right to be here!

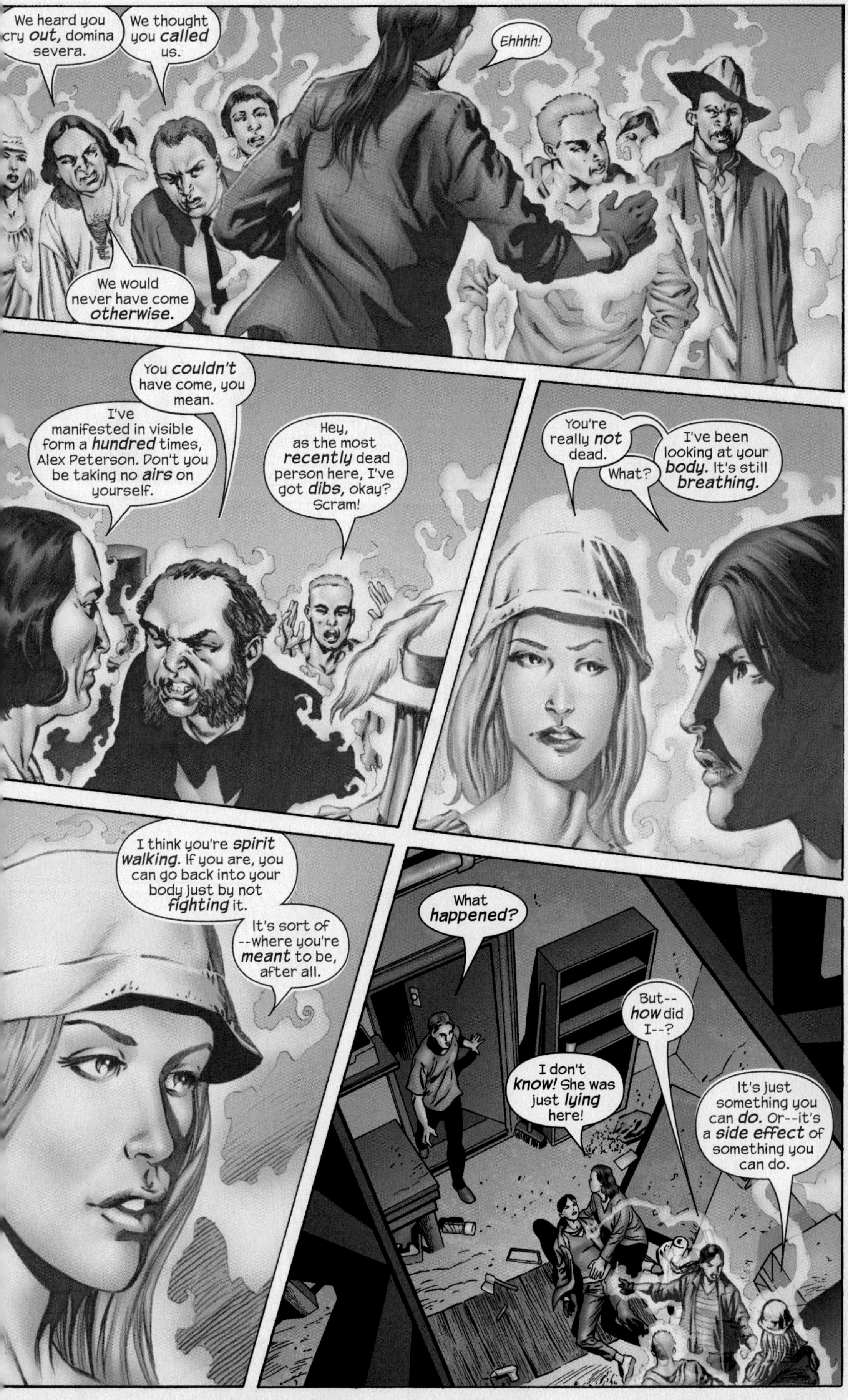
We heard you cry out, domina severa.
We thought you called us.
Ehhhh!
We would never have come otherwise.
You couldn't have come, you mean.
I've manifested in visible form a hundred times, Alex Peterson. Don't you be taking no airs on yourself.
Hey, as the most recently dead person here, I've got dibs, okay? Scram!
You're really not dead.
What?
I've been looking at your body. It's still breathing.
I think you're spirit walking. If you are, you can go back into your body just by not fighting it.
It's sort of --where you're meant to be, after all.
What happened?
But-- how did I--?
I don't know! She was just lying here!
It's just something you can do. Or--it's a side effect of something you can do.

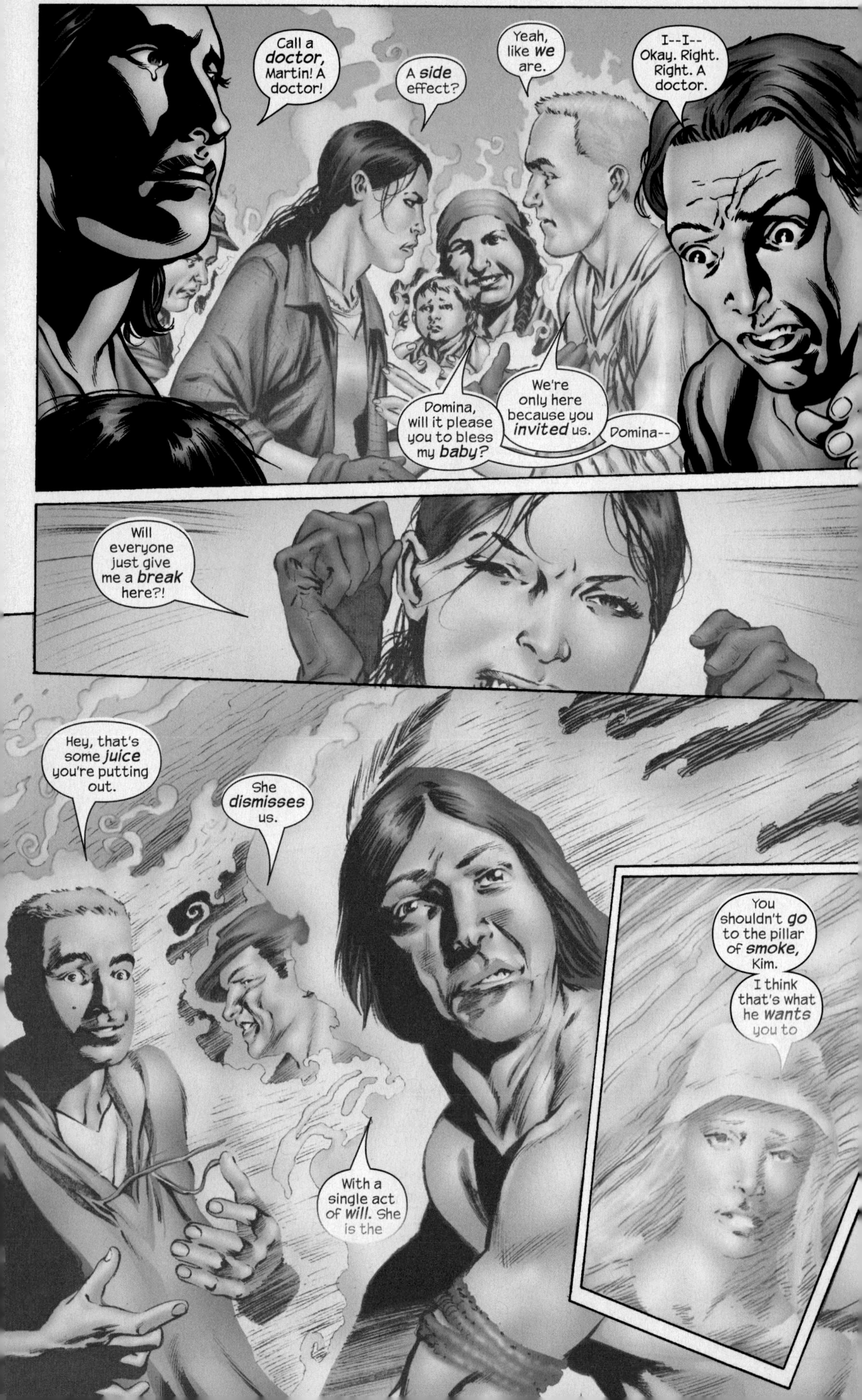
Call a doctor, Martin! A doctor!
A side effect?
Yeah, like we are.
I--I-- Okay. Right. Right. A doctor.
Domina, will it please you to bless my baby?
We're only here because you invited us.
Domina--
Will everyone just give me a break here?!
Hey, that's some juice you're putting out.
She dismisses us.
With a single act of will. She is the
You shouldn't go to the pillar of smoke, Kim.
I think that's what he wants you to

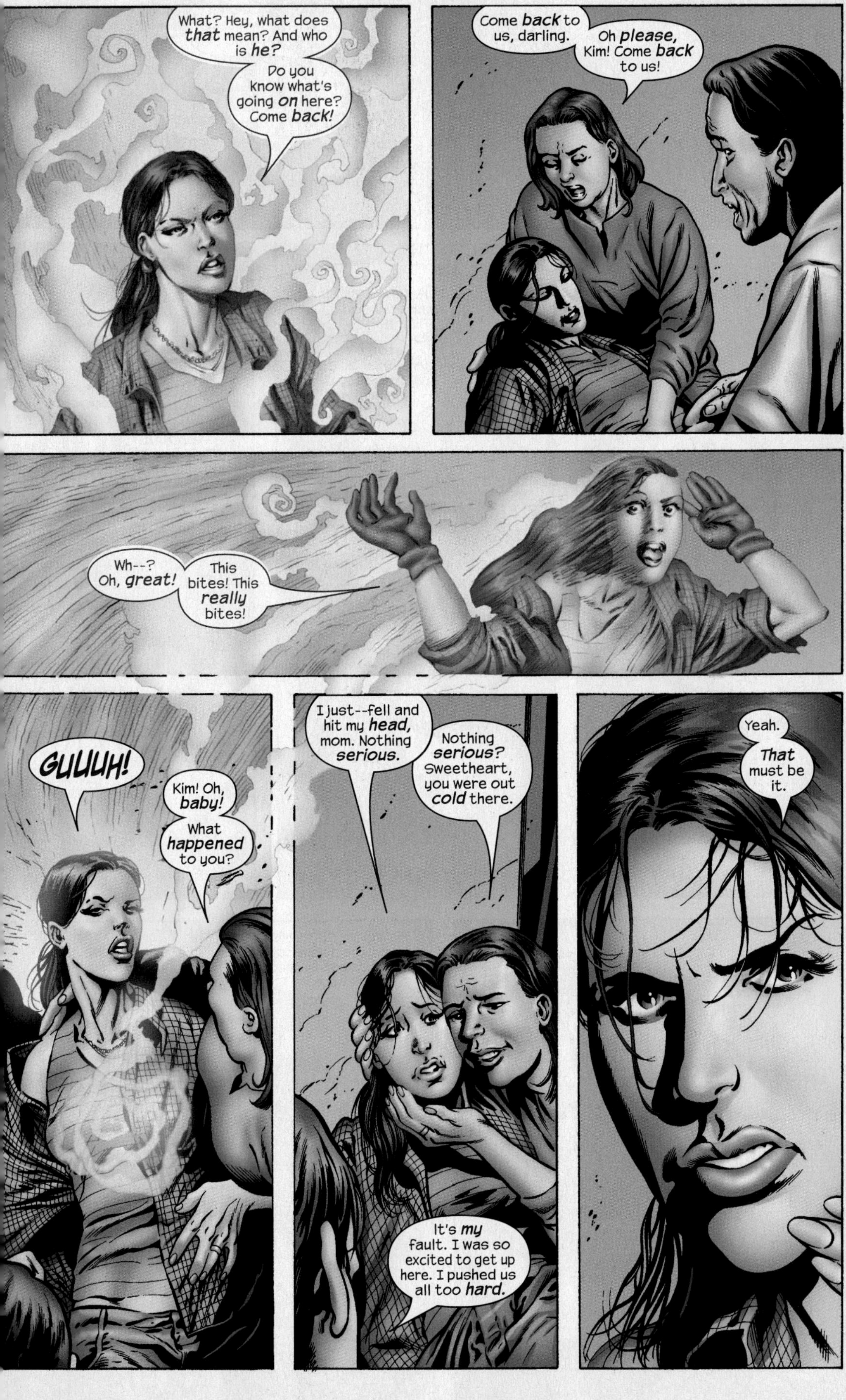
What? Hey, what does that mean? And who is he?
Do you know what's going on here? Come back!
Come back to us, darling.
Oh please, Kim! Come back to us!
Wh--? Oh, great!
This bites! This really bites!
GUUUH!
Kim! Oh, baby!
What happened to you?
I just--fell and hit my head, mom. Nothing serious.
Nothing serious? Sweetheart, you were out cold there.
It's my fault. I was so excited to get up here. I pushed us all too hard.
Yeah.
That must be it.

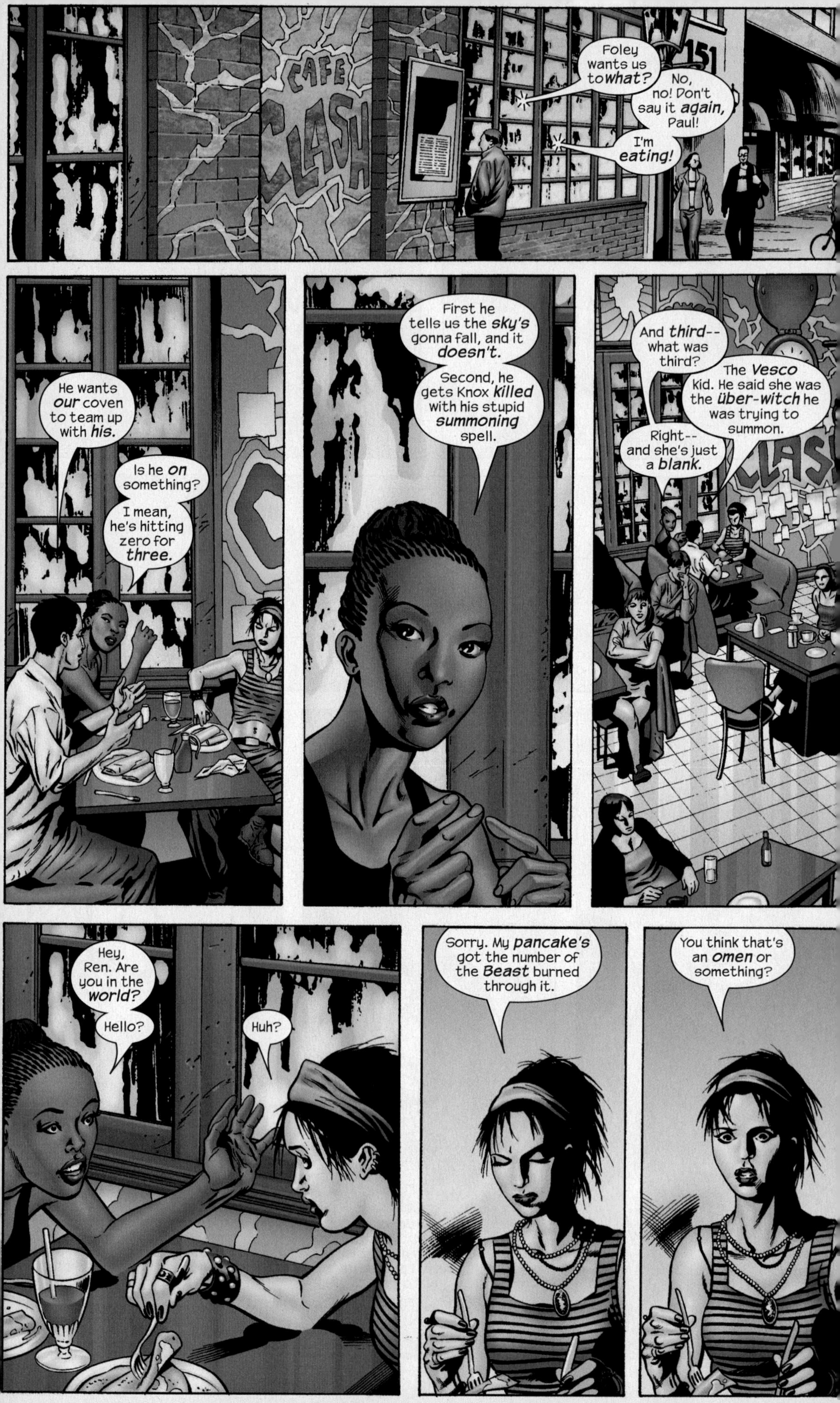
CAFE CLASH
151
Foley wants us to what?
No, no! Don't say it again, Paul!
I'm eating!
He wants our coven to team up with his.
Is he on something?
I mean, he's hitting zero for three.
First he tells us the sky's gonna fall, and it doesn't.
Second, he gets Knox killed with his stupid summoning spell.
And third-- what was third?
The Vesco kid. He said she was the über-witch he was trying to summon.
Right-- and she's just a blank.
Hey, Ren. Are you in the world?
Hello?
Huh?
Sorry. My pancake's got the number of the Beast burned through it.
You think that's an omen or something?

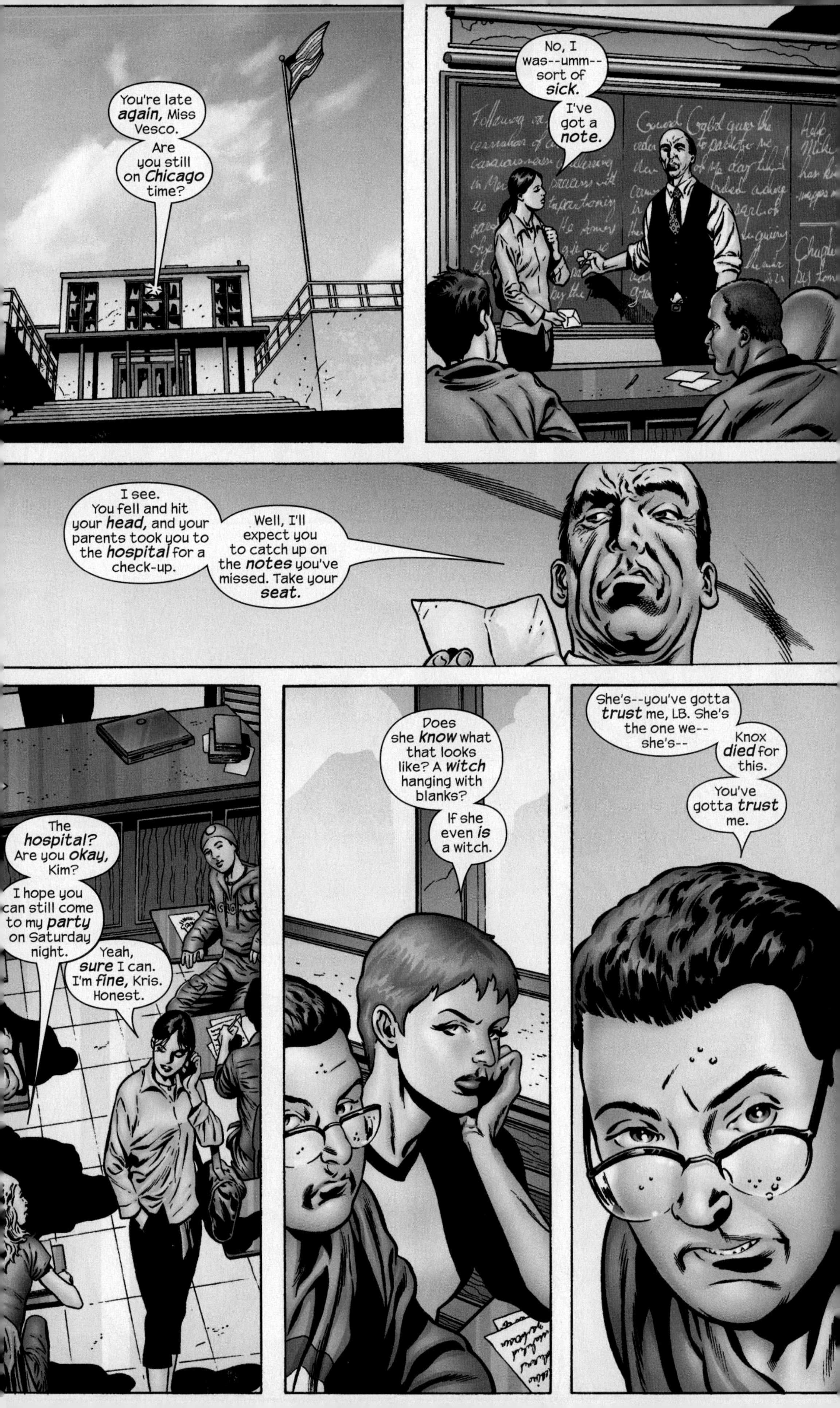

You're late **again,** Miss Vesco.
Are you still on *Chicago* time?
No, I was--umm--sort of **sick.**
I've got a **note.**
I see. You fell and hit your **head,** and your parents took you to the **hospital** for a check-up.
Well, I'll expect you to catch up on the **notes** you've missed. Take your **seat.**
The **hospital?** Are you **okay,** Kim?
I hope you can still come to my **party** on Saturday night.
Yeah, **sure** I can. I'm **fine,** Kris. Honest.
Does she **know** what that looks like? A **witch** hanging with blanks?
If she even **is** a witch.
She's--you've gotta **trust** me, LB. She's the one we--she's--
Knox **died** for this.
You've gotta **trust** me.

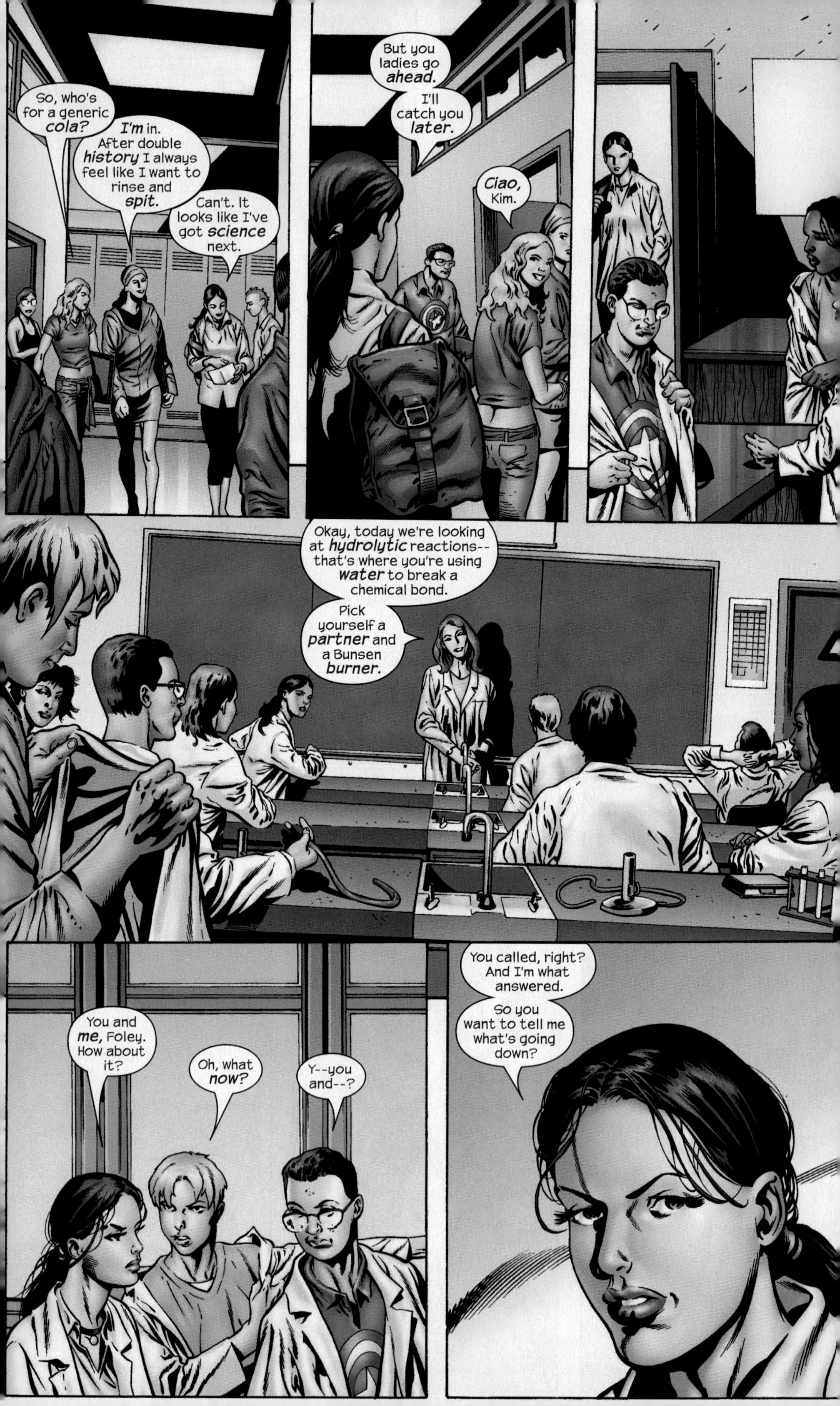

So, who's for a generic cola?
I'm in. After double history I always feel like I want to rinse and spit.
Can't. It looks like I've got science next.
But you ladies go ahead.
I'll catch you later.
Ciao, Kim.
Okay, today we're looking at hydrolytic reactions--that's where you're using water to break a chemical bond.
Pick yourself a partner and a Bunsen burner.
You and me, Foley. How about it?
Oh, what now?
Y--you and--?
You called, right? And I'm what answered.
So you want to tell me what's going down?

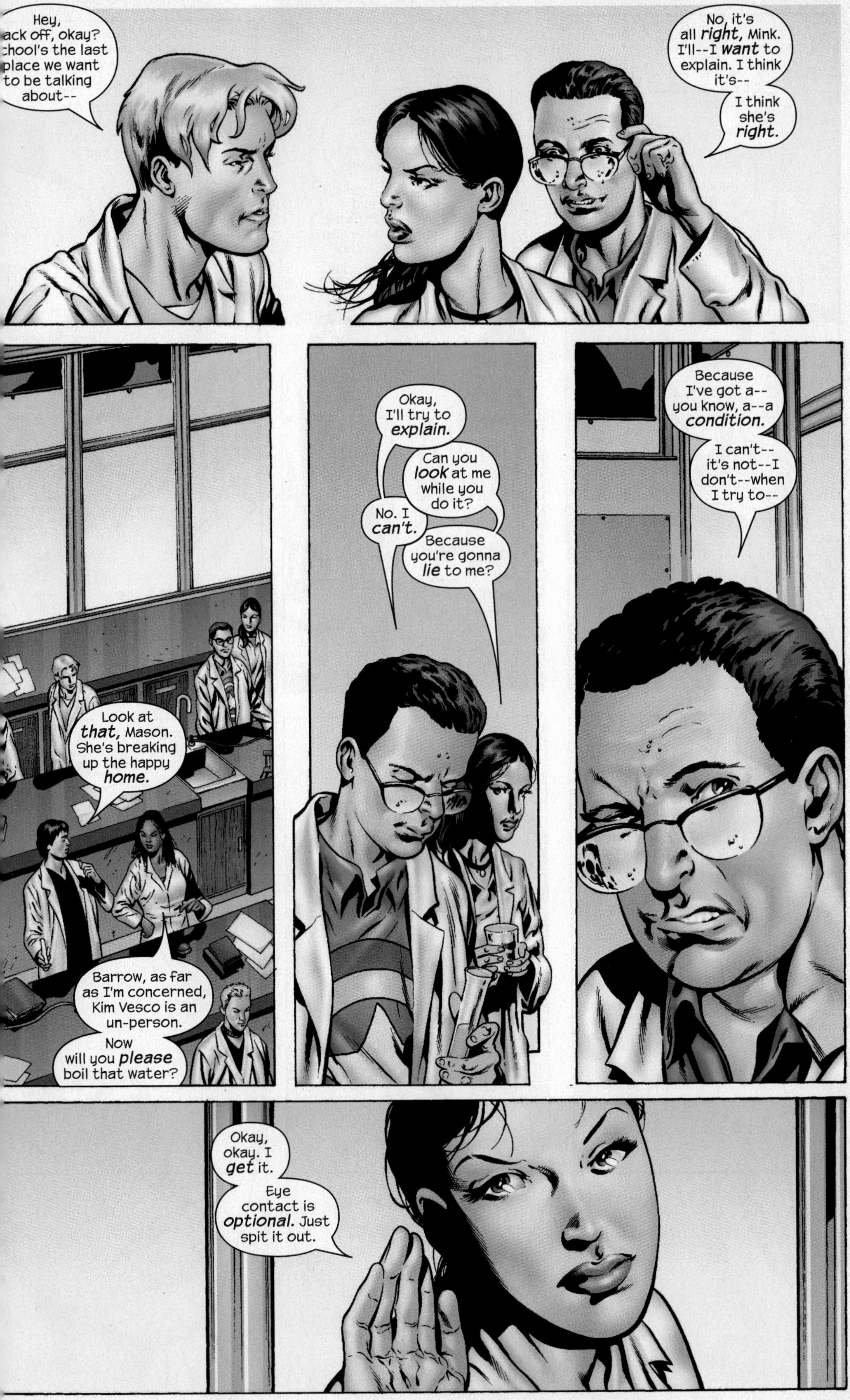

Hey, ack off, okay? chool's the last place we want to be talking about--
No, it's all right, Mink. I'll--I want to explain. I think it's--
I think she's right.
Look at that, Mason. She's breaking up the happy home.
Barrow, as far as I'm concerned, Kim Vesco is an un-person.
Now will you please boil that water?
Okay, I'll try to explain.
Can you look at me while you do it?
No. I can't.
Because you're gonna lie to me?
Because I've got a--you know, a--a condition.
I can't--it's not--I don't--when I try to--
Okay, okay. I get it.
Eye contact is optional. Just spit it out.

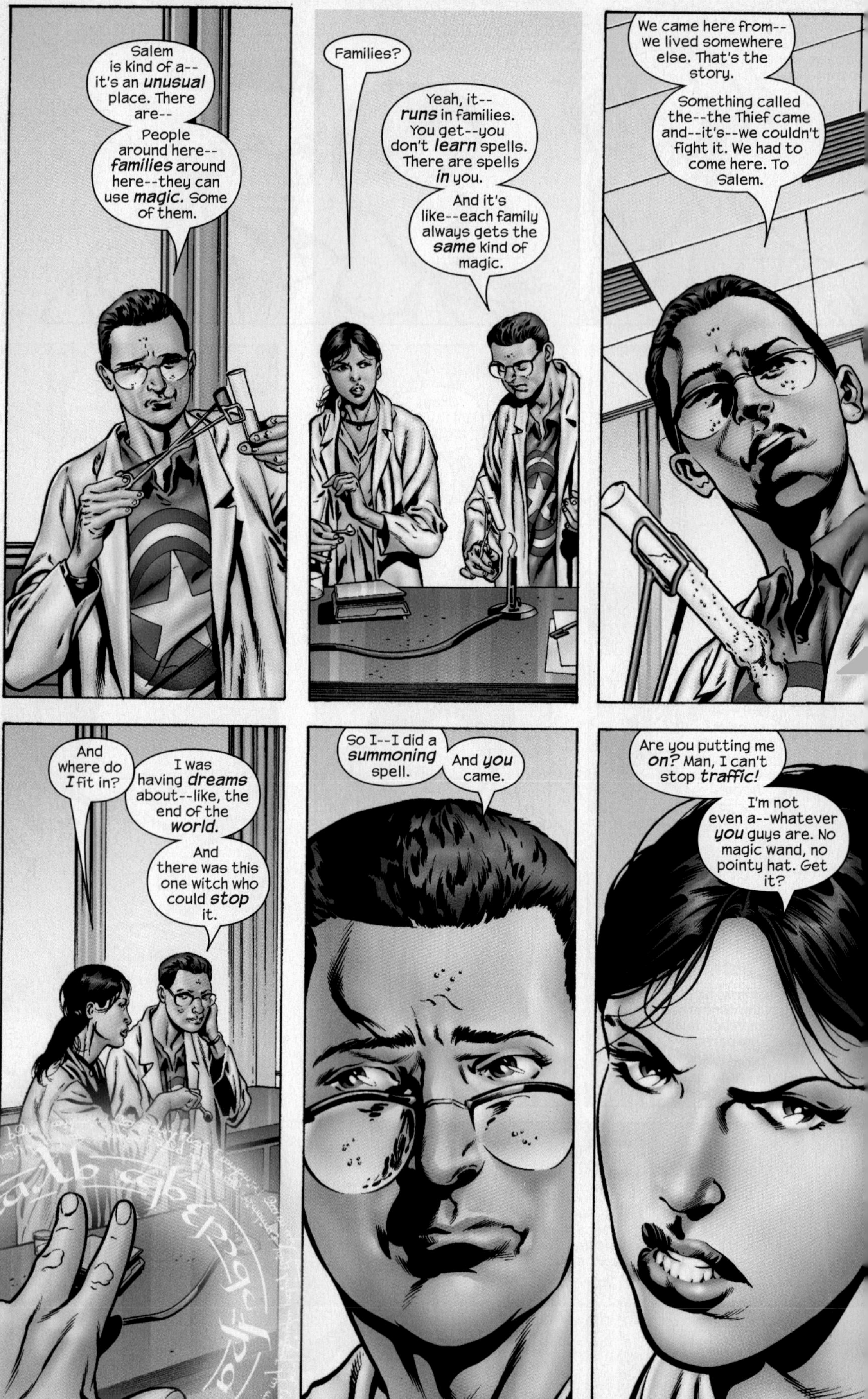
Salem is kind of a-- it's an unusual place. There are--
People around here-- families around here--they can use magic. Some of them.
Families?
Yeah, it-- runs in families. You get--you don't learn spells. There are spells in you.
And it's like--each family always gets the same kind of magic.
We came here from-- we lived somewhere else. That's the story.
Something called the--the Thief came and--it's--we couldn't fight it. We had to come here. To Salem.
And where do I fit in?
I was having dreams about--like, the end of the world.
And there was this one witch who could stop it.
So I--I did a summoning spell.
And you came.
Are you putting me on? Man, I can't stop traffic!
I'm not even a--whatever you guys are. No magic wand, no pointy hat. Get it?

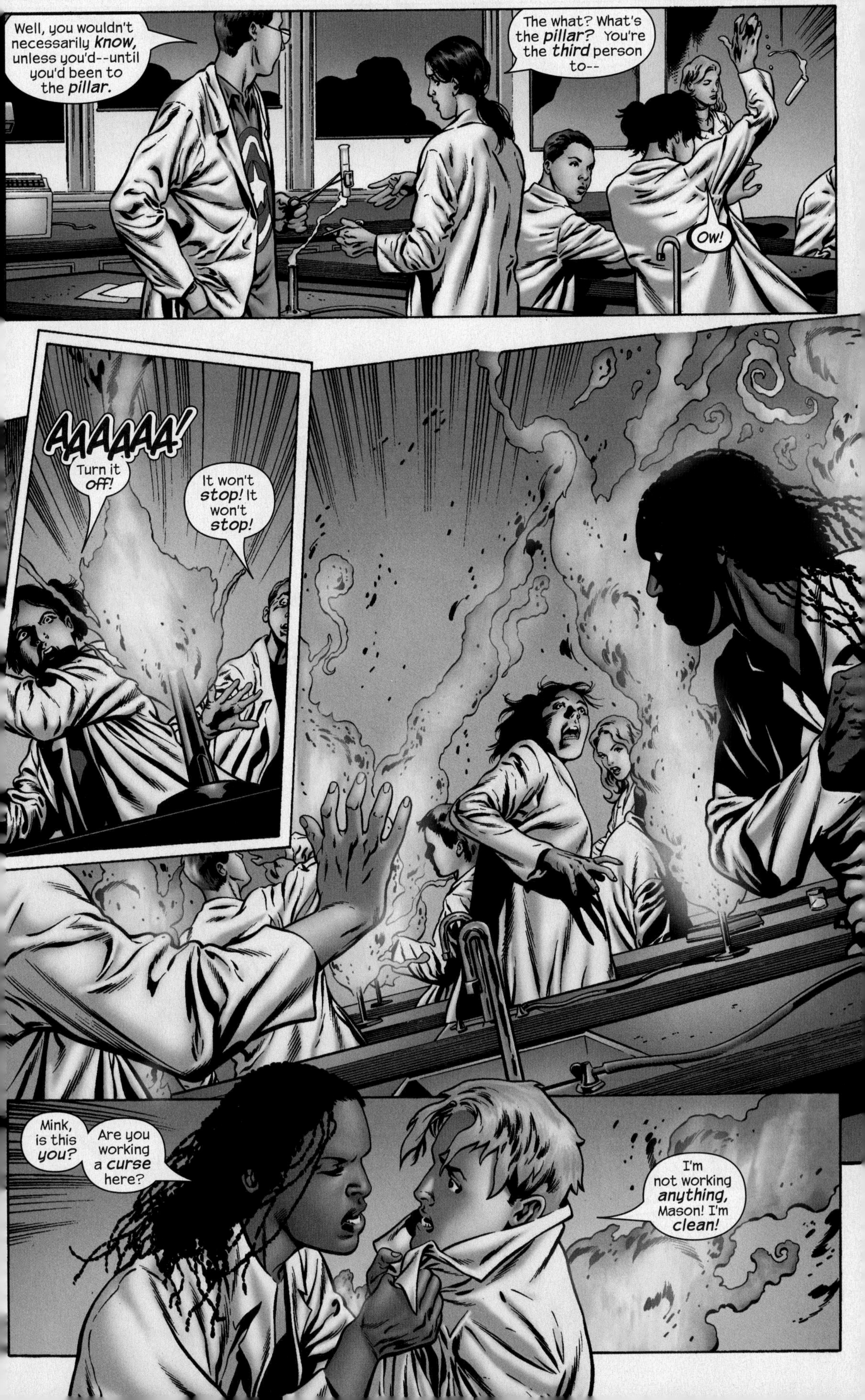

Well, you wouldn't necessarily know, unless you'd--until you'd been to the pillar.
The what? What's the pillar? You're the third person to--
Ow!
AAAAAA!
Turn it off!
It won't stop! It won't stop!
Mink, is this you?
Are you working a curse here?
I'm not working anything, Mason! I'm clean!

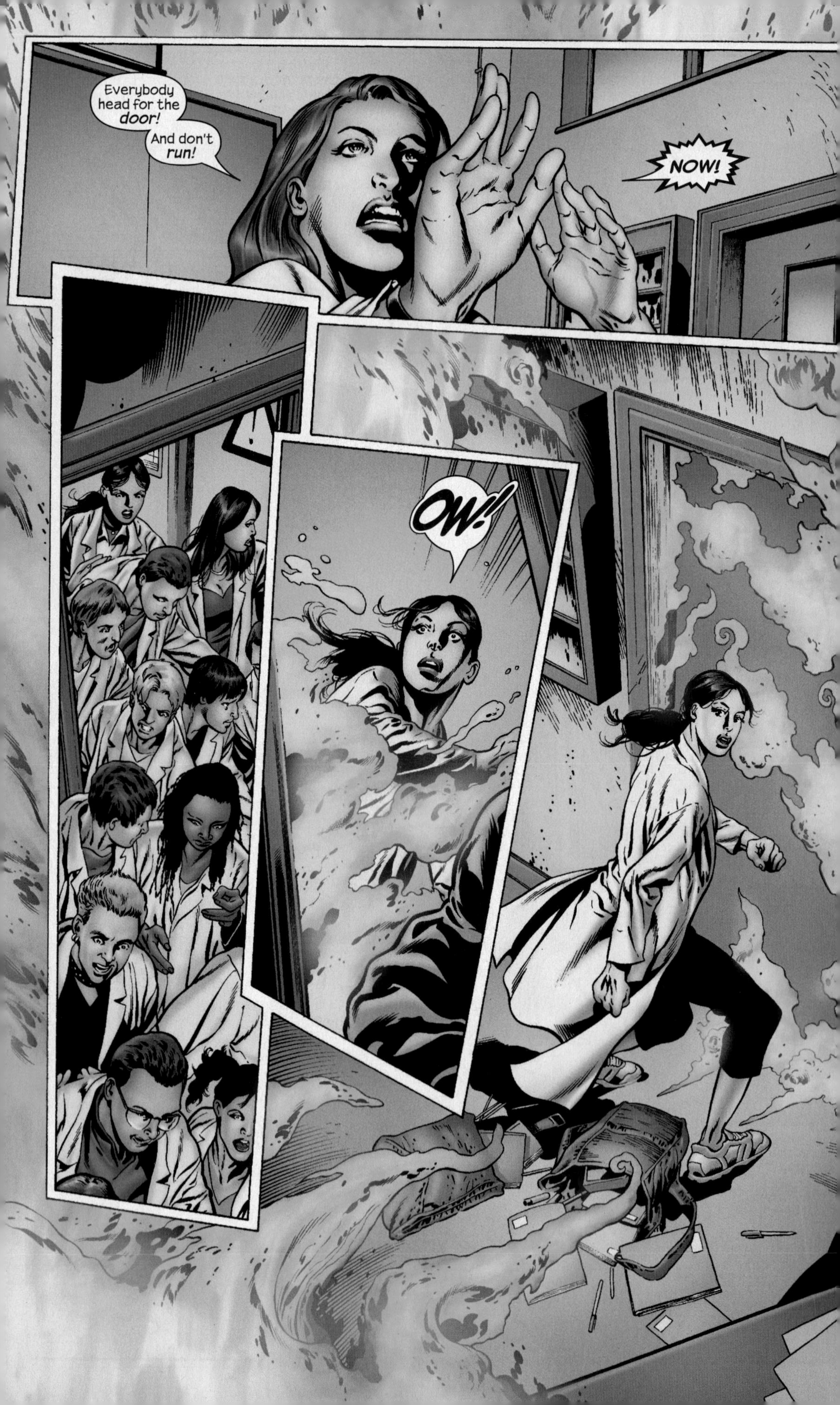

Everybody head for the *door!*
And don't *run!*
NOW!
OW!!

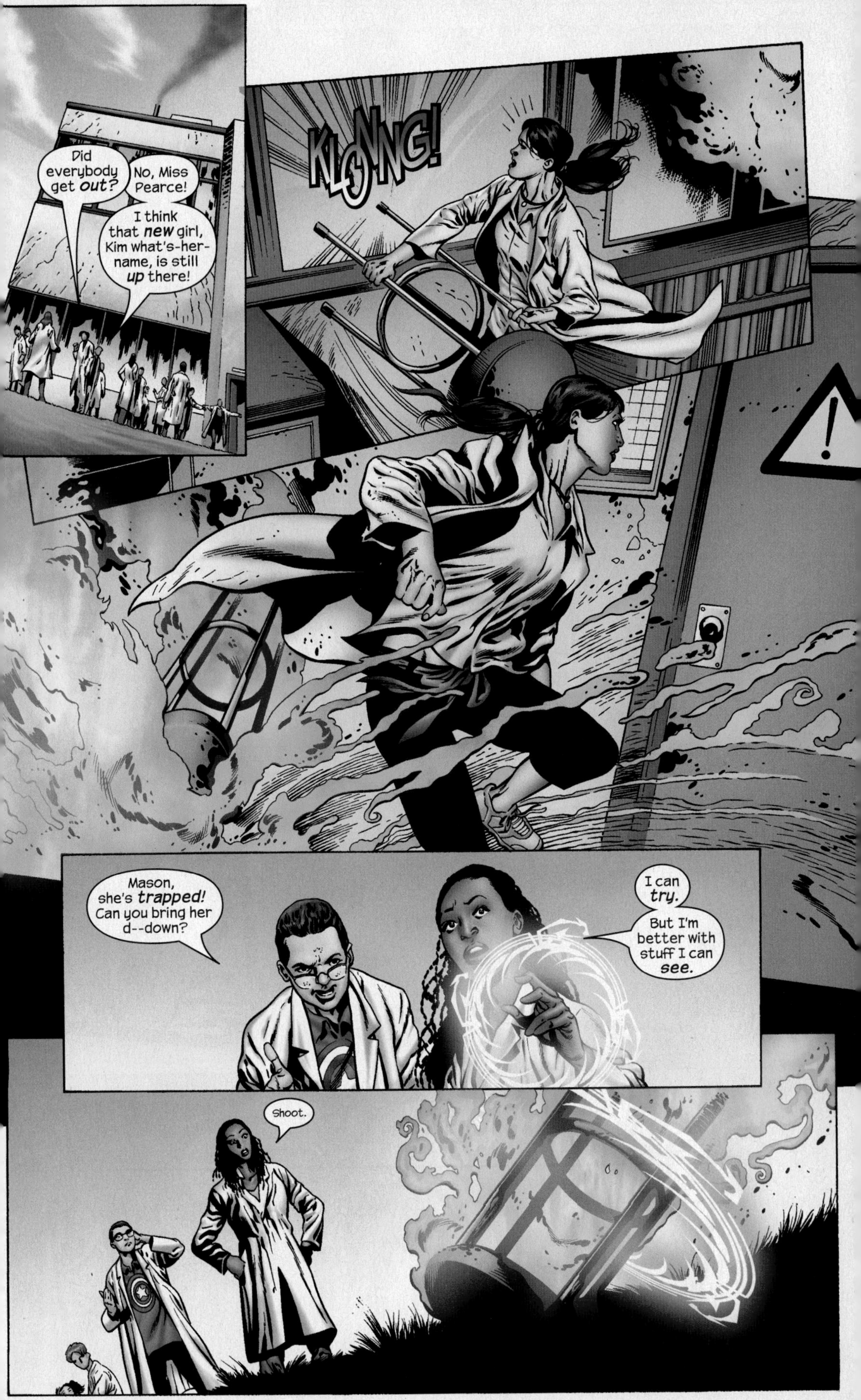
Did everybody get out?
No, Miss Pearce!
I think that new girl, Kim what's-her-name, is still up there!
KLONNG!
Mason, she's trapped! Can you bring her d--down?
I can try.
But I'm better with stuff I can see.
Shoot.

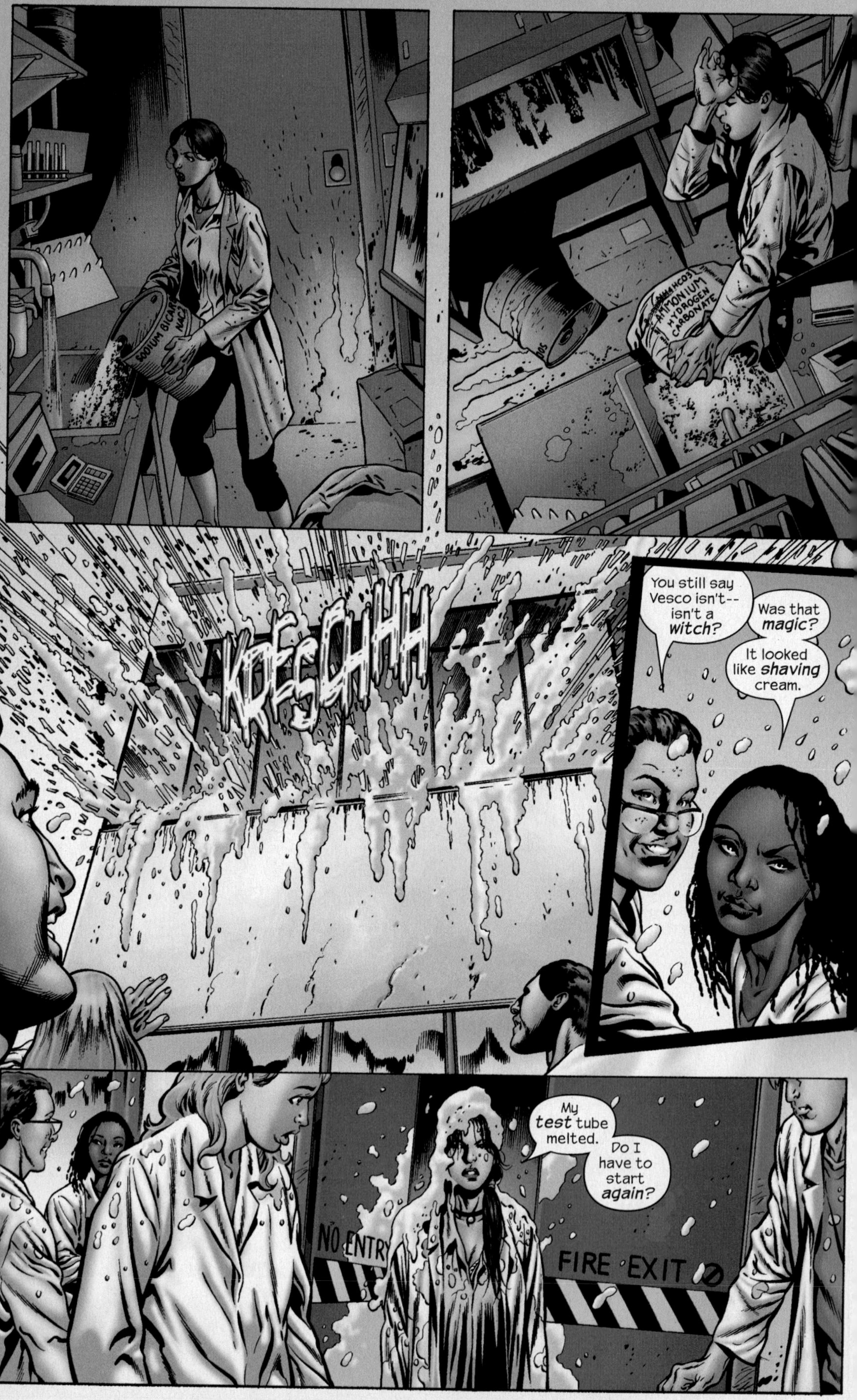
SODIUM BICAR
NAC
AMMONIUM HYDROGEN CARBONATE
KRESCHHH
You still say Vesco isn't-- isn't a witch?
Was that magic?
It looked like shaving cream.
My test tube melted.
Do I have to start again?
NO ENTRY
FIRE EXIT

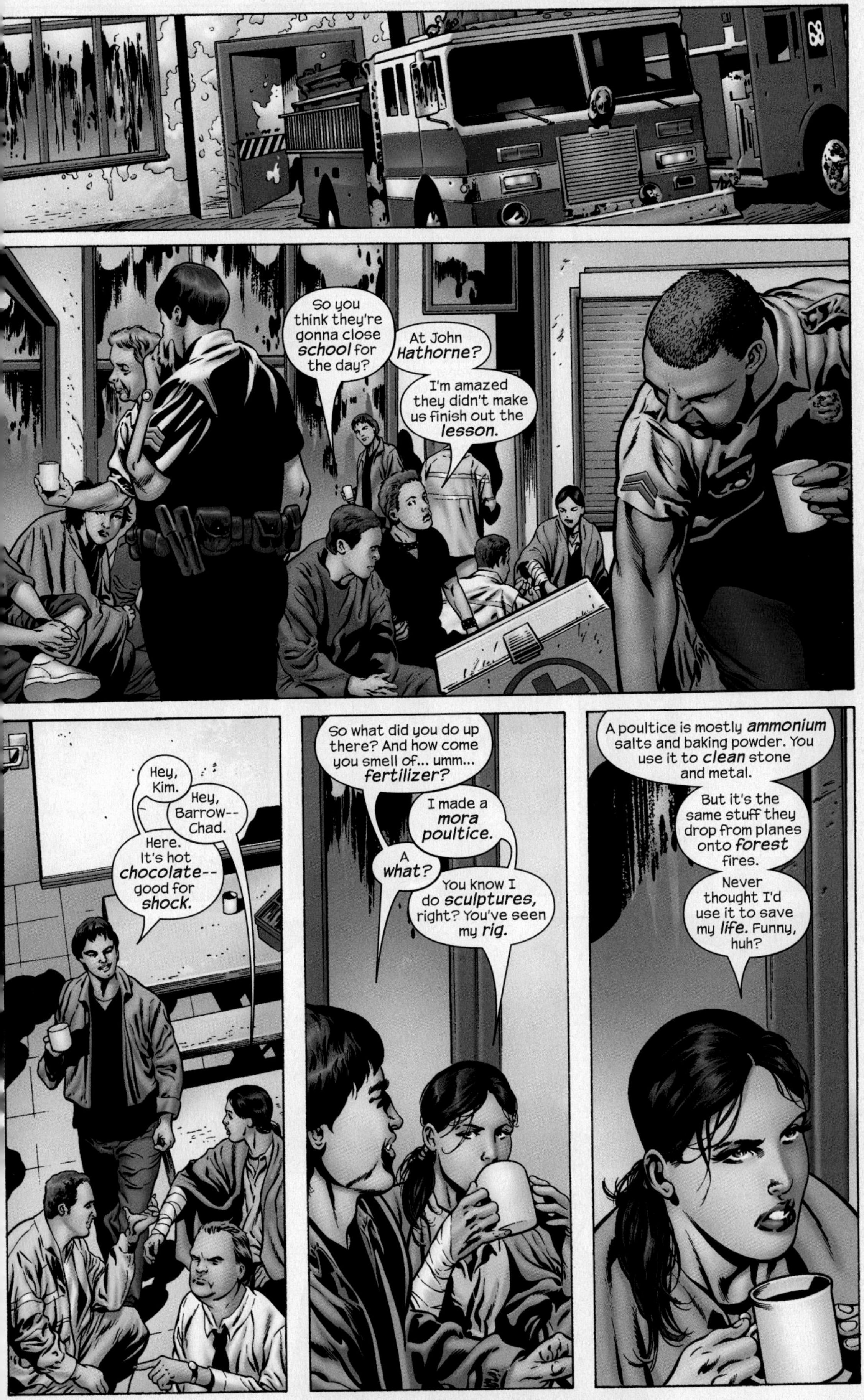
So you think they're gonna close school for the day?
At John Hathorne?
I'm amazed they didn't make us finish out the lesson.
Hey, Kim.
Hey, Barrow-- Chad.
Here. It's hot chocolate-- good for shock.
So what did you do up there? And how come you smell of... umm... fertilizer?
I made a mora poultice.
A what?
You know I do sculptures, right? You've seen my rig.
A poultice is mostly ammonium salts and baking powder. You use it to clean stone and metal.
But it's the same stuff they drop from planes onto forest fires.
Never thought I'd use it to save my life. Funny, huh?

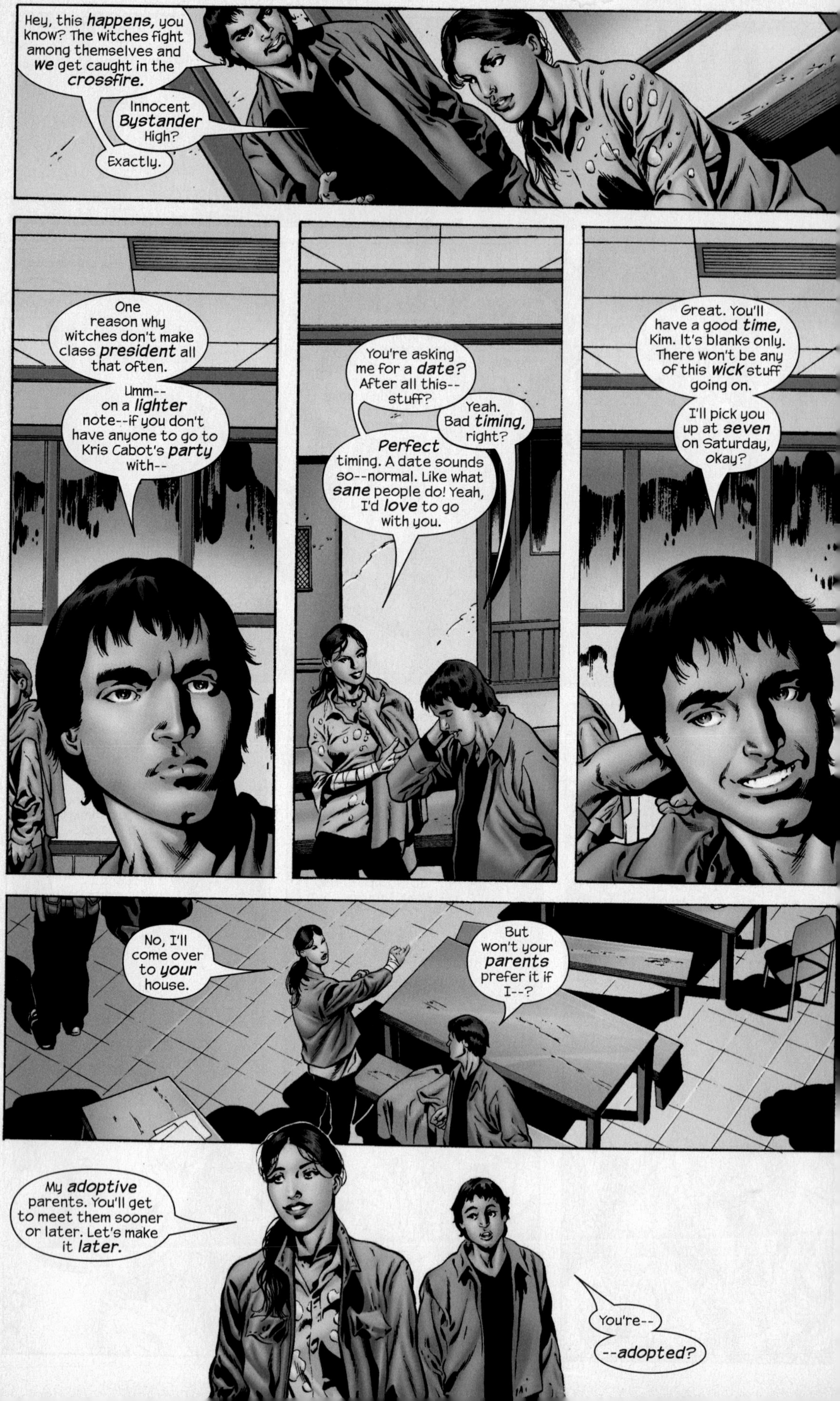

Hey, this happens, you know? The witches fight among themselves and we get caught in the crossfire.
Innocent Bystander High?
Exactly.
One reason why witches don't make class president all that often.
Umm-- on a lighter note--if you don't have anyone to go to Kris Cabot's party with--
You're asking me for a date? After all this--stuff?
Yeah. Bad timing, right?
Perfect timing. A date sounds so--normal. Like what sane people do! Yeah, I'd love to go with you.
Great. You'll have a good time, Kim. It's blanks only. There won't be any of this wick stuff going on.
I'll pick you up at seven on Saturday, okay?
No, I'll come over to your house.
But won't your parents prefer it if I--?
My adoptive parents. You'll get to meet them sooner or later. Let's make it later.
You're--
--adopted?

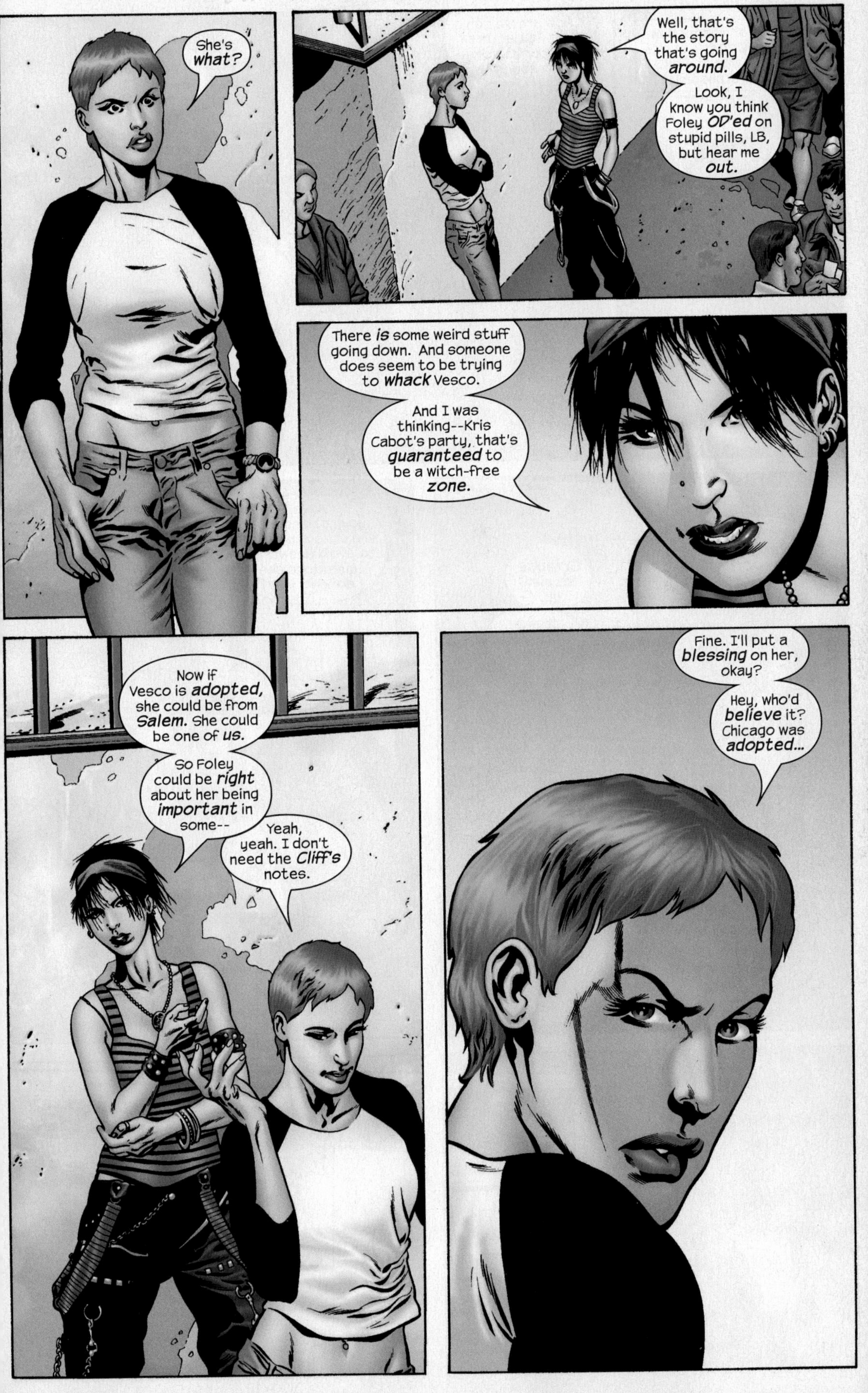
She's what?
Well, that's the story that's going around.
Look, I know you think Foley OD'ed on stupid pills, LB, but hear me out.
There is some weird stuff going down. And someone does seem to be trying to whack Vesco.
And I was thinking--Kris Cabot's party, that's guaranteed to be a witch-free zone.
Now if Vesco is adopted, she could be from Salem. She could be one of us.
So Foley could be right about her being important in some--
Yeah, yeah. I don't need the Cliff's notes.
Fine. I'll put a blessing on her, okay?
Hey, who'd believe it? Chicago was adopted...

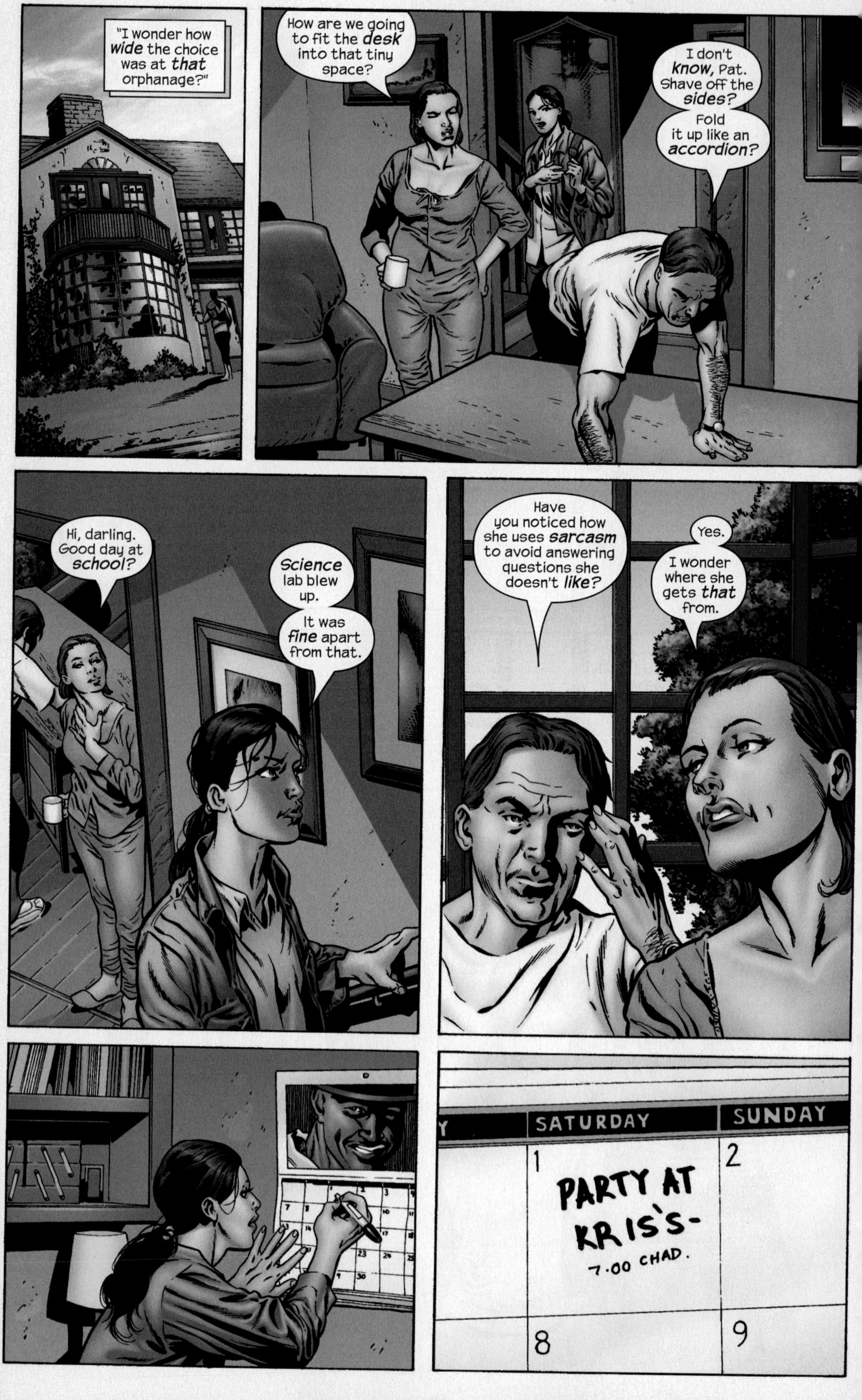
"I wonder how wide the choice was at that orphanage?"
How are we going to fit the desk into that tiny space?
I don't know, Pat. Shave off the sides?
Fold it up like an accordion?
Hi, darling. Good day at school?
Science lab blew up.
It was fine apart from that.
Have you noticed how she uses sarcasm to avoid answering questions she doesn't like?
Yes.
I wonder where she gets that from.
SATURDAY
SUNDAY
1
2
PARTY AT KRIS'S-
7.00 CHAD.
8
9

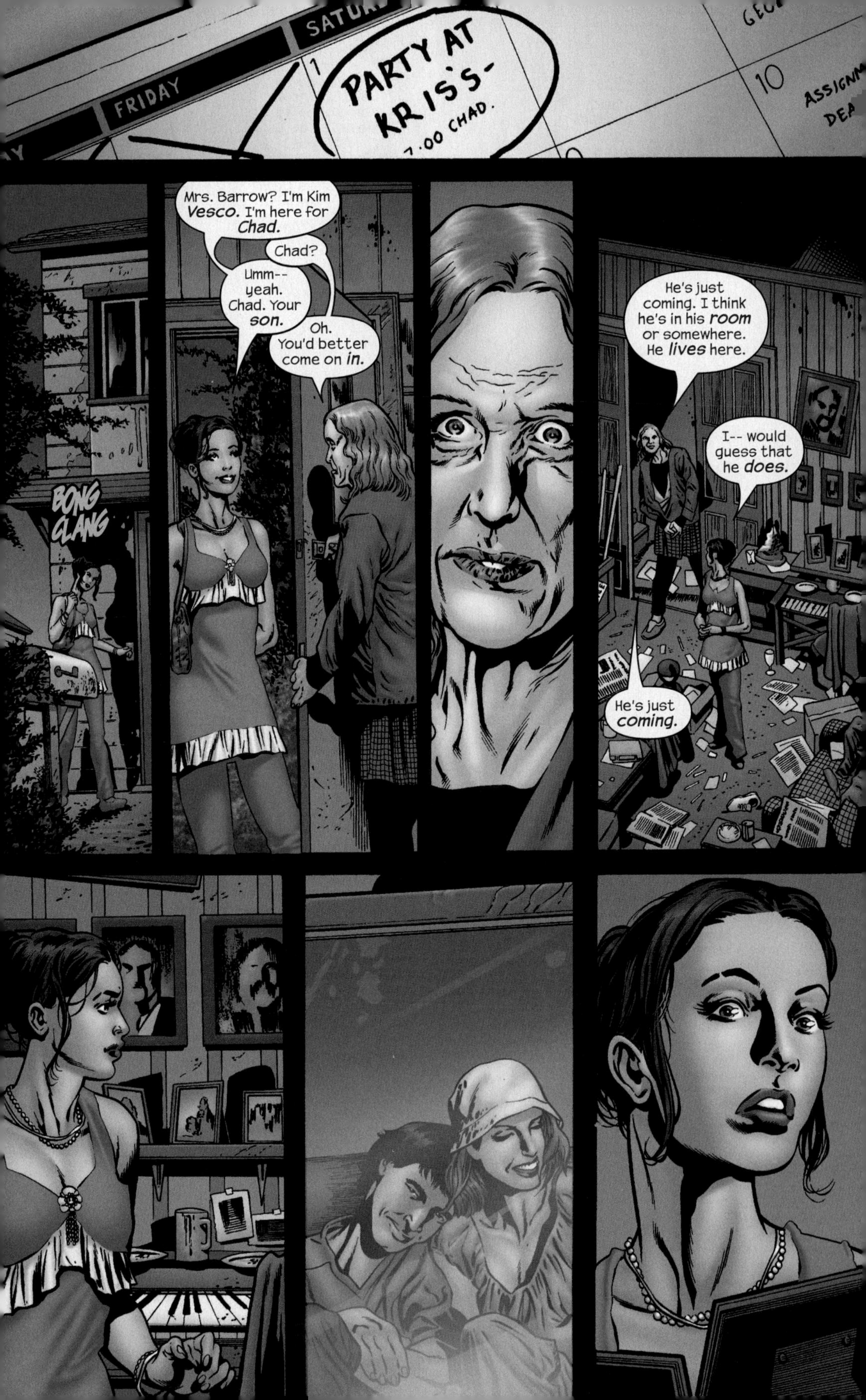
SATUR
FRIDAY
1
PARTY AT KRIS'S-
7:00 CHAD.
10
ASSIGNM
DEA
Mrs. Barrow? I'm Kim Vesco. I'm here for Chad.
Chad?
Umm-- yeah. Chad. Your son.
Oh. You'd better come on in.
BONG CLANG
He's just coming. I think he's in his room or somewhere. He lives here.
I-- would guess that he does.
He's just coming.

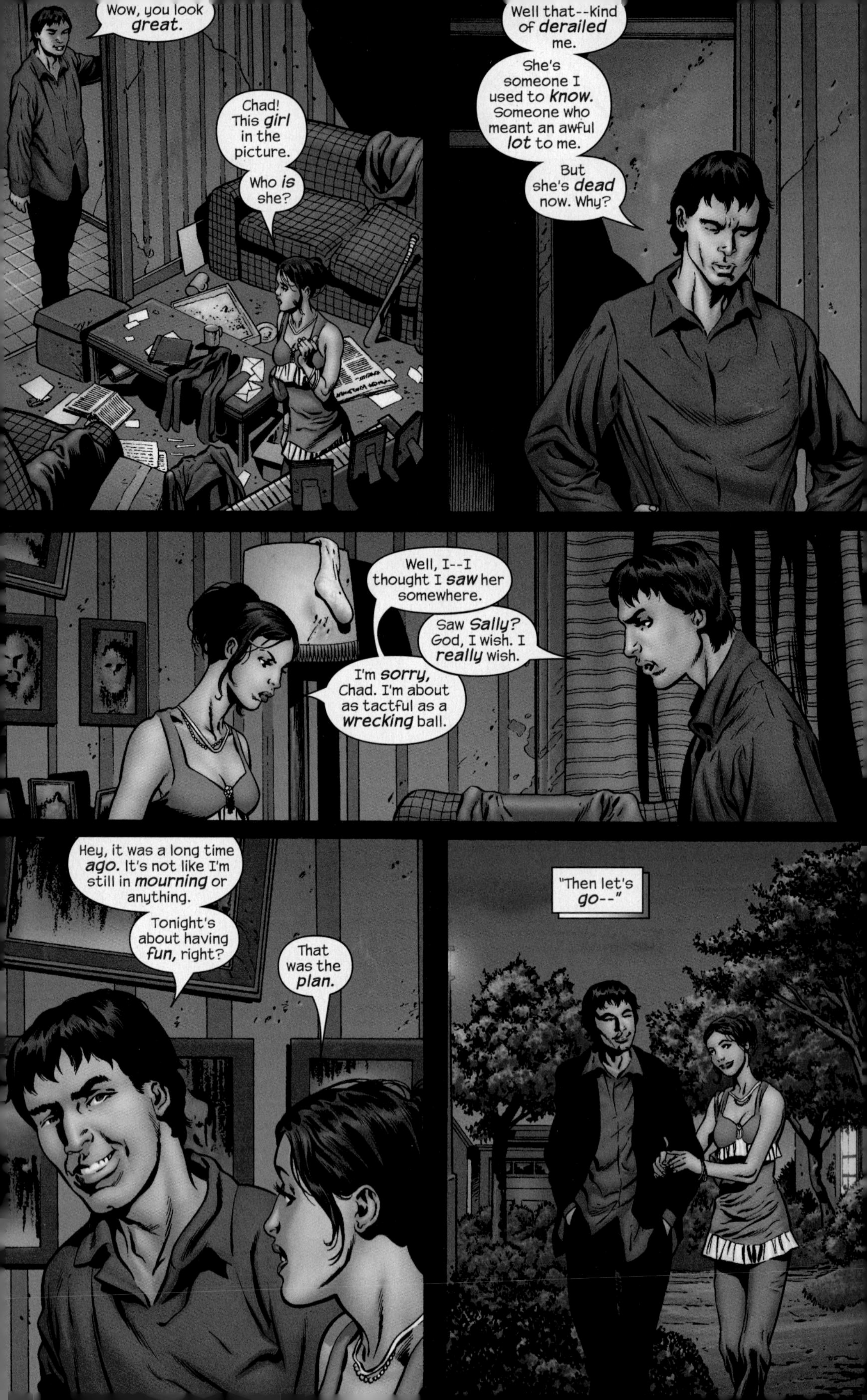

Wow, you look great.
Chad! This girl in the picture.
Who is she?
Well that--kind of derailed me.
She's someone I used to know. Someone who meant an awful lot to me.
But she's dead now. Why?
Well, I--I thought I saw her somewhere.
Saw Sally? God, I wish. I really wish.
I'm sorry, Chad. I'm about as tactful as a wrecking ball.
Hey, it was a long time ago. It's not like I'm still in mourning or anything.
Tonight's about having fun, right?
That was the plan.
"Then let's go--"

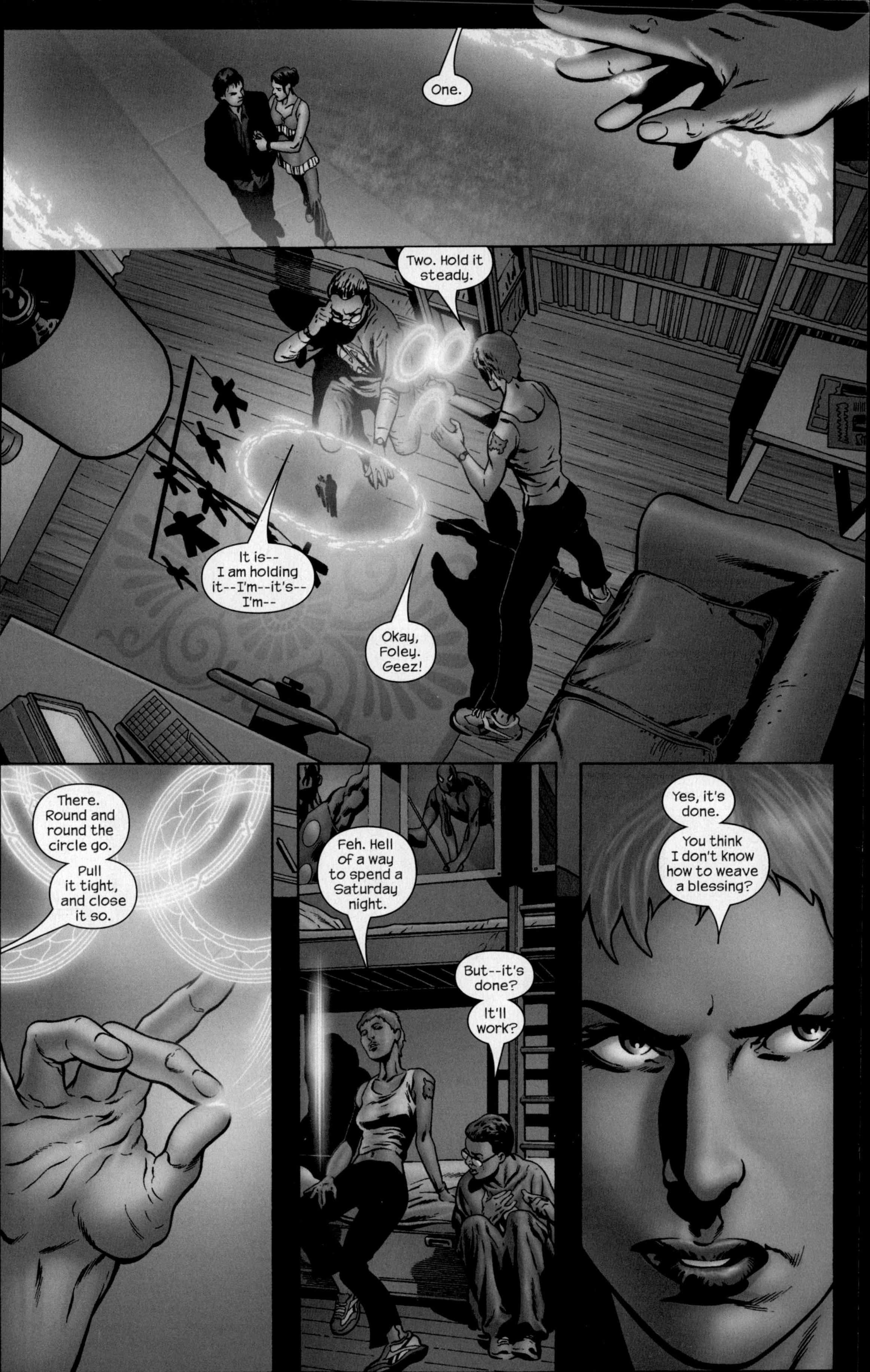
One.
Two. Hold it steady.
It is-- I am holding it--I'm--it's-- I'm--
Okay, Foley. Geez!
There. Round and round the circle go.
Pull it tight, and close it so.
Feh. Hell of a way to spend a Saturday night.
But--it's done?
It'll work?
Yes, it's done.
You think I don't know how to weave a blessing?

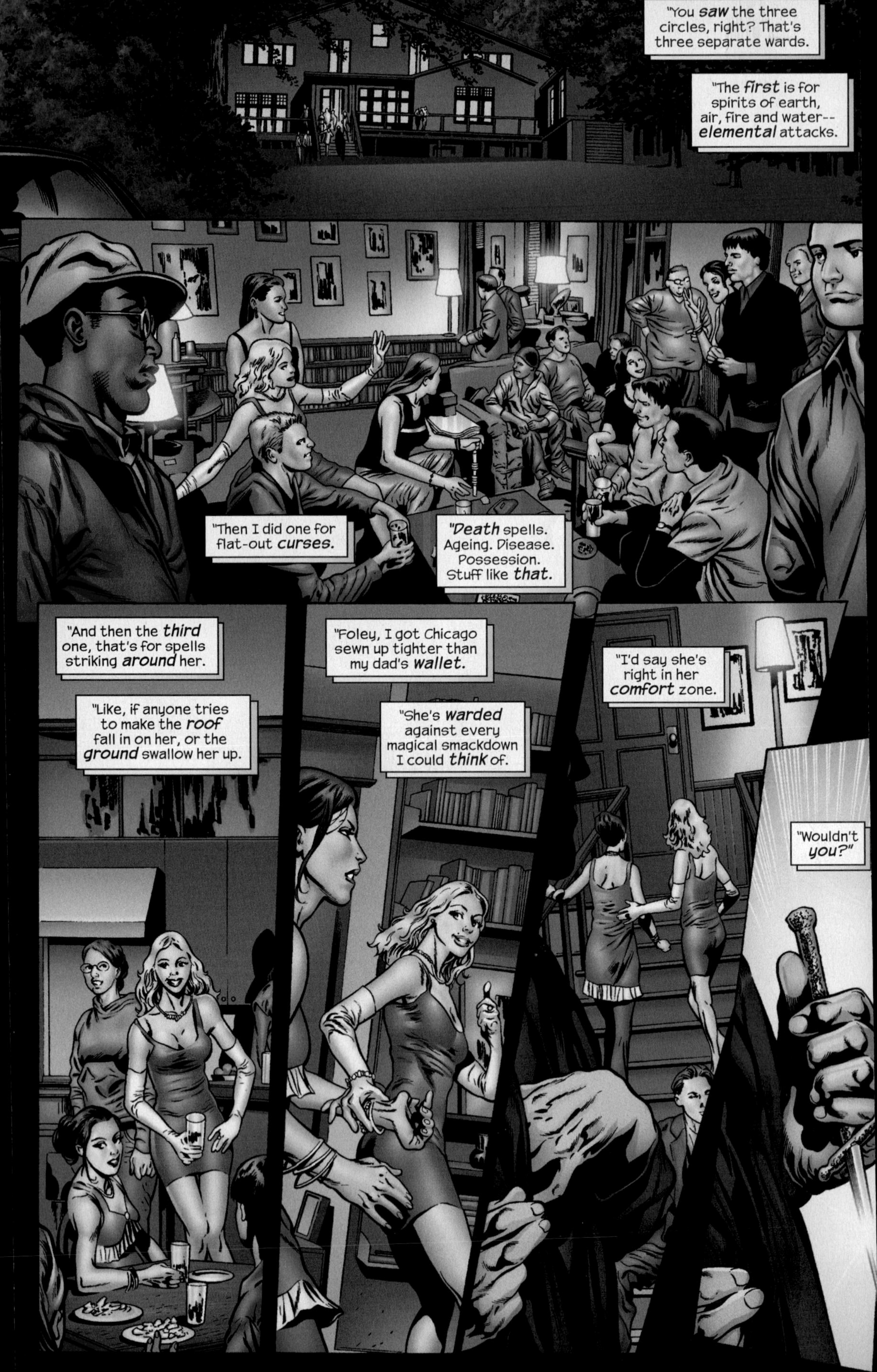
"You saw the three circles, right? That's three separate wards.
"The first is for spirits of earth, air, fire and water-- elemental attacks.
"Then I did one for flat-out curses.
"Death spells. Ageing. Disease. Possession. Stuff like that.
"And then the third one, that's for spells striking around her.
"Like, if anyone tries to make the roof fall in on her, or the ground swallow her up.
"Foley, I got Chicago sewn up tighter than my dad's wallet.
"She's warded against every magical smackdown I could think of.
"I'd say she's right in her comfort zone.
"Wouldn't you?"

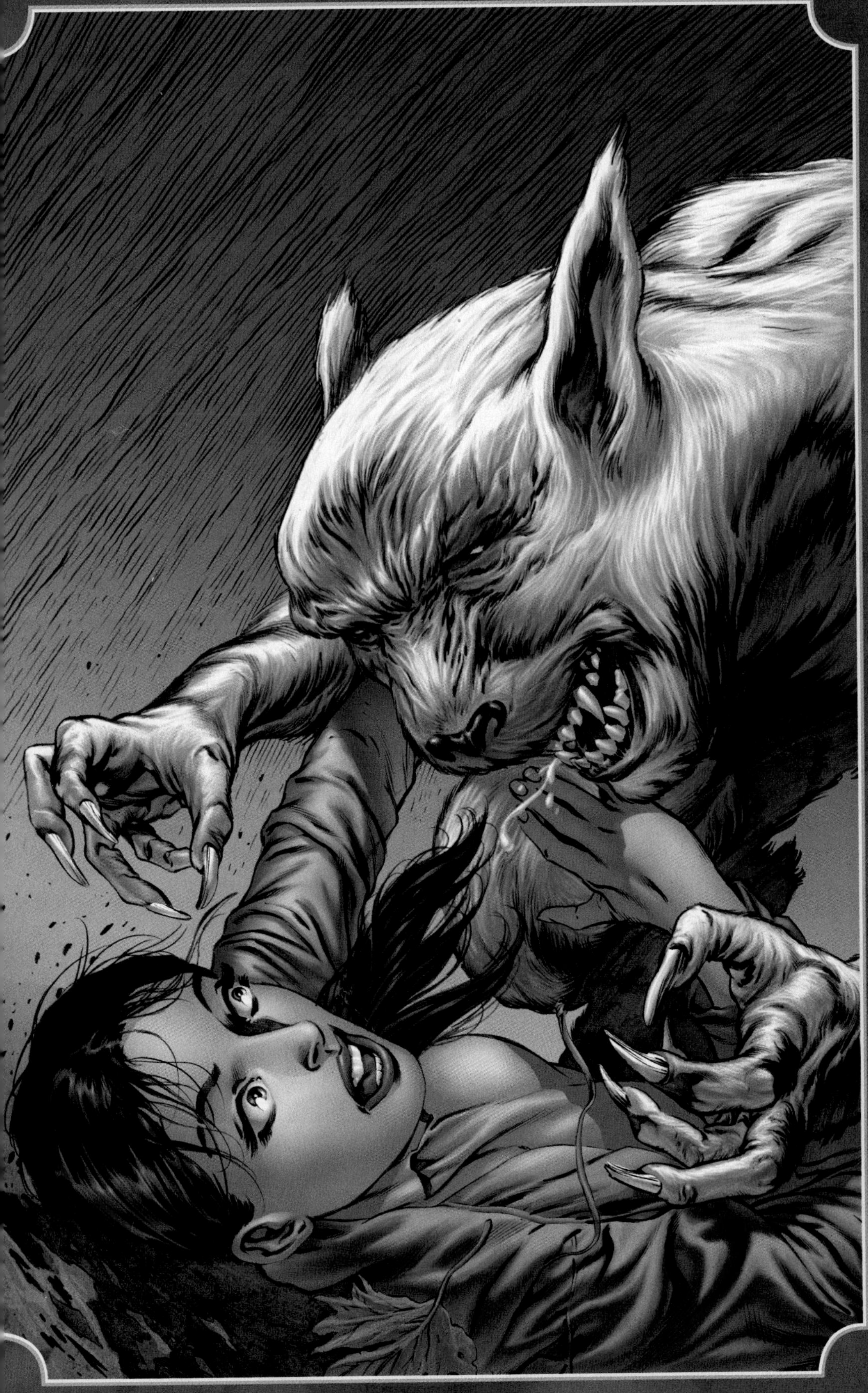

3

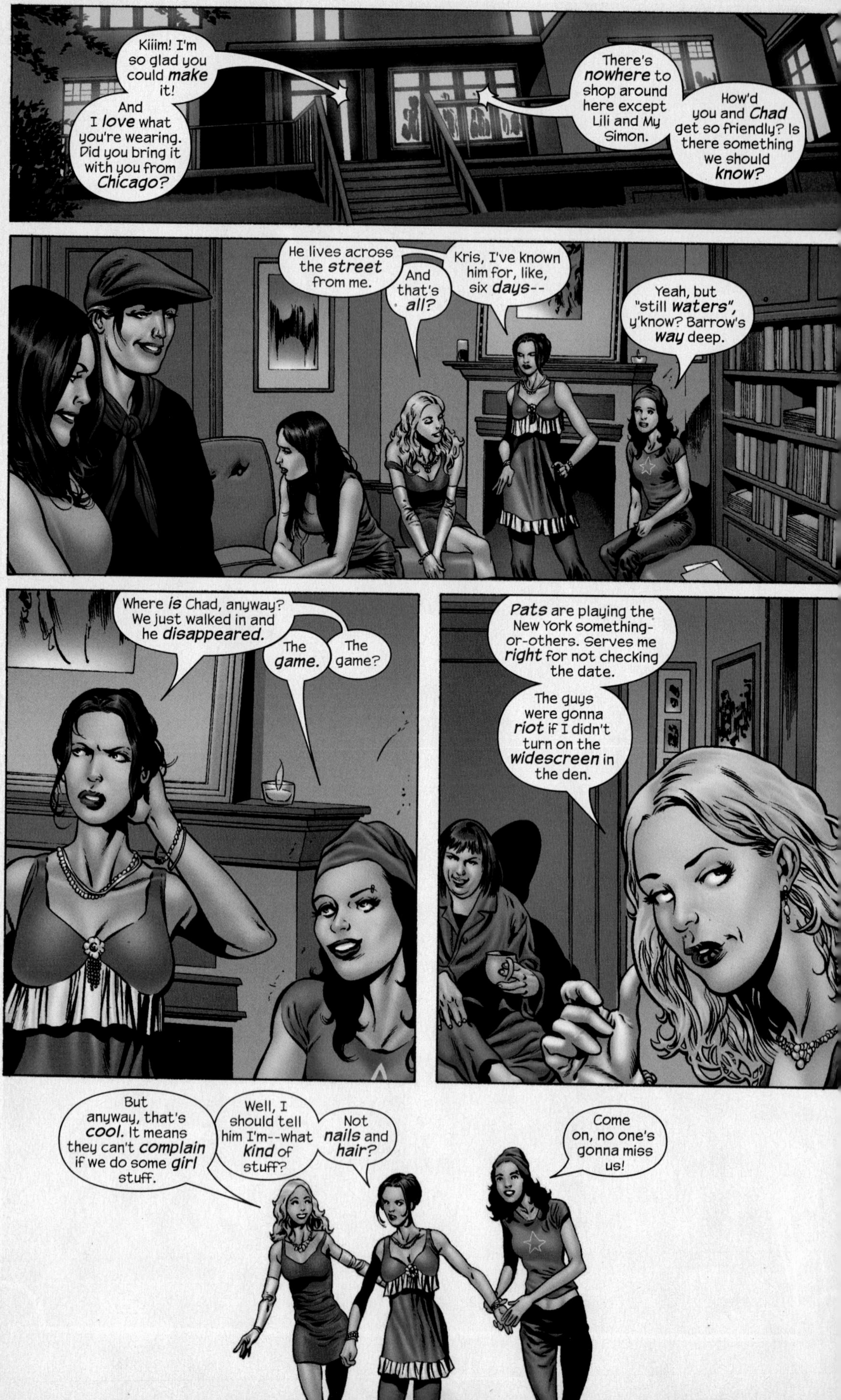

Kiiim! I'm so glad you could make it!
And I love what you're wearing. Did you bring it with you from Chicago?
There's nowhere to shop around here except Lili and My Simon.
How'd you and Chad get so friendly? Is there something we should know?
He lives across the street from me.
And that's all?
Kris, I've known him for, like, six days--
Yeah, but "still waters", y'know? Barrow's way deep.
Where is Chad, anyway? We just walked in and he disappeared.
The game.
The game?
Pats are playing the New York something-or-others. Serves me right for not checking the date.
The guys were gonna riot if I didn't turn on the widescreen in the den.
But anyway, that's cool. It means they can't complain if we do some girl stuff.
Well, I should tell him I'm--what kind of stuff?
Not nails and hair?
Come on, no one's gonna miss us!

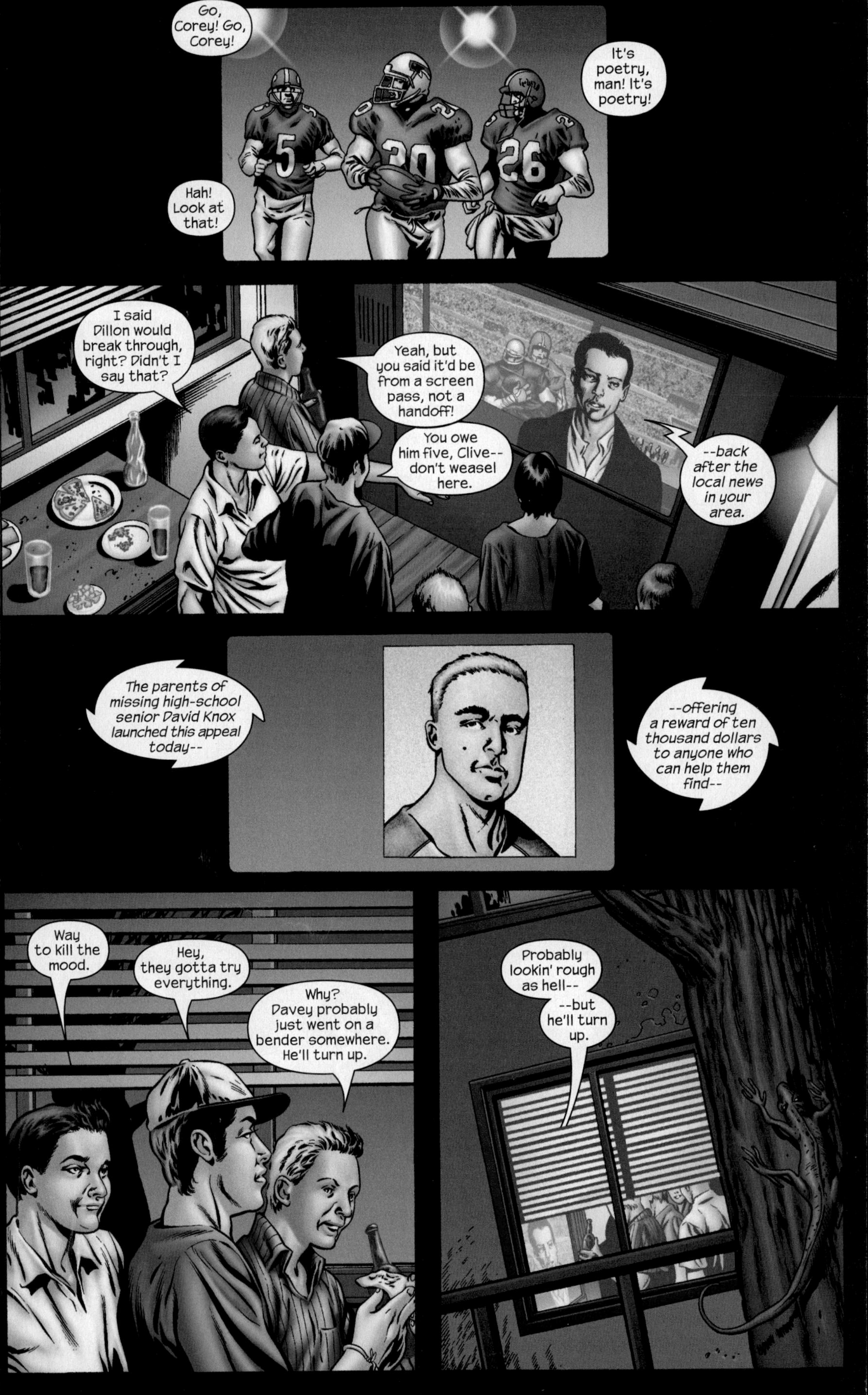
Go, Corey! Go, Corey!
It's poetry, man! It's poetry!
Hah! Look at that!
I said Dillon would break through, right? Didn't I say that?
Yeah, but you said it'd be from a screen pass, not a handoff!
You owe him five, Clive-- don't weasel here.
--back after the local news in your area.
The parents of missing high-school senior David Knox launched this appeal today--
--offering a reward of ten thousand dollars to anyone who can help them find--
Way to kill the mood.
Hey, they gotta try everything.
Why? Davey probably just went on a bender somewhere. He'll turn up.
Probably lookin' rough as hell--
--but he'll turn up.

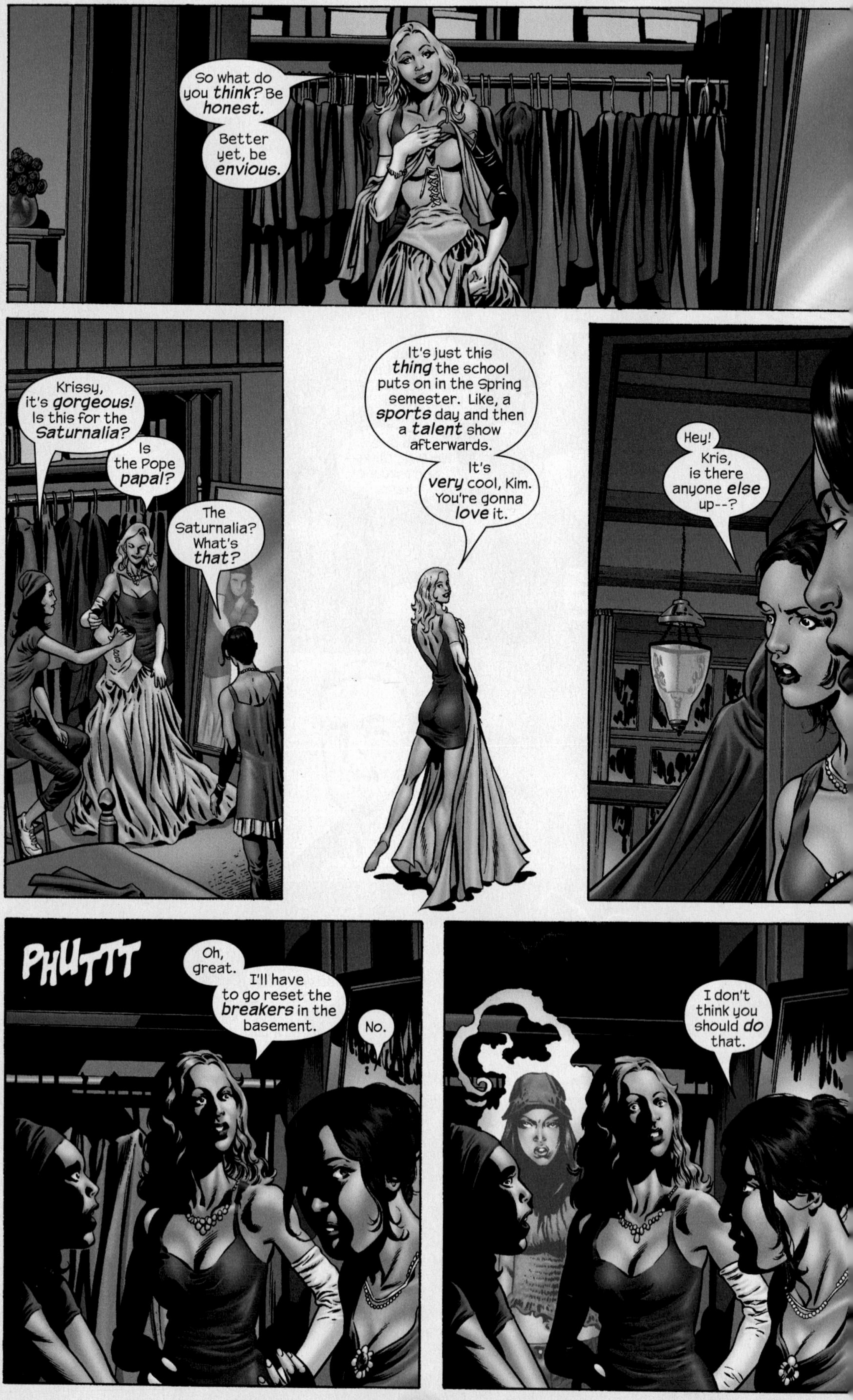
So what do you think? Be honest.
Better yet, be envious.
Krissy, it's gorgeous! Is this for the Saturnalia?
Is the Pope papal?
The Saturnalia? What's that?
It's just this thing the school puts on in the Spring semester. Like, a sports day and then a talent show afterwards.
It's very cool, Kim. You're gonna love it.
Hey! Kris, is there anyone else up--?
PHUTTT
Oh, great.
I'll have to go reset the breakers in the basement.
No.
I don't think you should do that.

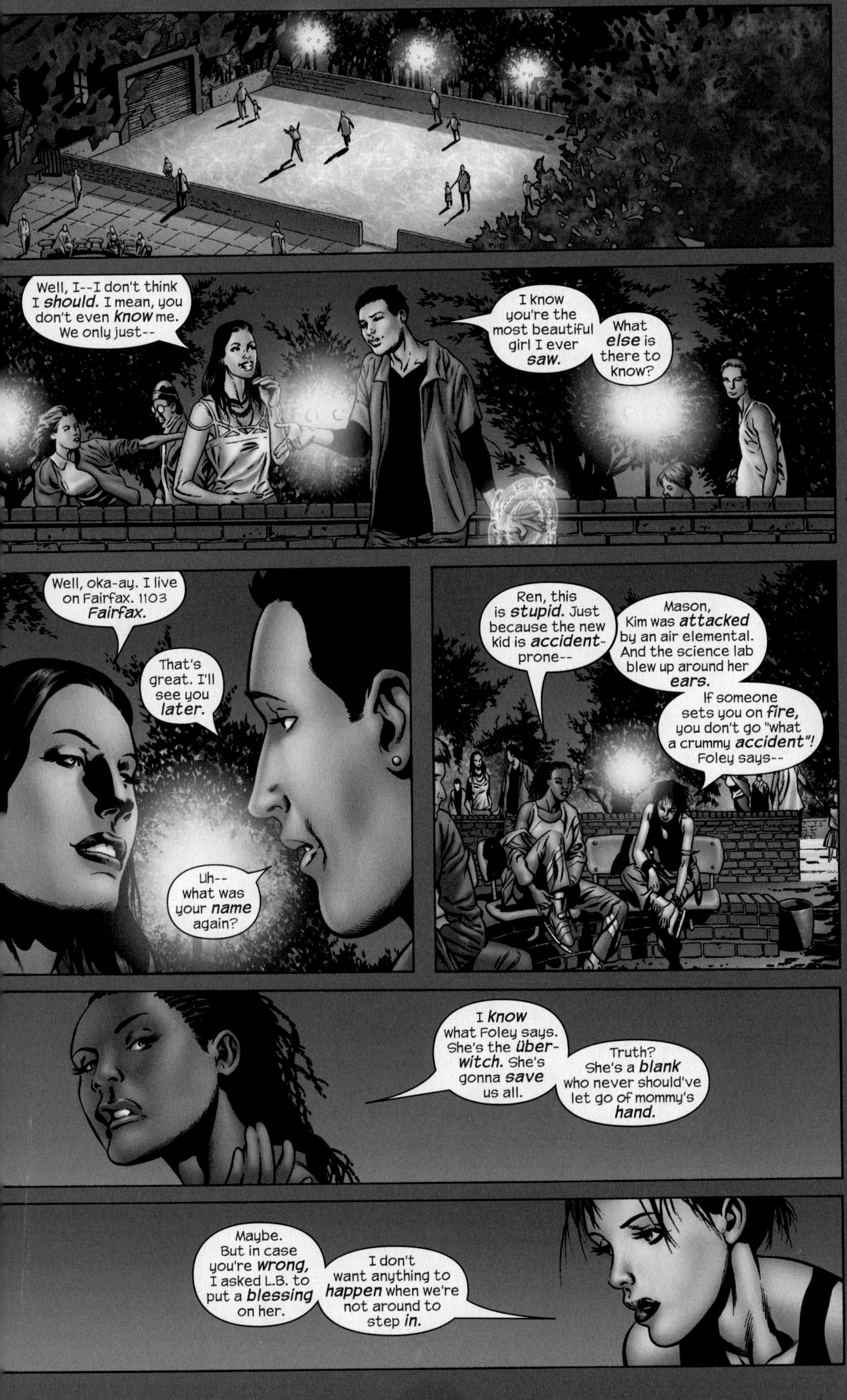

Well, I--I don't think I should. I mean, you don't even know me. We only just--
I know you're the most beautiful girl I ever saw.
What else is there to know?
Well, oka-ay. I live on Fairfax. 1103 Fairfax.
That's great. I'll see you later.
Uh-- what was your name again?
Ren, this is stupid. Just because the new kid is accident-prone--
Mason, Kim was attacked by an air elemental. And the science lab blew up around her ears.
If someone sets you on fire, you don't go "what a crummy accident"! Foley says--
I know what Foley says. She's the über-witch. She's gonna save us all.
Truth? She's a blank who never should've let go of mommy's hand.
Maybe. But in case you're wrong, I asked L.B. to put a blessing on her.
I don't want anything to happen when we're not around to step in.

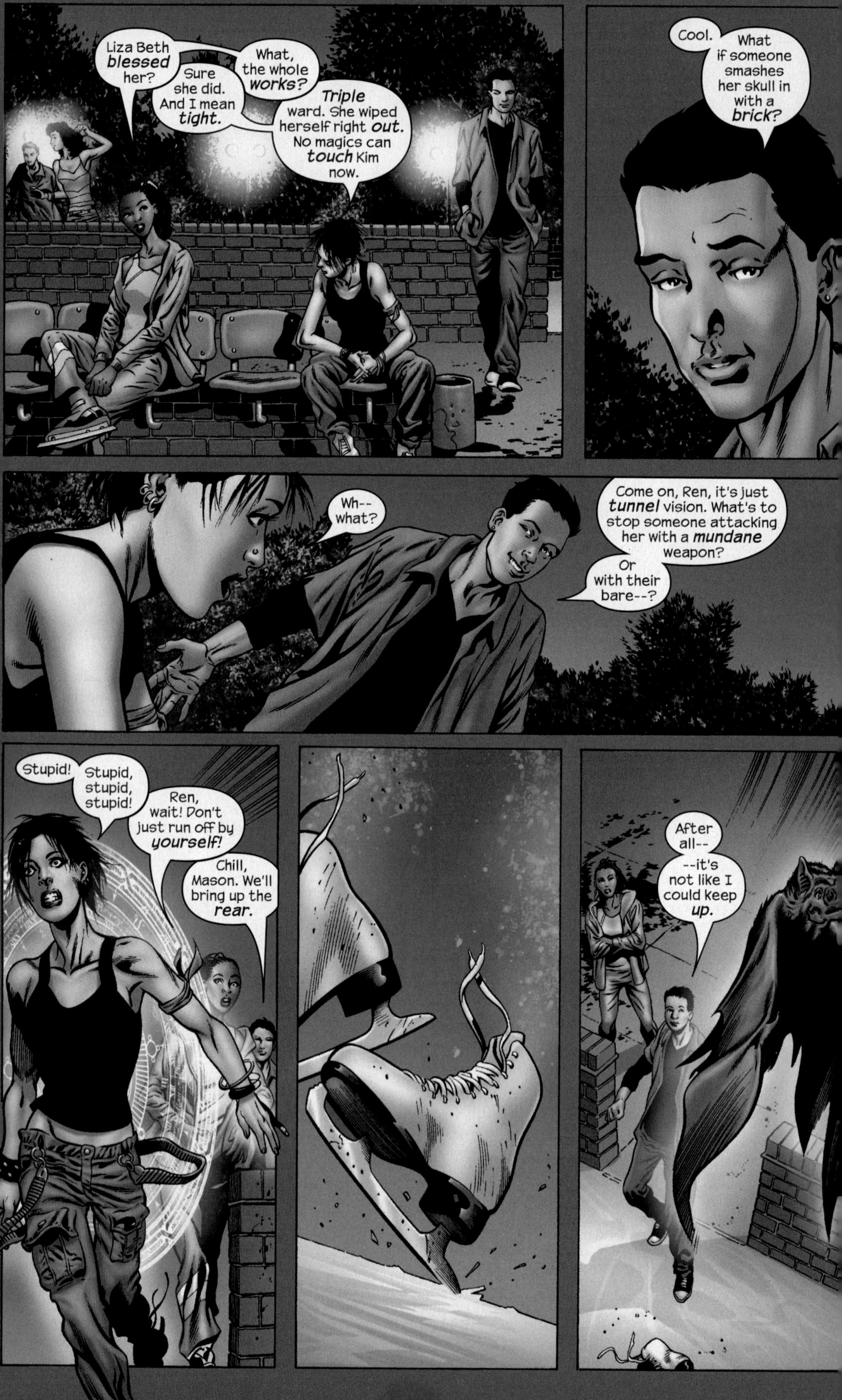

Liza Beth *blessed* her?
What, the whole *works?*
Sure she did. And I mean *tight.*
Triple ward. She wiped herself right *out.* No magics can *touch* Kim now.
Cool.
What if someone smashes her skull in with a *brick?*
Wh-- what?
Come on, Ren, it's just *tunnel* vision. What's to stop someone attacking her with a *mundane* weapon?
Or with their bare--?
Stupid!
Stupid, stupid, stupid!
Ren, wait! Don't just run off by *yourself!*
Chill, Mason. We'll bring up the *rear.*
After all--
--it's not like I could keep *up.*

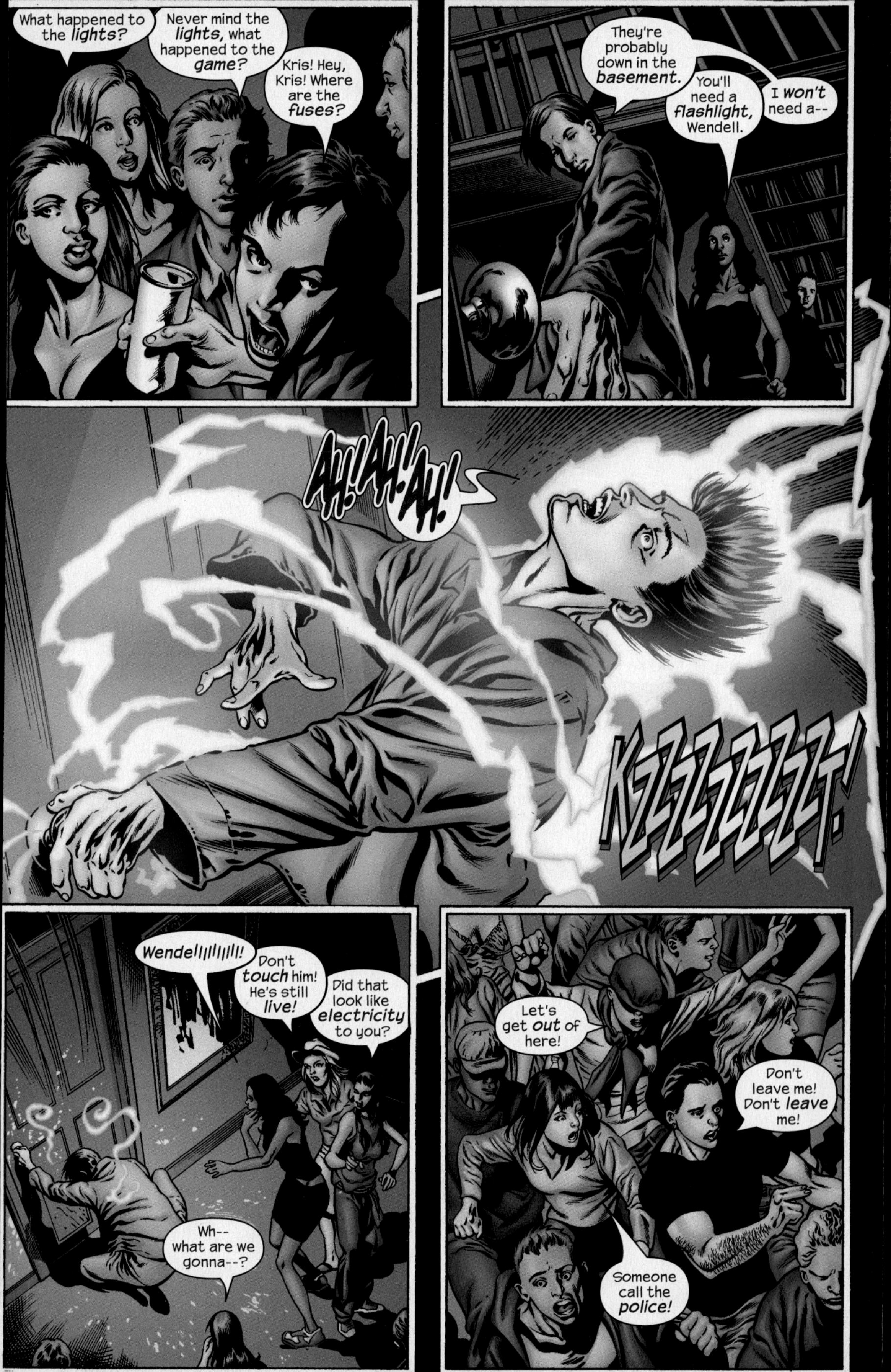
What happened to the lights?
Never mind the lights, what happened to the game?
Kris! Hey, Kris! Where are the fuses?
They're probably down in the basement.
You'll need a flashlight, Wendell.
I won't need a--
AH!-AH!-AH!
KZZZZZZZT!
Wendellllllll!
Don't touch him! He's still live!
Did that look like electricity to you?
Wh-- what are we gonna--?
Let's get out of here!
Don't leave me! Don't leave me!
Someone call the police!

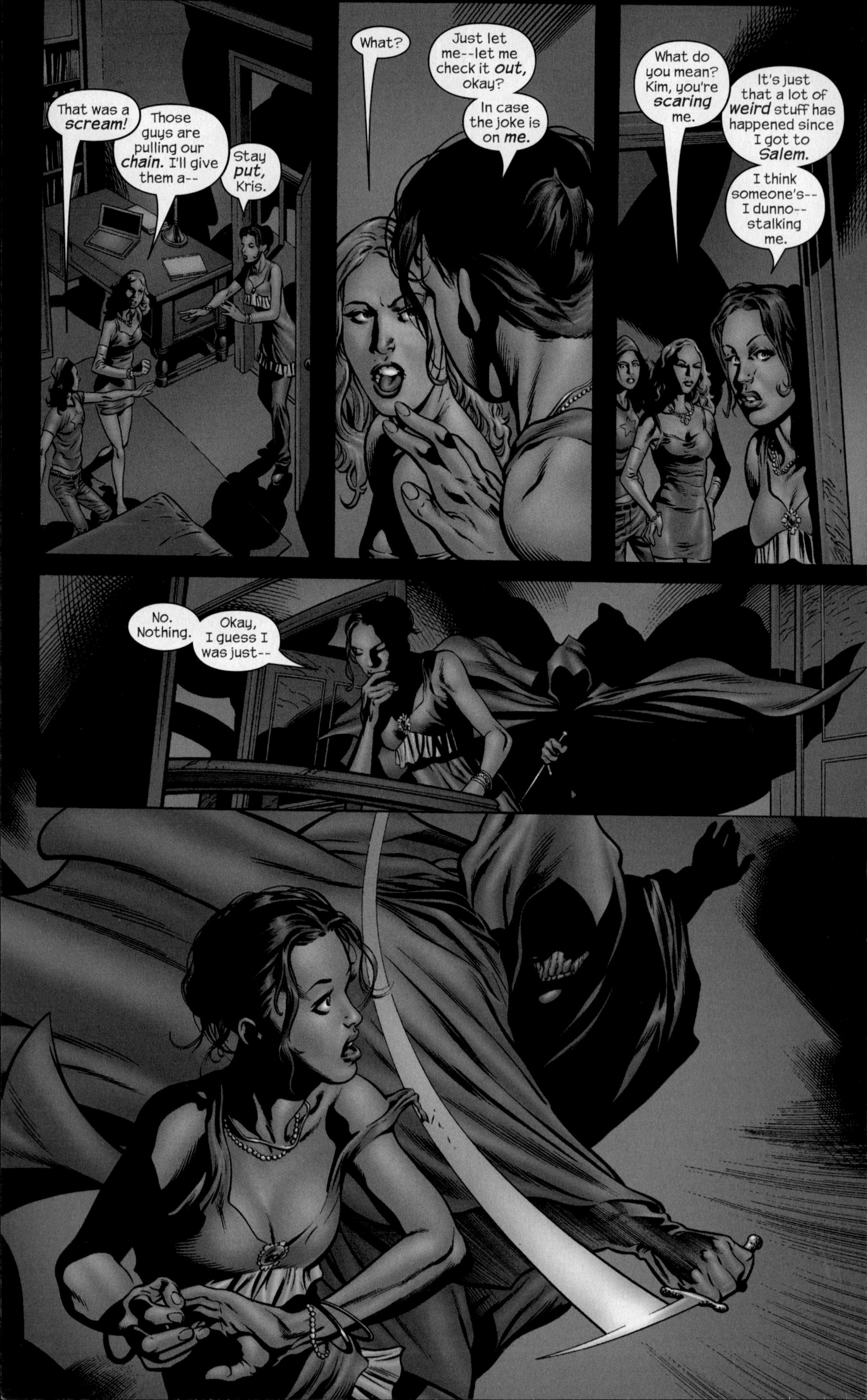
That was a scream!
Those guys are pulling our chain. I'll give them a--
Stay put, Kris.
What?
Just let me--let me check it out, okay?
In case the joke is on me.
What do you mean? Kim, you're scaring me.
It's just that a lot of weird stuff has happened since I got to Salem.
I think someone's-- I dunno-- stalking me.
No. Nothing.
Okay, I guess I was just--

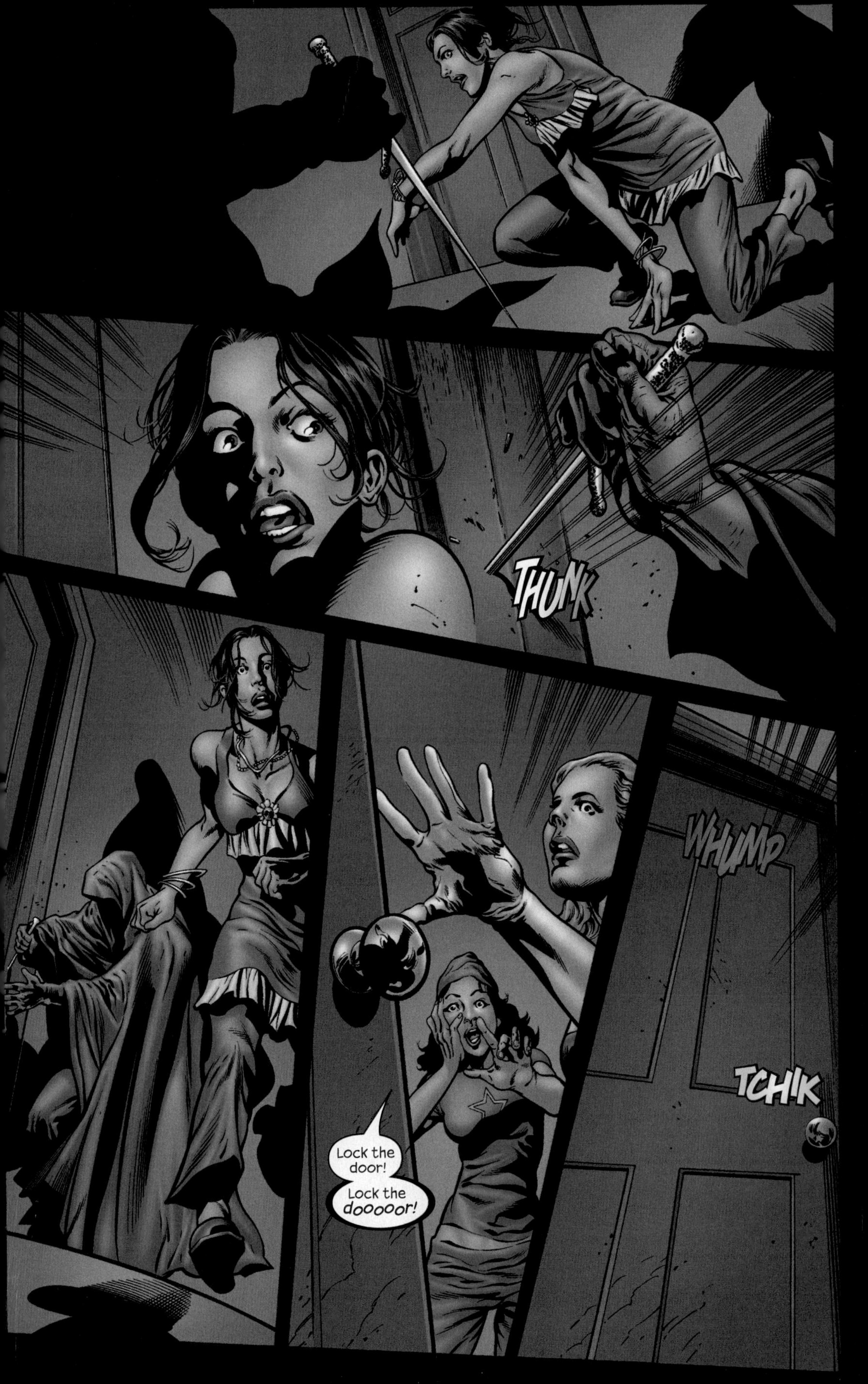
THUNK
WHUMP
TCHIK
Lock the door!
Lock the dooooor!

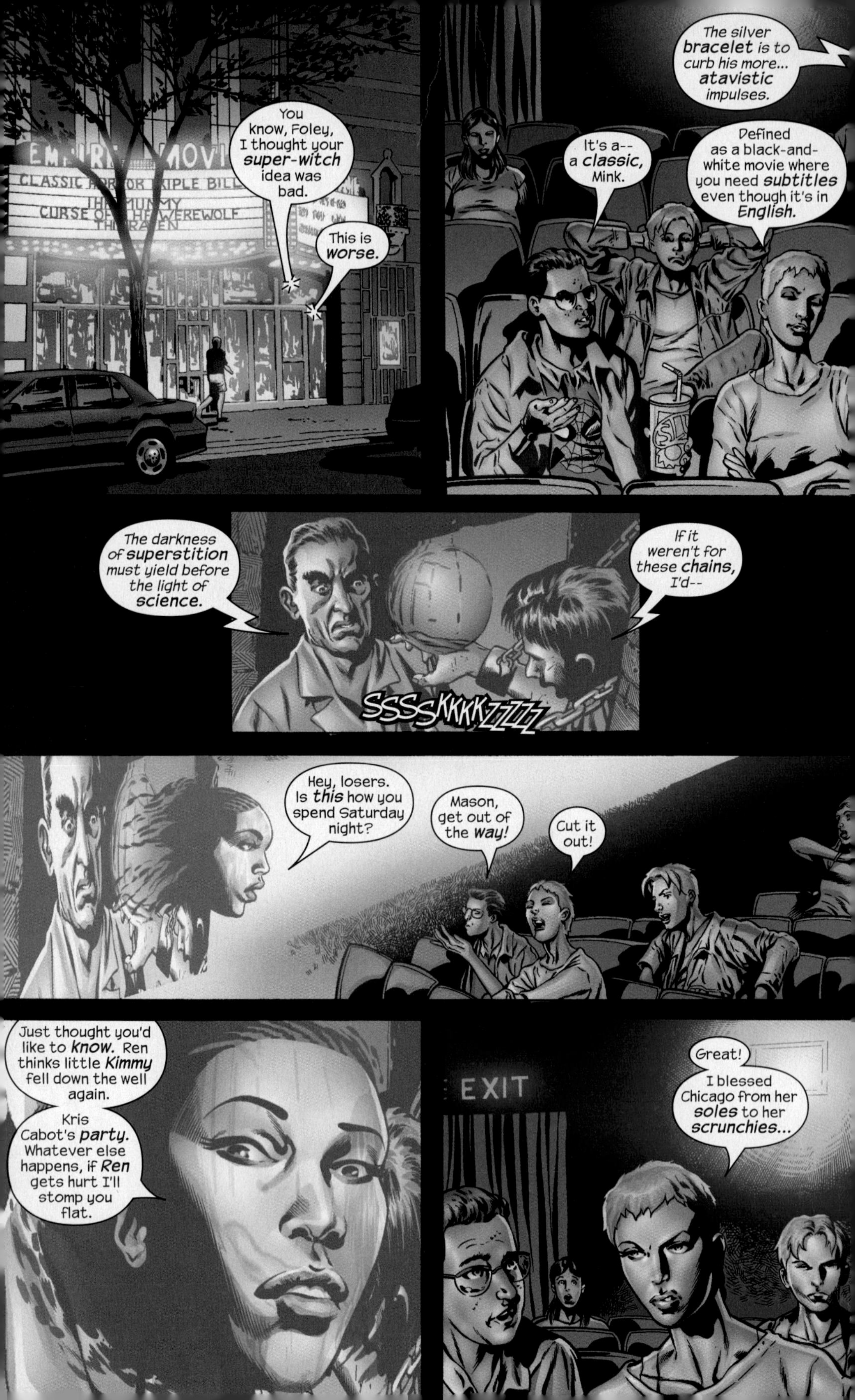

EMPIRE MOVIE
CLASSIC HORROR TRIPLE BILL
THE MUMMY
CURSE OF THE WEREWOLF
THE RAVEN
You know, Foley, I thought your super-witch idea was bad.
This is worse.
The silver bracelet is to curb his more... atavistic impulses.
It's a-- a classic, Mink.
Defined as a black-and-white movie where you need subtitles even though it's in English.
The darkness of superstition must yield before the light of science.
If it weren't for these chains, I'd--
SSSSKKKZZZZZ
Hey, losers. Is this how you spend Saturday night?
Mason, get out of the way!
Cut it out!
Just thought you'd like to know. Ren thinks little Kimmy fell down the well again.
Kris Cabot's party. Whatever else happens, if Ren gets hurt I'll stomp you flat.
EXIT
Great!
I blessed Chicago from her soles to her scrunchies...

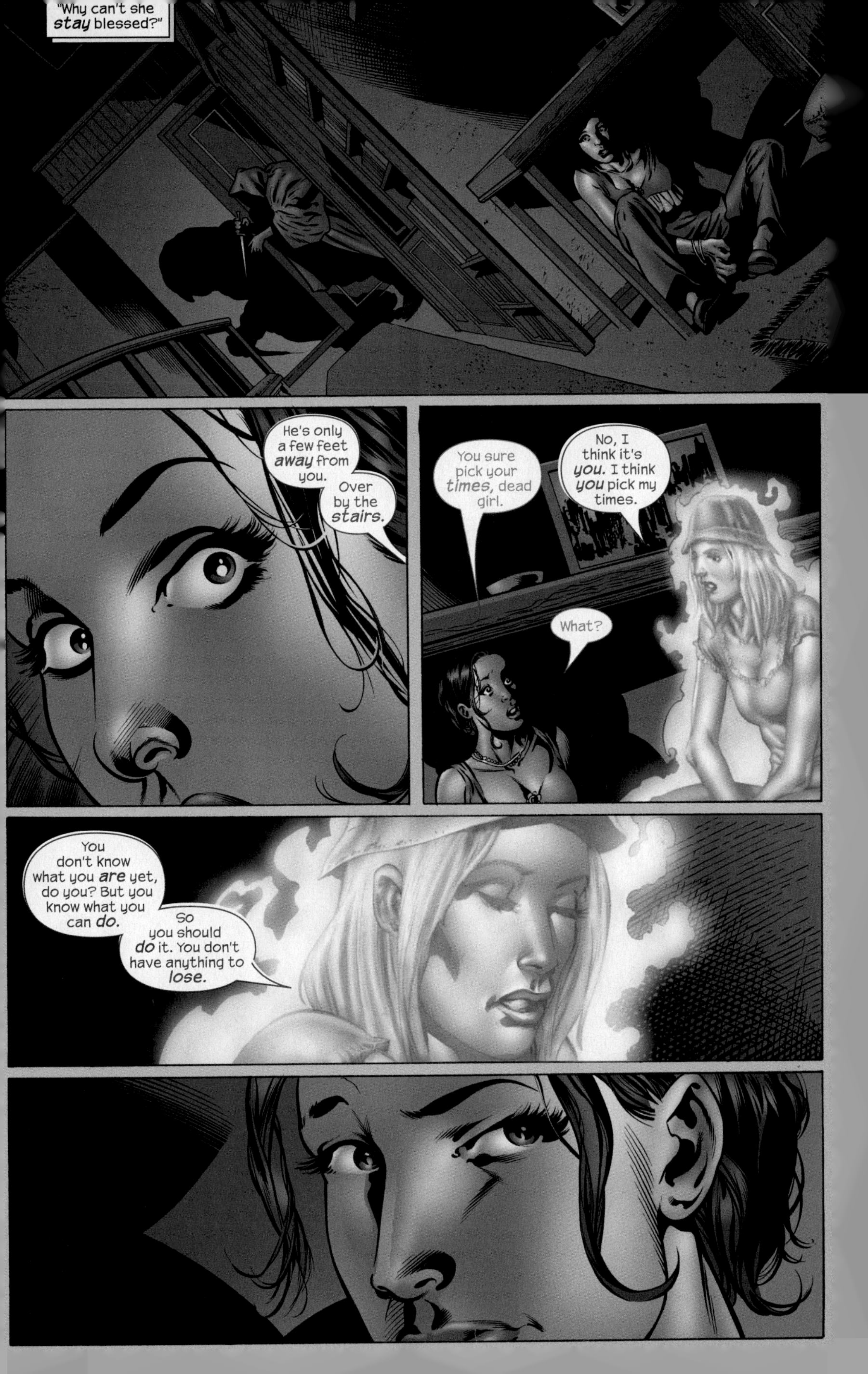
"Why can't she stay blessed?"
He's only a few feet away from you.
Over by the stairs.
You sure pick your times, dead girl.
No, I think it's you. I think you pick my times.
What?
You don't know what you are yet, do you? But you know what you can do.
So you should do it. You don't have anything to lose.

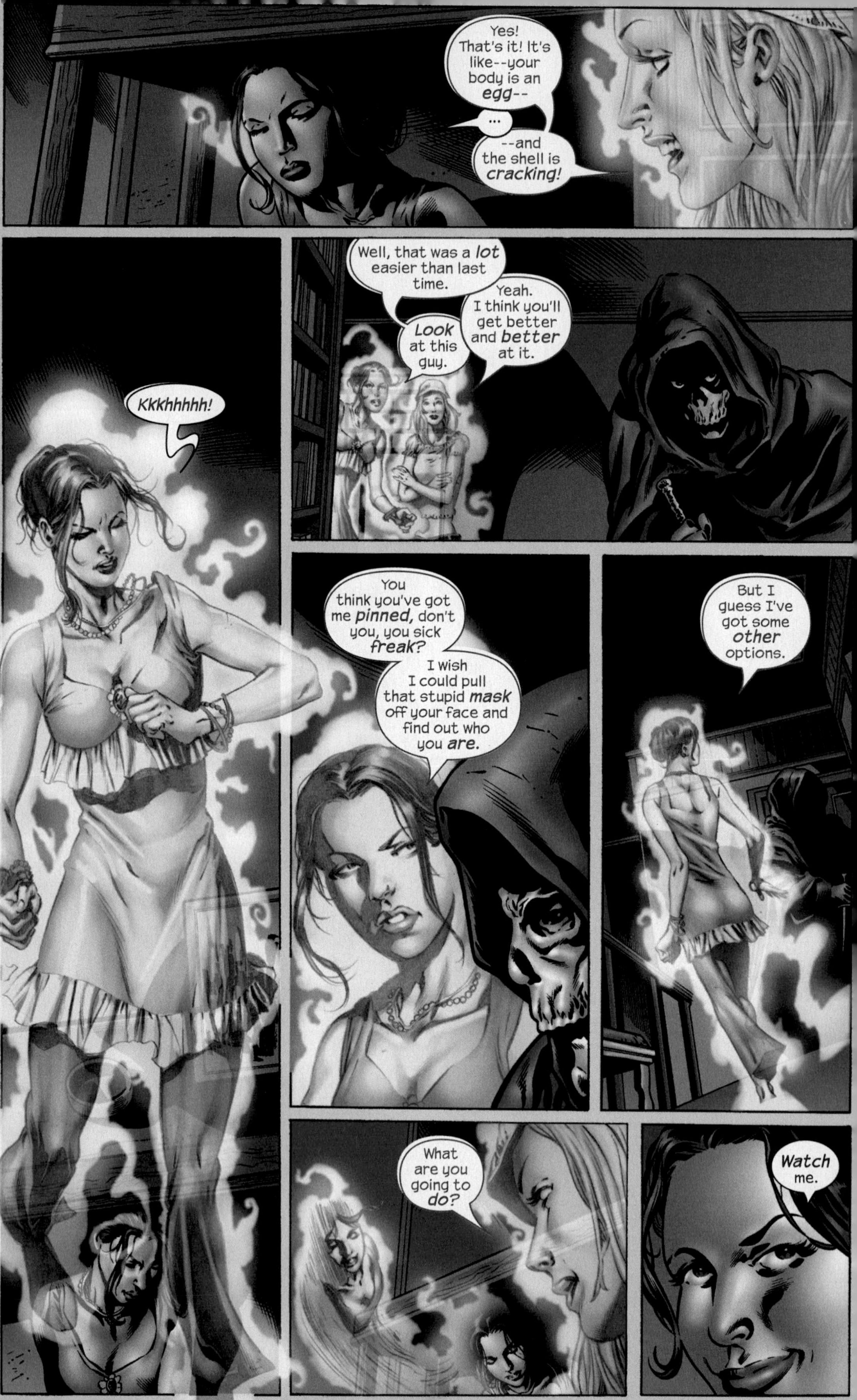
Yes! That's it! It's like--your body is an *egg*--
...
--and the shell is *cracking!*
Well, that was a *lot* easier than last time.
Yeah. I think you'll get better and *better* at it.
Look at this guy.
Kkkhhhhh!
You think you've got me *pinned,* don't you, you sick *freak?*
I wish I could pull that stupid *mask* off your face and find out who you *are.*
But I guess I've got some *other* options.
What are you going to *do?*
Watch me.

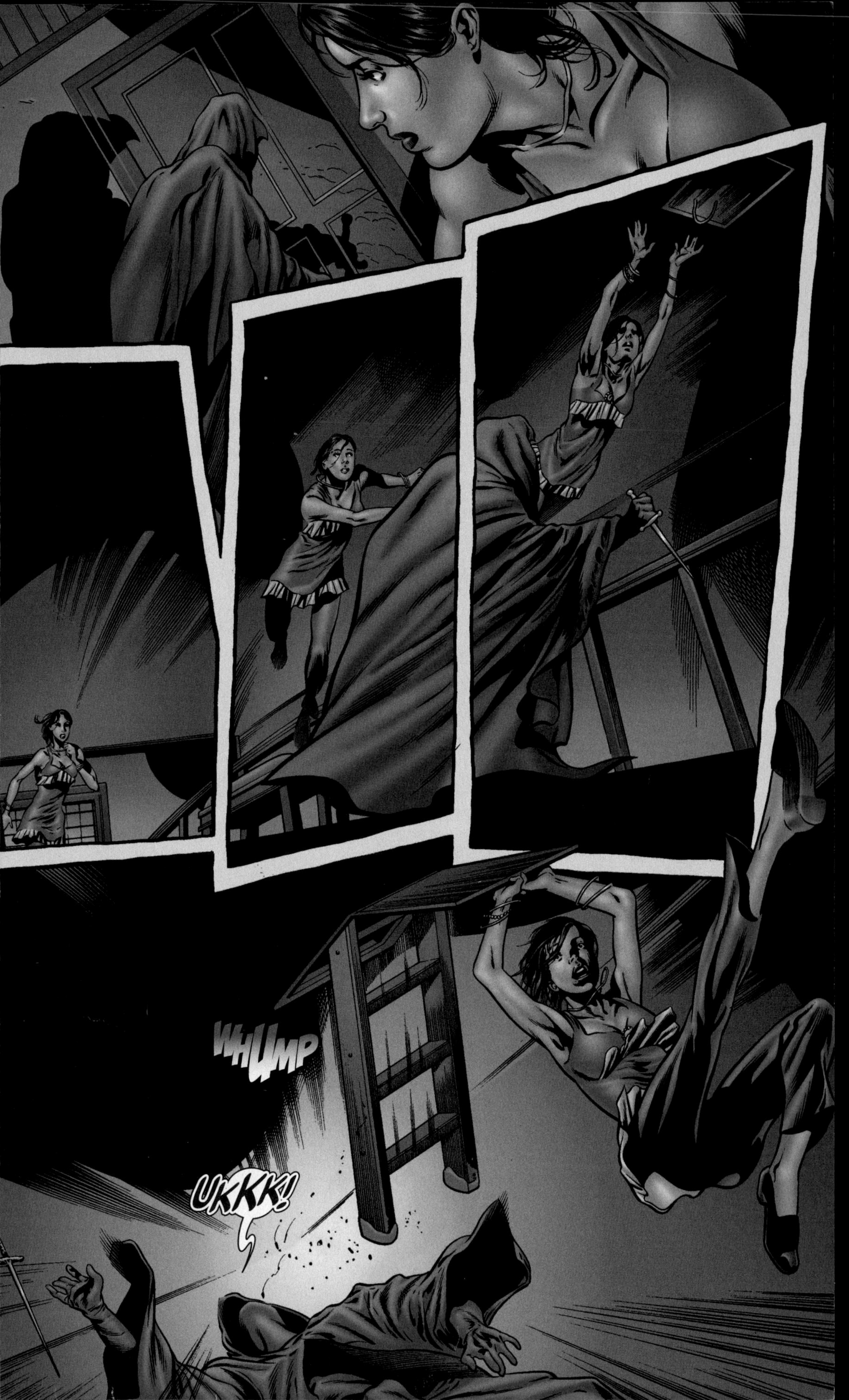
WHUMP
UKKK!

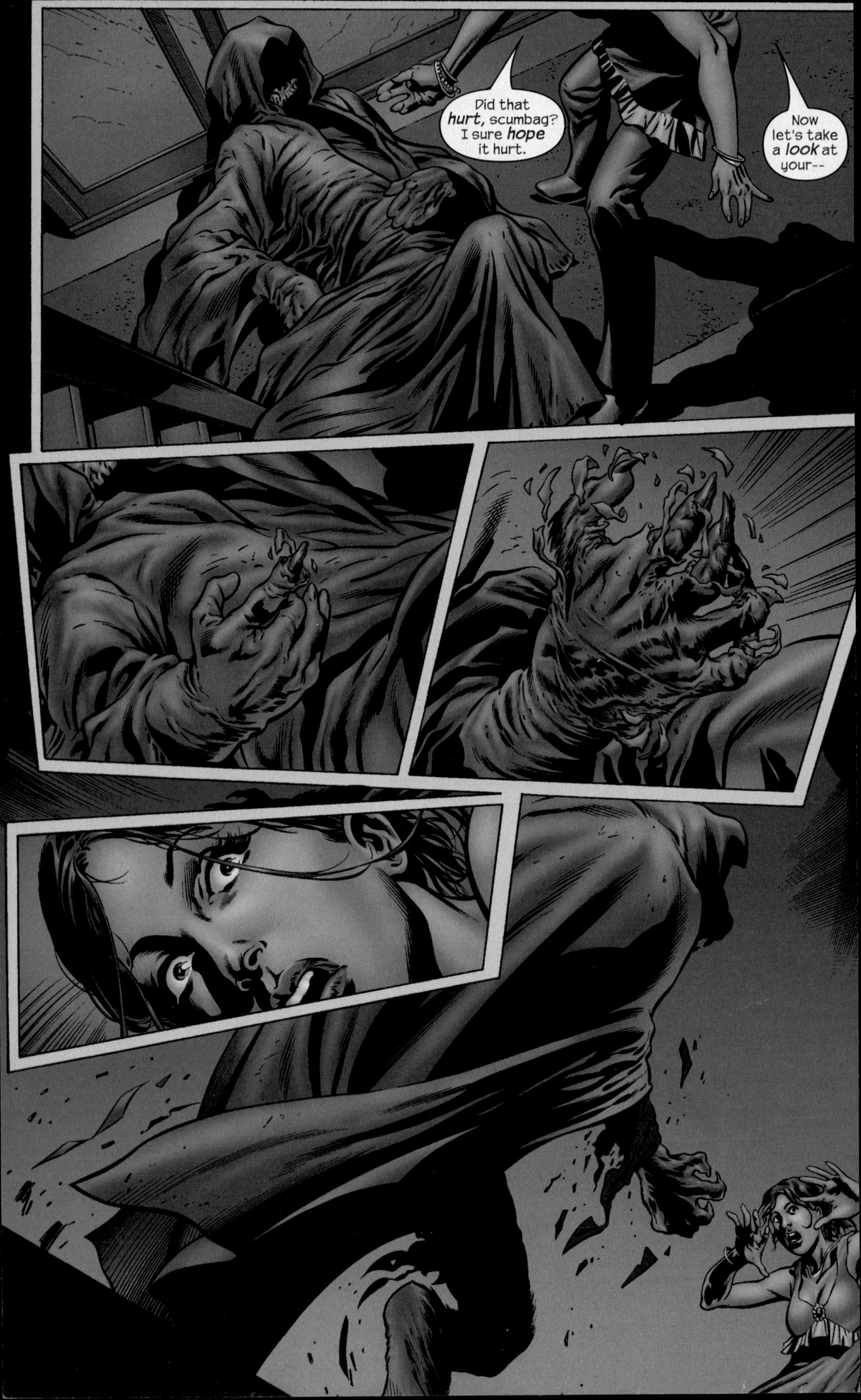
Did that **hurt,** scumbag? I sure **hope** it hurt.
Now let's take a **look** at your--

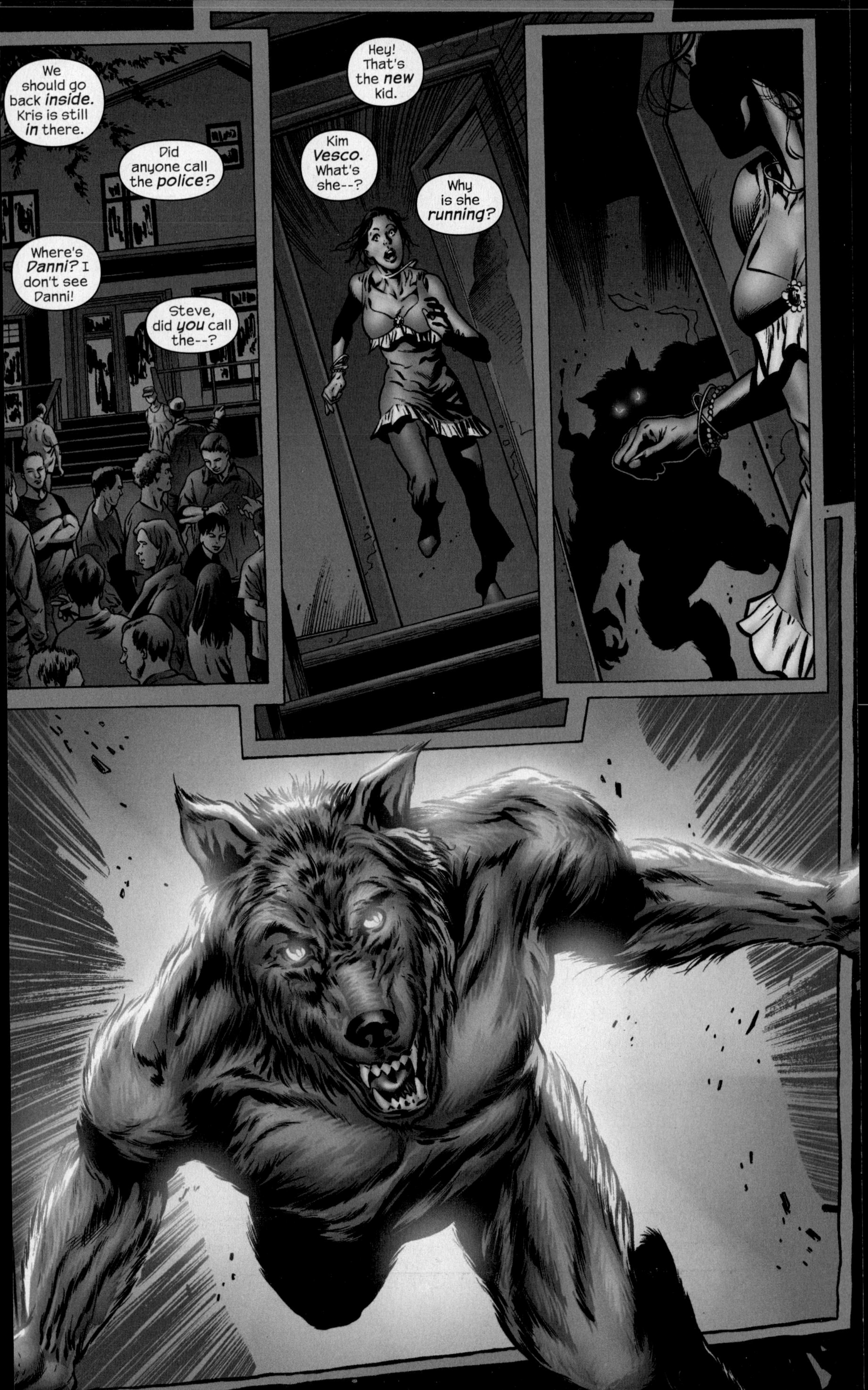
We should go back *inside.* Kris is still *in* there.
Did anyone call the *police?*
Where's *Danni?* I don't see Danni!
Steve, did *you* call the--?
Hey! That's the *new* kid.
Kim *Vesco.* What's she--?
Why is she *running?*

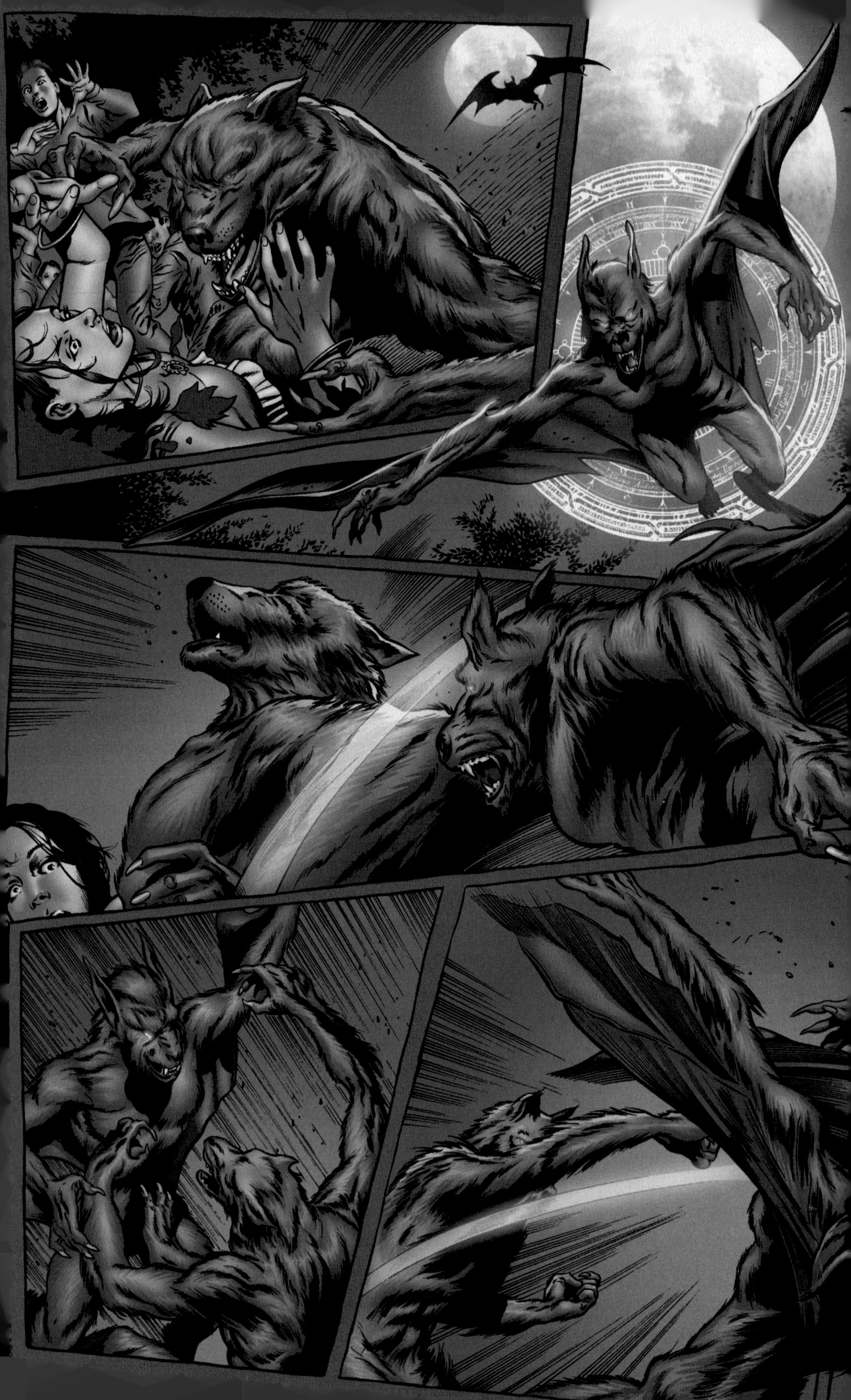

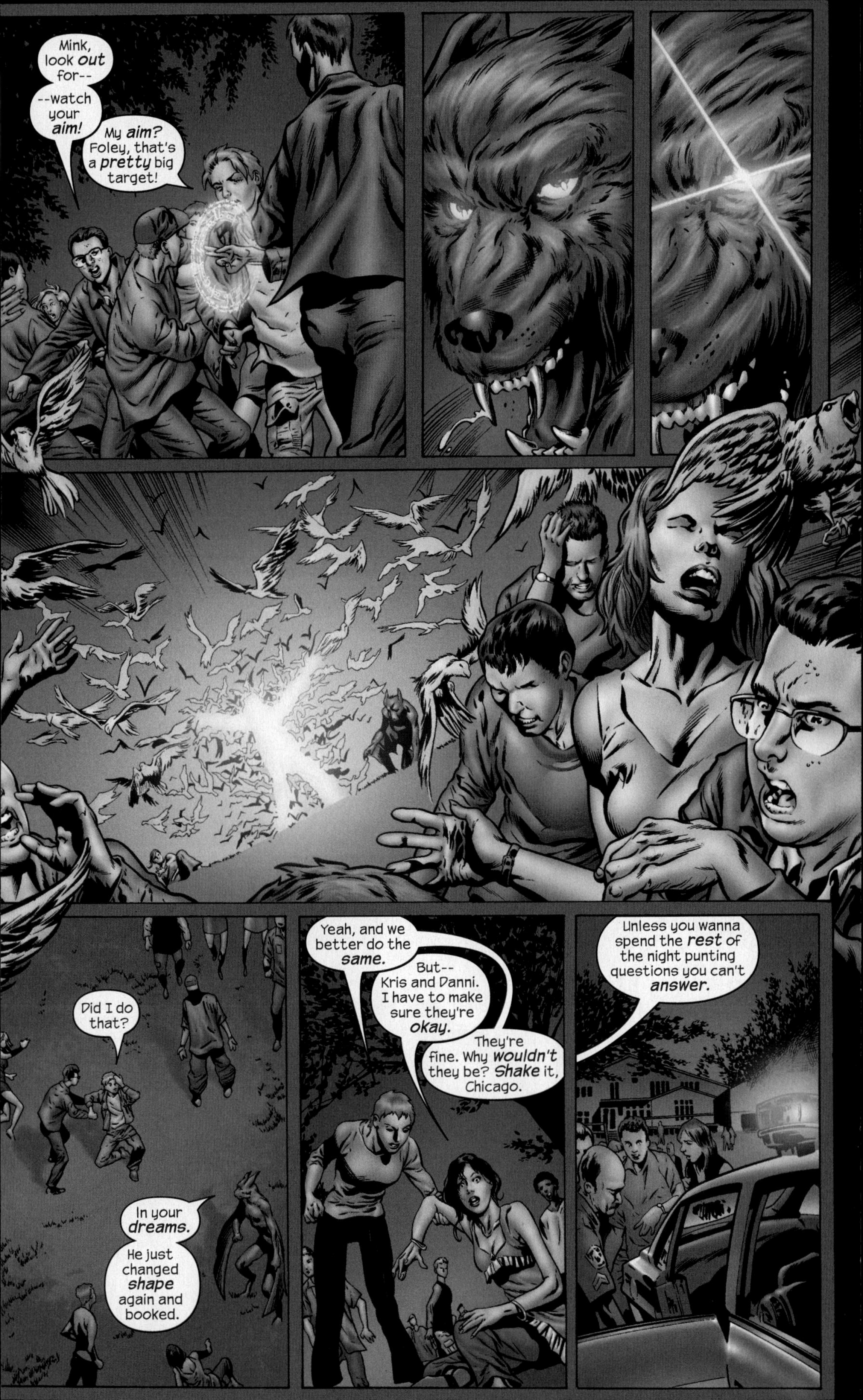

Mink, look out for--
--watch your aim!
My aim? Foley, that's a pretty big target!
Did I do that?
In your dreams.
He just changed shape again and booked.
Yeah, and we better do the same.
But-- Kris and Danni. I have to make sure they're okay.
They're fine. Why wouldn't they be? Shake it, Chicago.
Unless you wanna spend the rest of the night punting questions you can't answer.

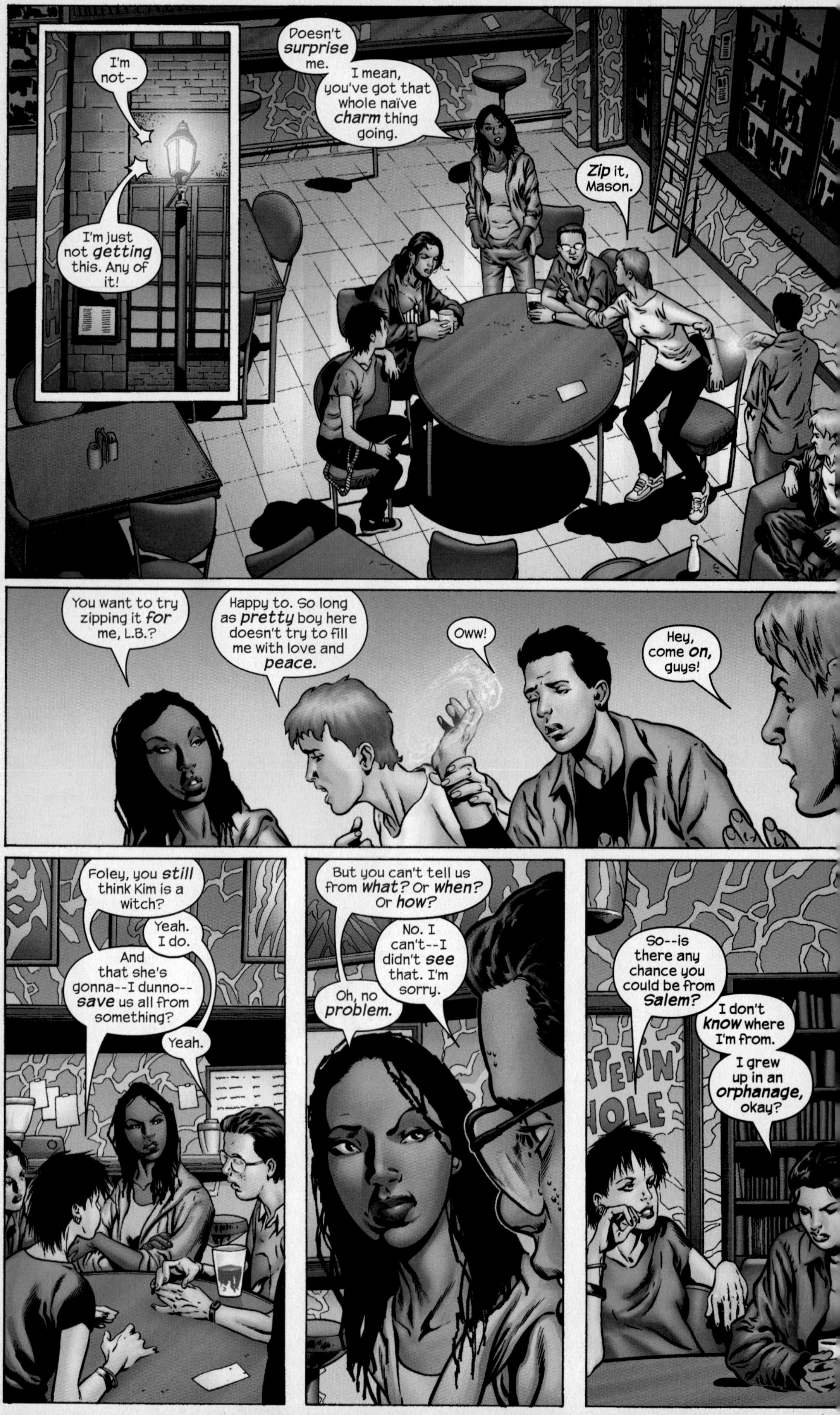
I'm not--
I'm just not getting this. Any of it!
Doesn't surprise me.
I mean, you've got that whole naïve charm thing going.
Zip it, Mason.
You want to try zipping it for me, L.B.?
Happy to. So long as pretty boy here doesn't try to fill me with love and peace.
Oww!
Hey, come on, guys!
Foley, you still think Kim is a witch?
Yeah. I do.
And that she's gonna--I dunno--save us all from something?
Yeah.
But you can't tell us from what? Or when? Or how?
No. I can't--I didn't see that. I'm sorry.
Oh, no problem.
So--is there any chance you could be from Salem?
I don't know where I'm from.
I grew up in an orphanage, okay?

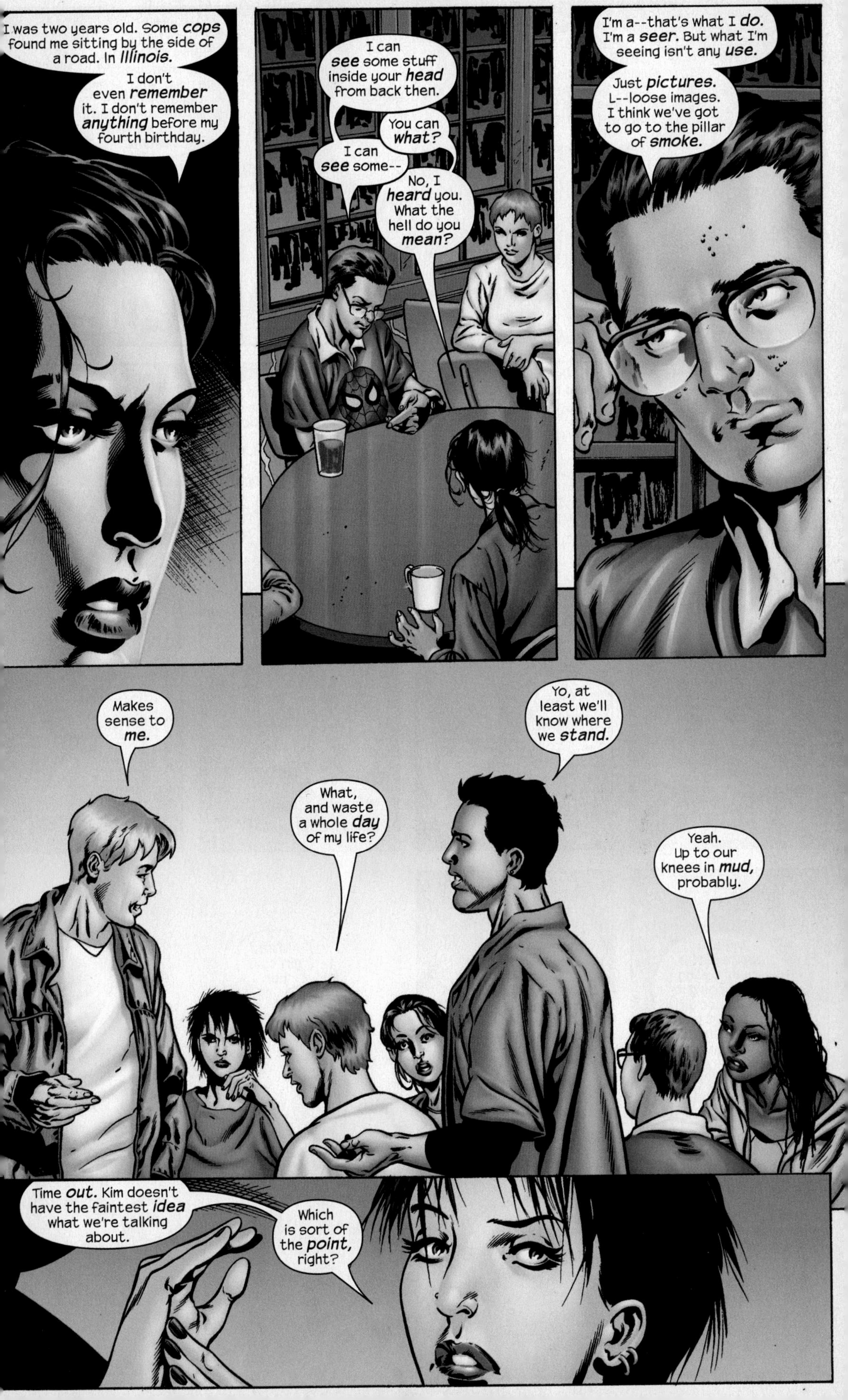
I was two years old. Some cops found me sitting by the side of a road. In Illinois.
I don't even remember it. I don't remember anything before my fourth birthday.
I can see some stuff inside your head from back then.
You can what?
I can see some--
No, I heard you. What the hell do you mean?
I'm a--that's what I do. I'm a seer. But what I'm seeing isn't any use.
Just pictures. L--loose images. I think we've got to go to the pillar of smoke.
Makes sense to me.
What, and waste a whole day of my life?
Yo, at least we'll know where we stand.
Yeah. Up to our knees in mud, probably.
Time out. Kim doesn't have the faintest idea what we're talking about.
Which is sort of the point, right?

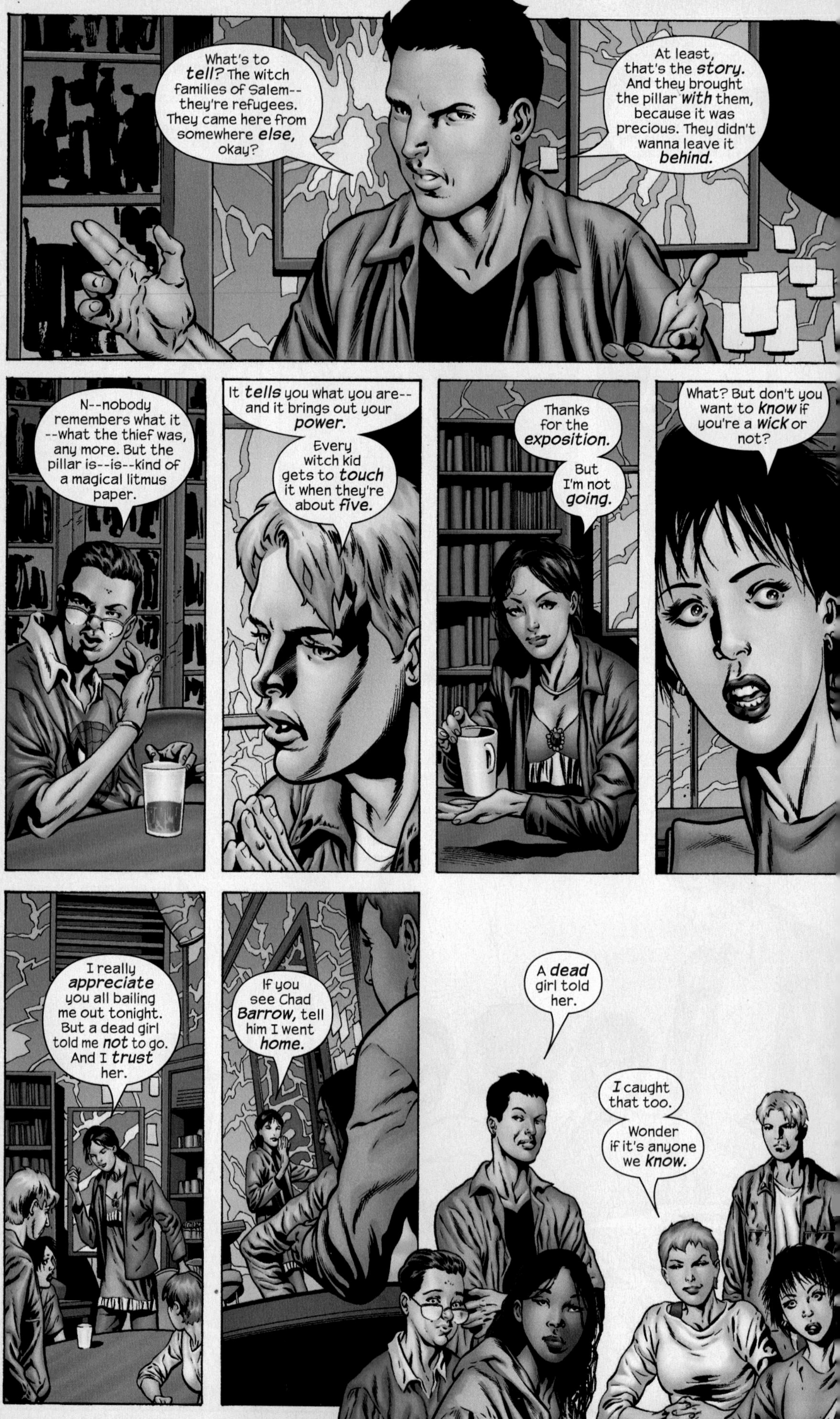
What's to tell? The witch families of Salem--they're refugees. They came here from somewhere else, okay?
At least, that's the story. And they brought the pillar with them, because it was precious. They didn't wanna leave it behind.
N--nobody remembers what it --what the thief was, any more. But the pillar is--is--kind of a magical litmus paper.
It tells you what you are--and it brings out your power.
Every witch kid gets to touch it when they're about five.
Thanks for the exposition.
But I'm not going.
What? But don't you want to know if you're a wick or not?
I really appreciate you all bailing me out tonight. But a dead girl told me not to go. And I trust her.
If you see Chad Barrow, tell him I went home.
A dead girl told her.
I caught that too.
Wonder if it's anyone we know.

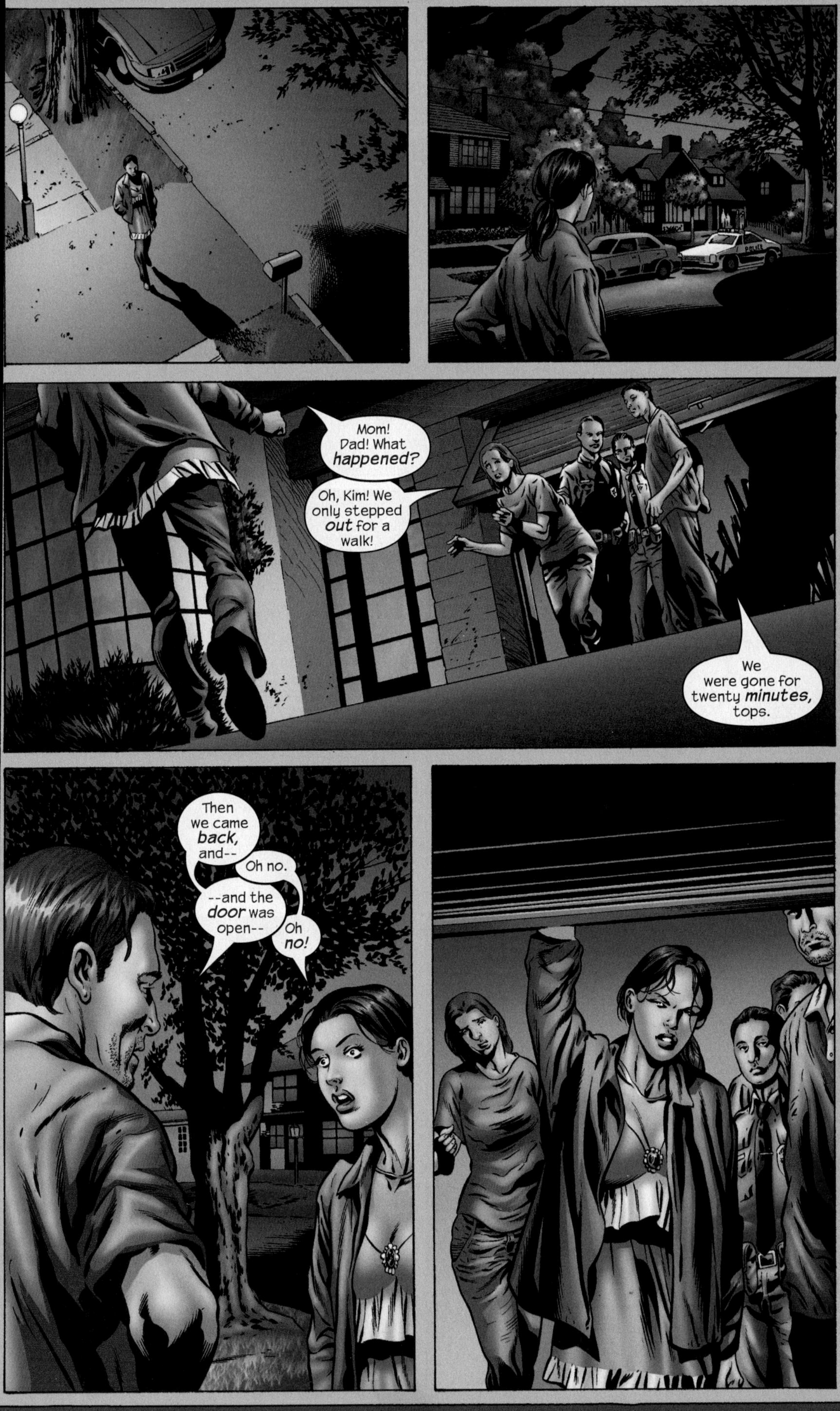
Mom! Dad! What *happened?*
Oh, Kim! We only stepped *out* for a walk!
We were gone for twenty *minutes,* tops.
Then we came *back,* and--
Oh no.
--and the *door* was open--
Oh *no!*

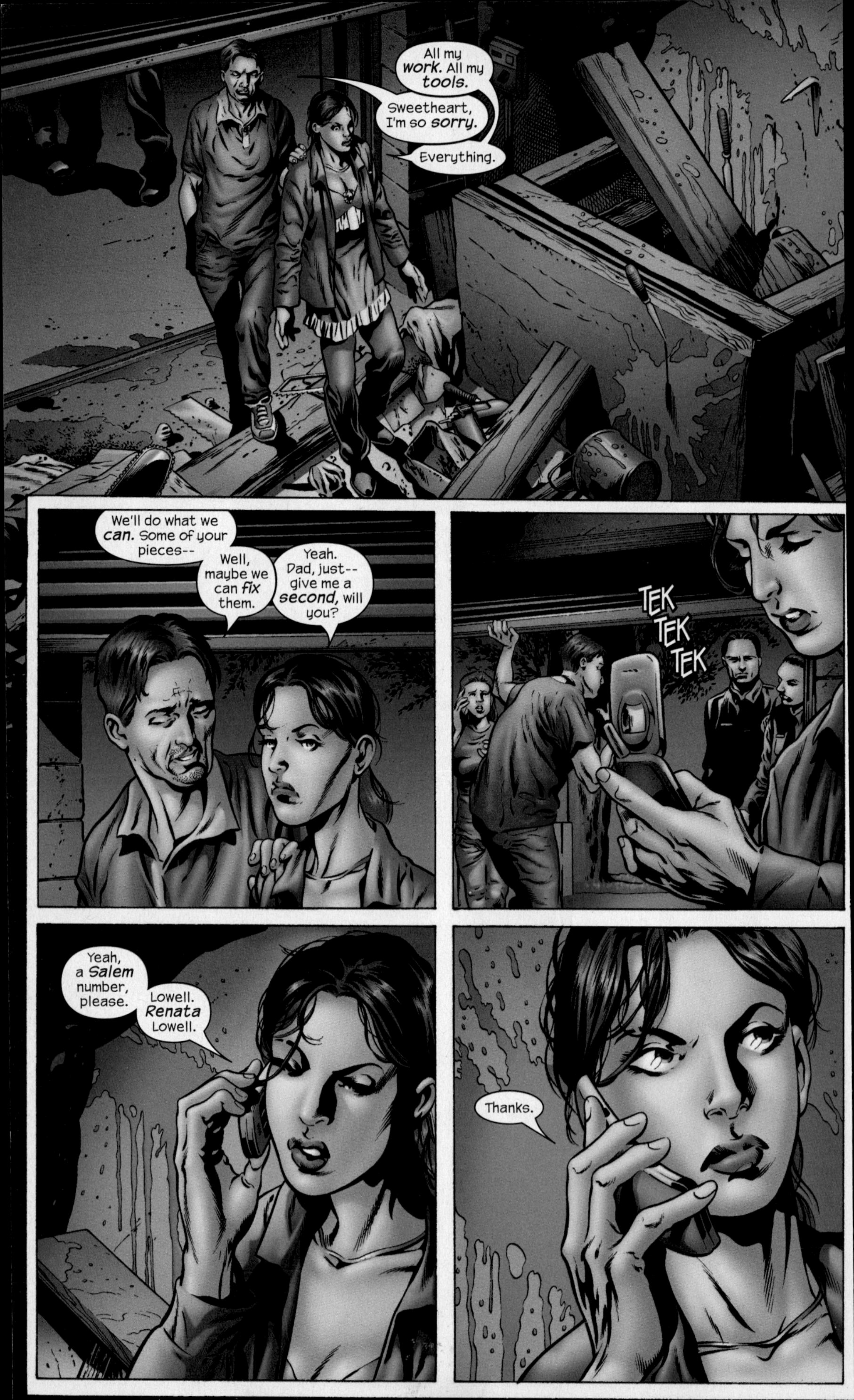
All my work. All my tools.
Sweetheart, I'm so sorry.
Everything.
We'll do what we can. Some of your pieces--
Well, maybe we can fix them.
Yeah. Dad, just-- give me a second, will you?
TEK TEK TEK
Yeah, a Salem number, please.
Lowell. Renata Lowell.
Thanks.

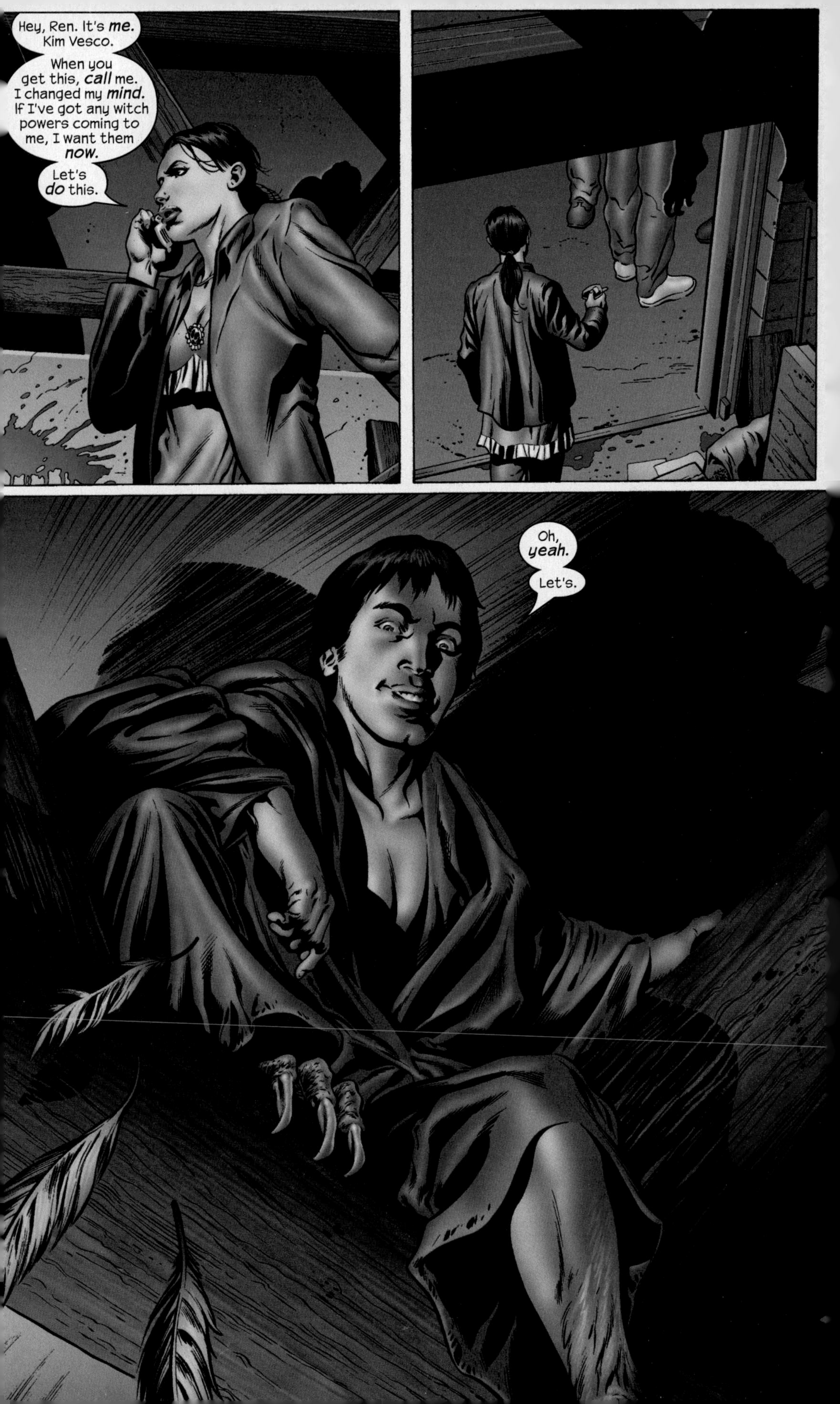
Hey, Ren. It's **me.** Kim Vesco.
When you get this, ***call*** me. I changed my ***mind.*** If I've got any witch powers coming to me, I want them ***now.***
Let's ***do*** this.
Oh, ***yeah.***
Let's.

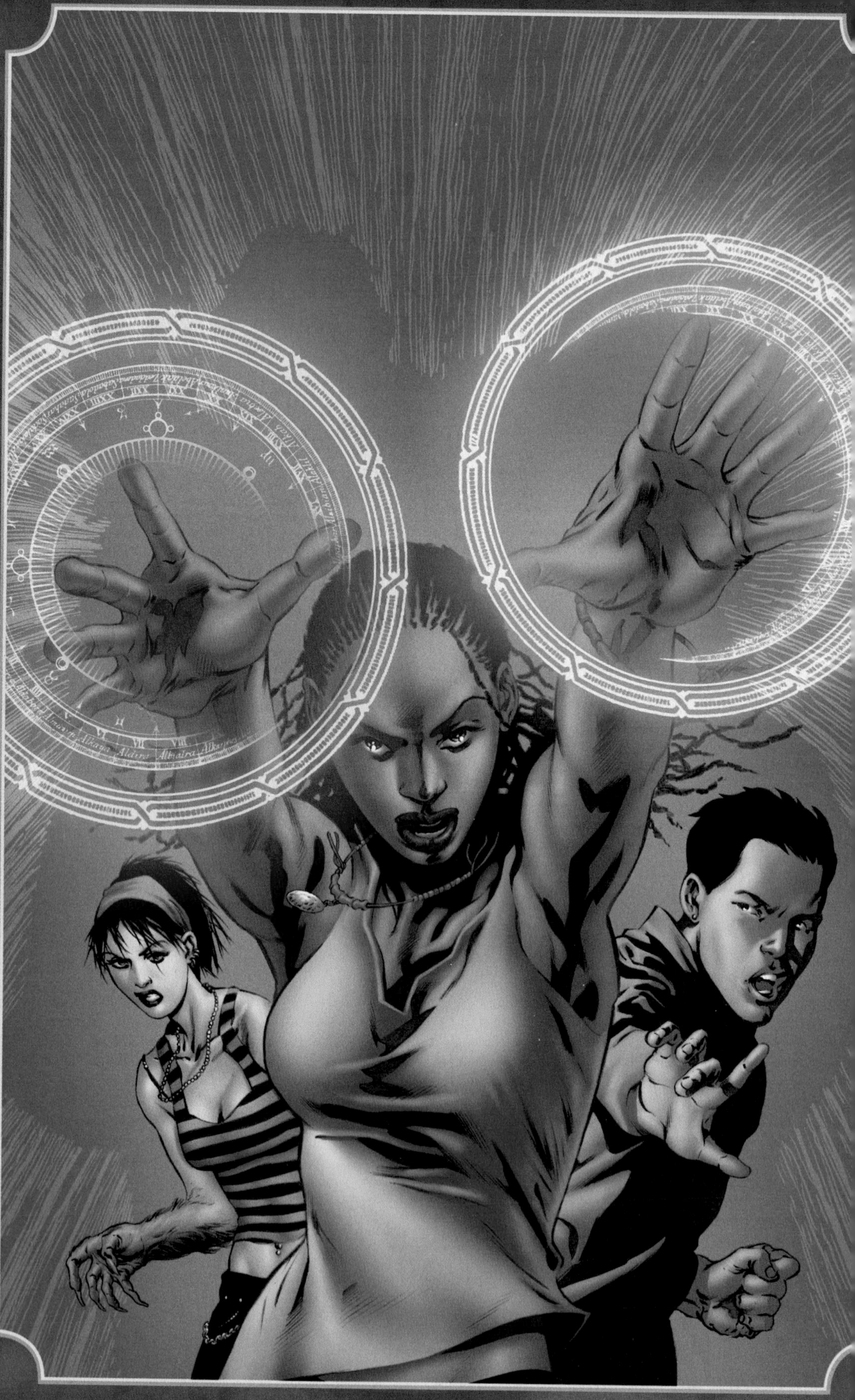

4

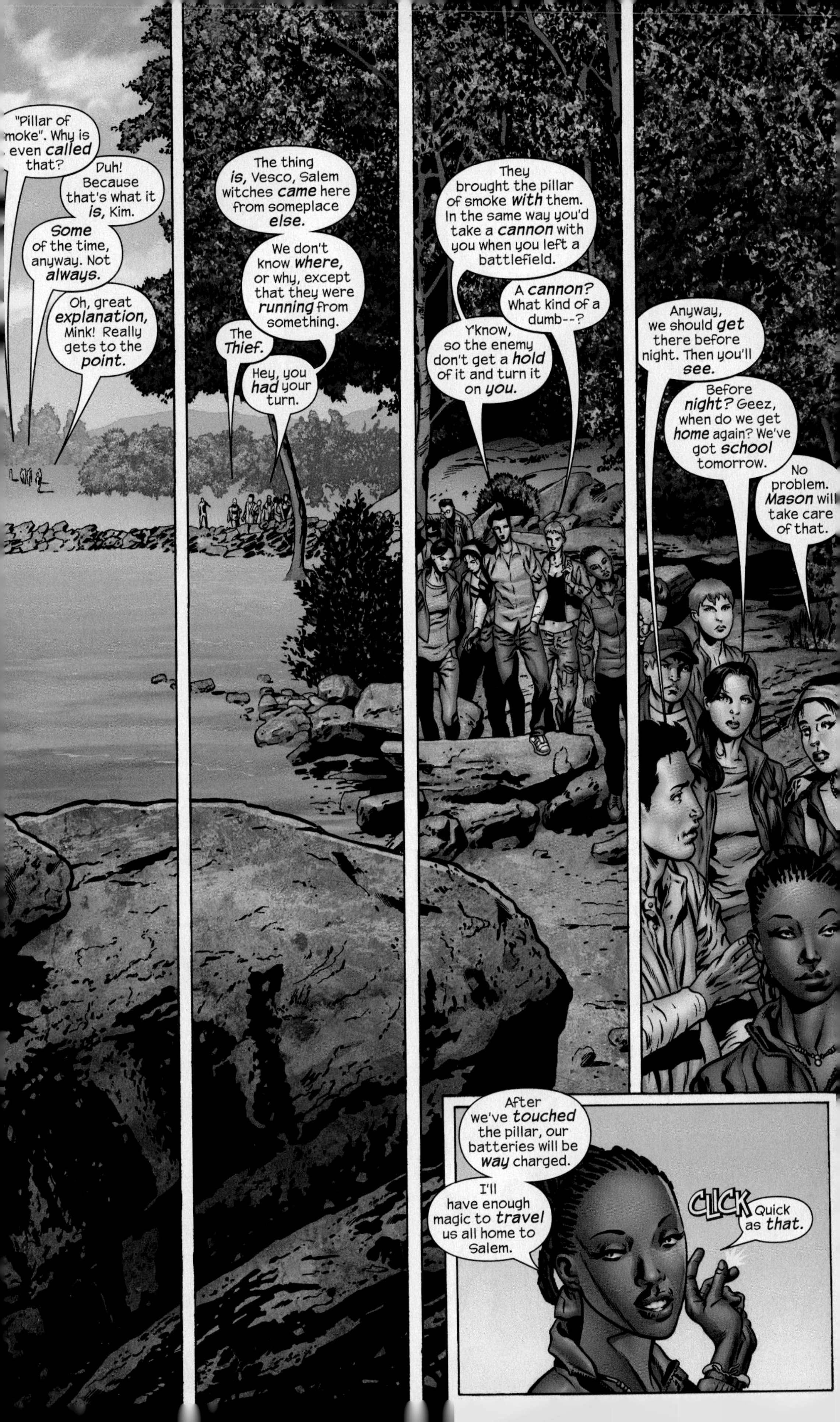
"Pillar of moke". Why is even called that?
Duh! Because that's what it is, Kim.
Some of the time, anyway. Not always.
Oh, great explanation, Mink! Really gets to the point.
The thing is, Vesco, Salem witches came here from someplace else.
We don't know where, or why, except that they were running from something.
The Thief.
Hey, you had your turn.
They brought the pillar of smoke with them. In the same way you'd take a cannon with you when you left a battlefield.
A cannon? What kind of a dumb--?
Y'know, so the enemy don't get a hold of it and turn it on you.
Anyway, we should get there before night. Then you'll see.
Before night? Geez, when do we get home again? We've got school tomorrow.
No problem. Mason will take care of that.
After we've touched the pillar, our batteries will be way charged.
I'll have enough magic to travel us all home to Salem.
CLICK
Quick as that.

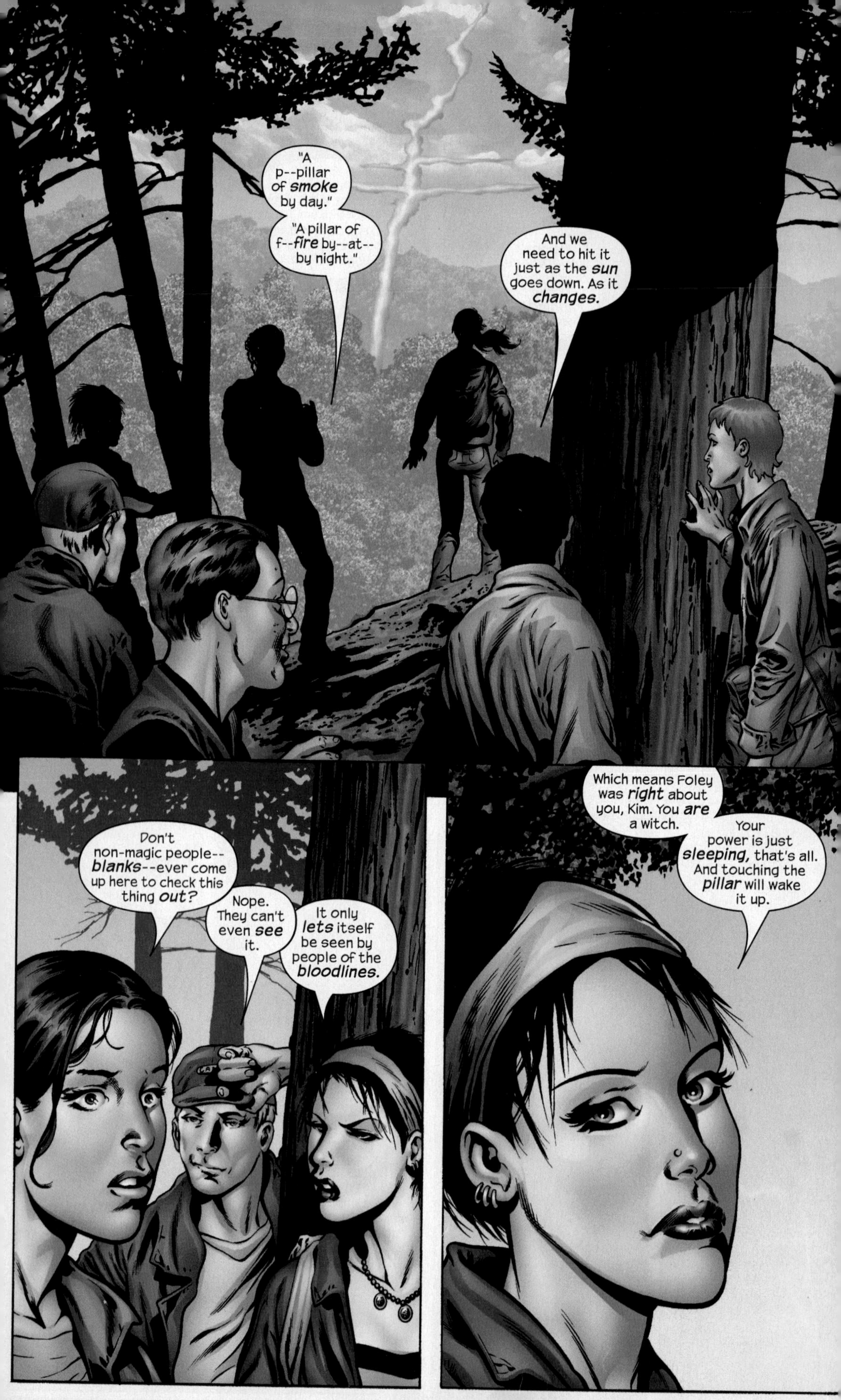
"A p--pillar of smoke by day."
"A pillar of f--fire by--at--by night."
And we need to hit it just as the sun goes down. As it changes.
Don't non-magic people--blanks--ever come up here to check this thing out?
Nope. They can't even see it.
It only lets itself be seen by people of the bloodlines.
Which means Foley was right about you, Kim. You are a witch.
Your power is just sleeping, that's all. And touching the pillar will wake it up.

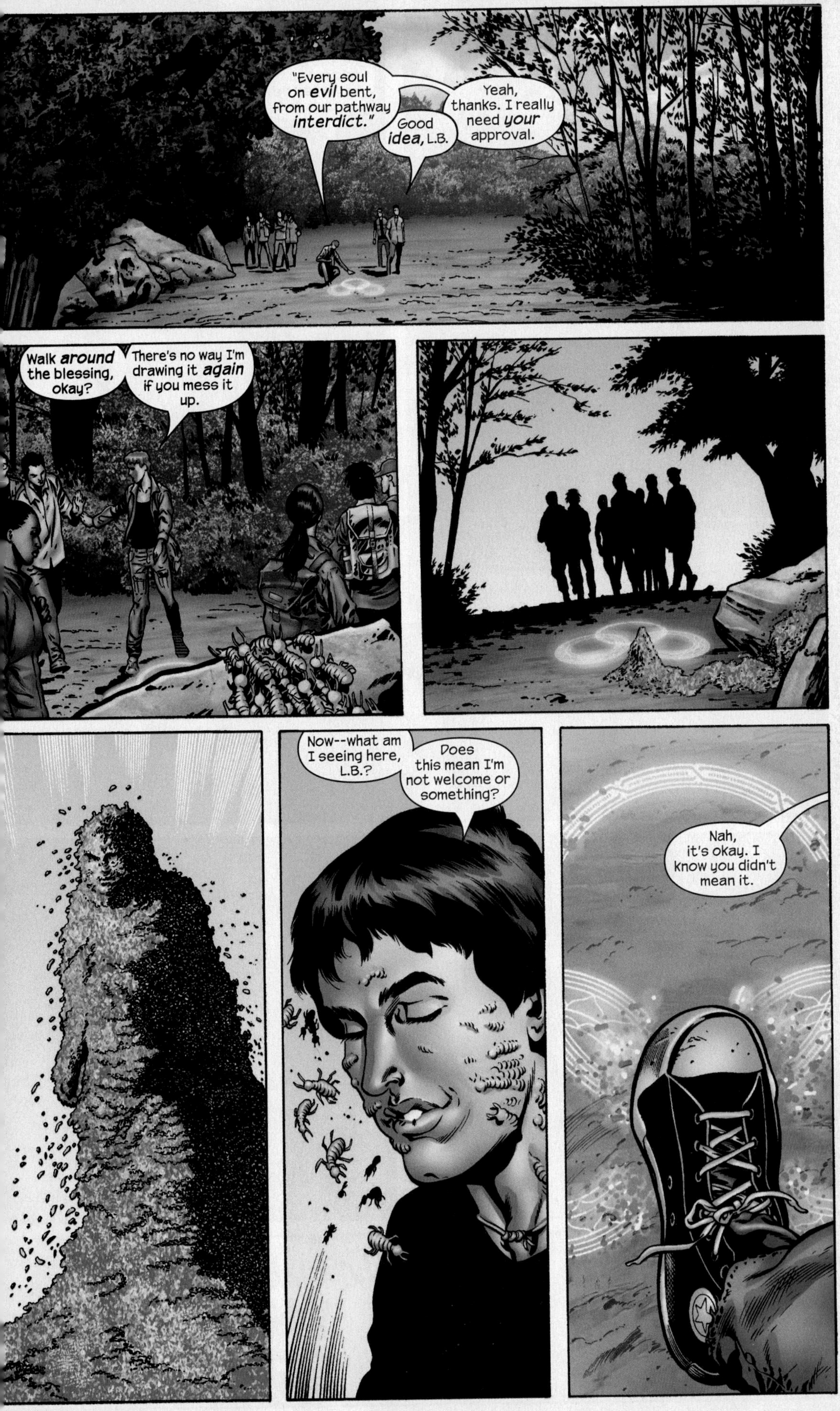
"Every soul on evil bent, from our pathway interdict."
Good idea, L.B.
Yeah, thanks. I really need your approval.
Walk around the blessing, okay?
There's no way I'm drawing it again if you mess it up.
Now--what am I seeing here, L.B.?
Does this mean I'm not welcome or something?
Nah, it's okay. I know you didn't mean it.

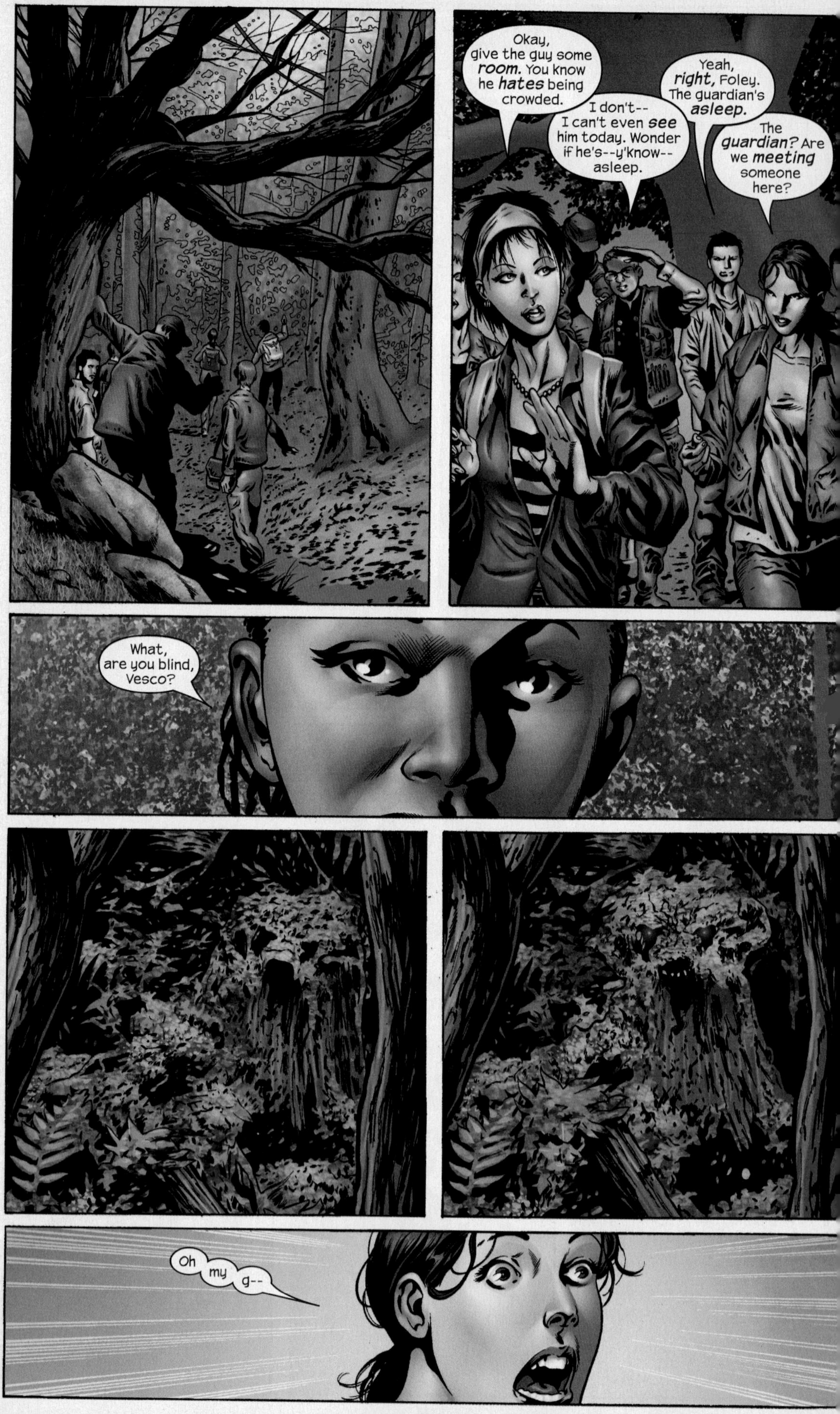
Okay, give the guy some room. You know he hates being crowded.
I don't-- I can't even see him today. Wonder if he's--y'know-- asleep.
Yeah, right, Foley. The guardian's asleep.
The guardian? Are we meeting someone here?
What, are you blind, Vesco?
Oh my g--

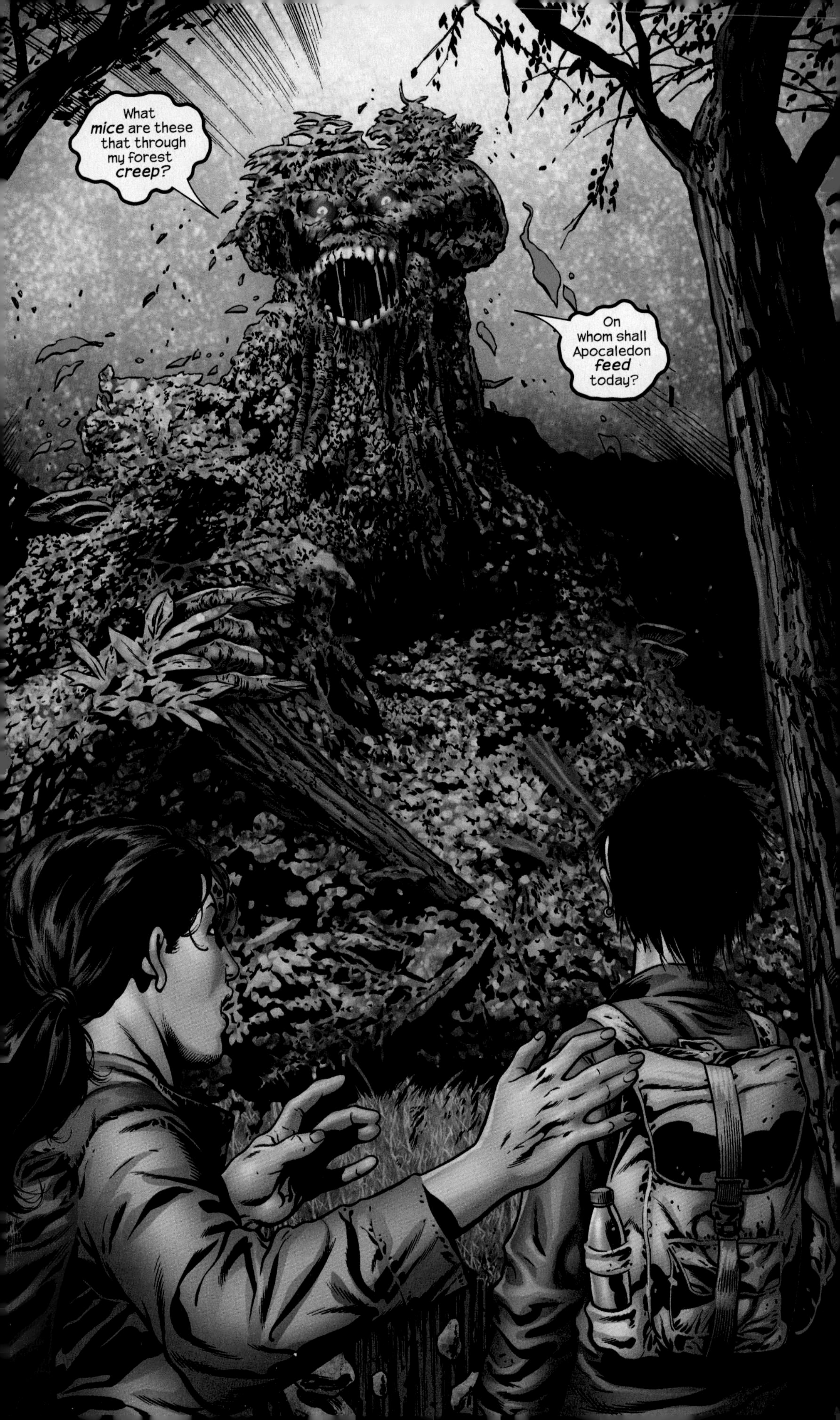
What *mice* are these that through my forest *creep?*
On whom shall Apocaledon *feed* today?

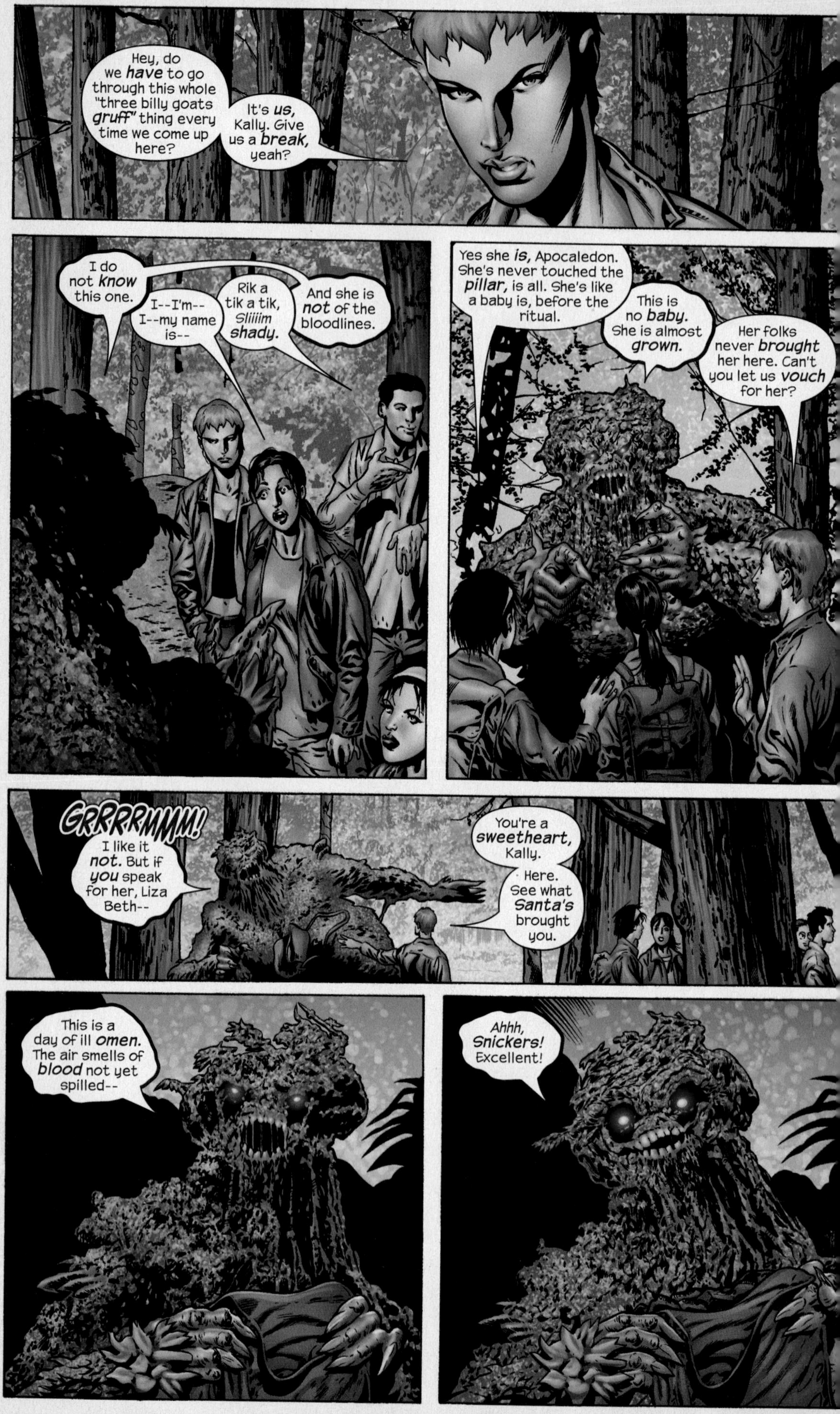

Hey, do we have to go through this whole "three billy goats gruff" thing every time we come up here?
It's us, Kally. Give us a break, yeah?
I do not know this one.
I--I'm-- I--my name is--
Rik a tik a tik, Sliiiim shady.
And she is not of the bloodlines.
Yes she is, Apocaledon. She's never touched the pillar, is all. She's like a baby is, before the ritual.
This is no baby. She is almost grown.
Her folks never brought her here. Can't you let us vouch for her?
GRRRRMMM!
I like it not. But if you speak for her, Liza Beth--
You're a sweetheart, Kally.
Here. See what Santa's brought you.
This is a day of ill omen. The air smells of blood not yet spilled--
Ahhh, Snickers! Excellent!

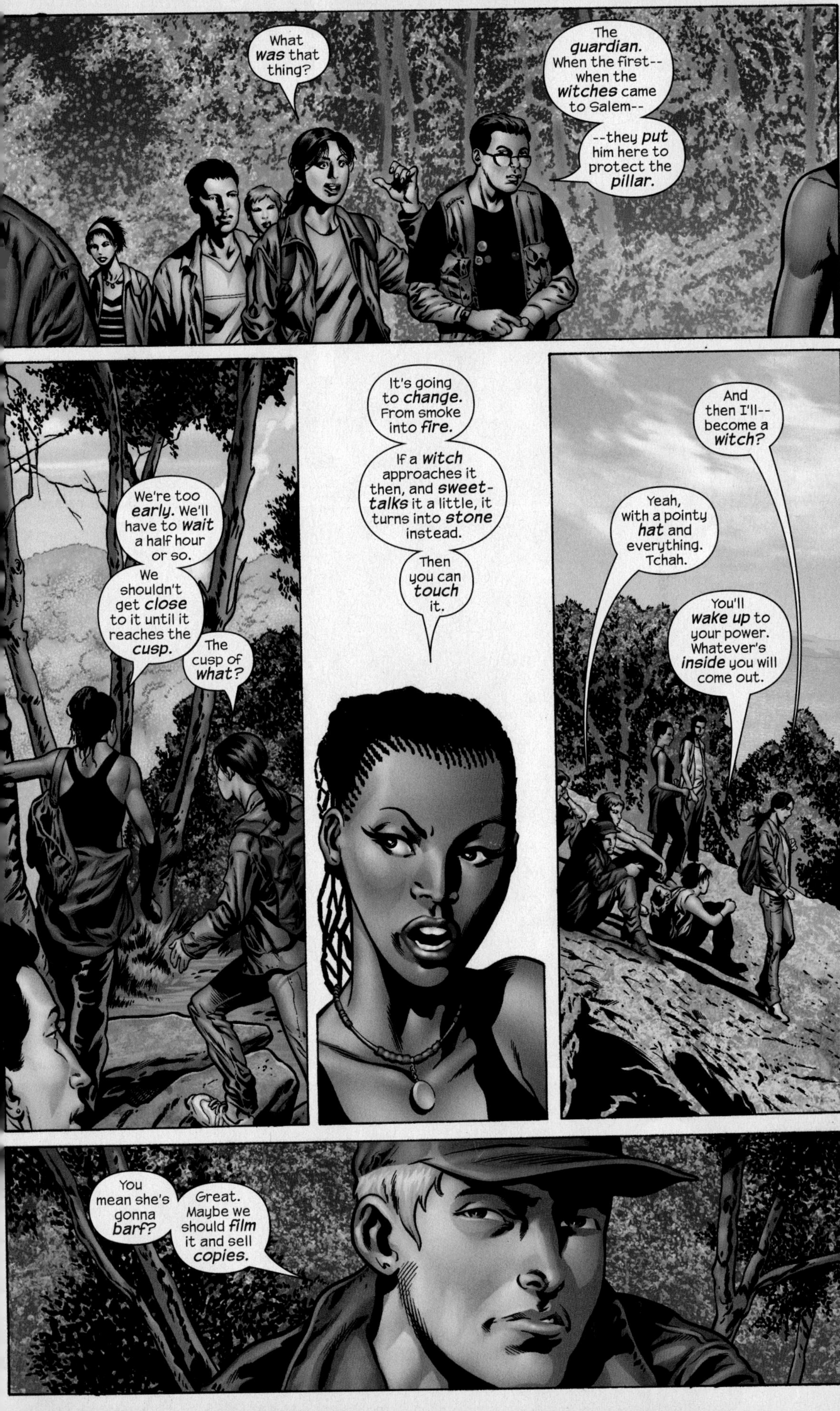
What was that thing?
The guardian. When the first-- when the witches came to Salem--
--they put him here to protect the pillar.
We're too early. We'll have to wait a half hour or so.
We shouldn't get close to it until it reaches the cusp.
The cusp of what?
It's going to change. From smoke into fire.
If a witch approaches it then, and sweet-talks it a little, it turns into stone instead.
Then you can touch it.
And then I'll-- become a witch?
Yeah, with a pointy hat and everything. Tchah.
You'll wake up to your power. Whatever's inside you will come out.
You mean she's gonna barf?
Great. Maybe we should film it and sell copies.

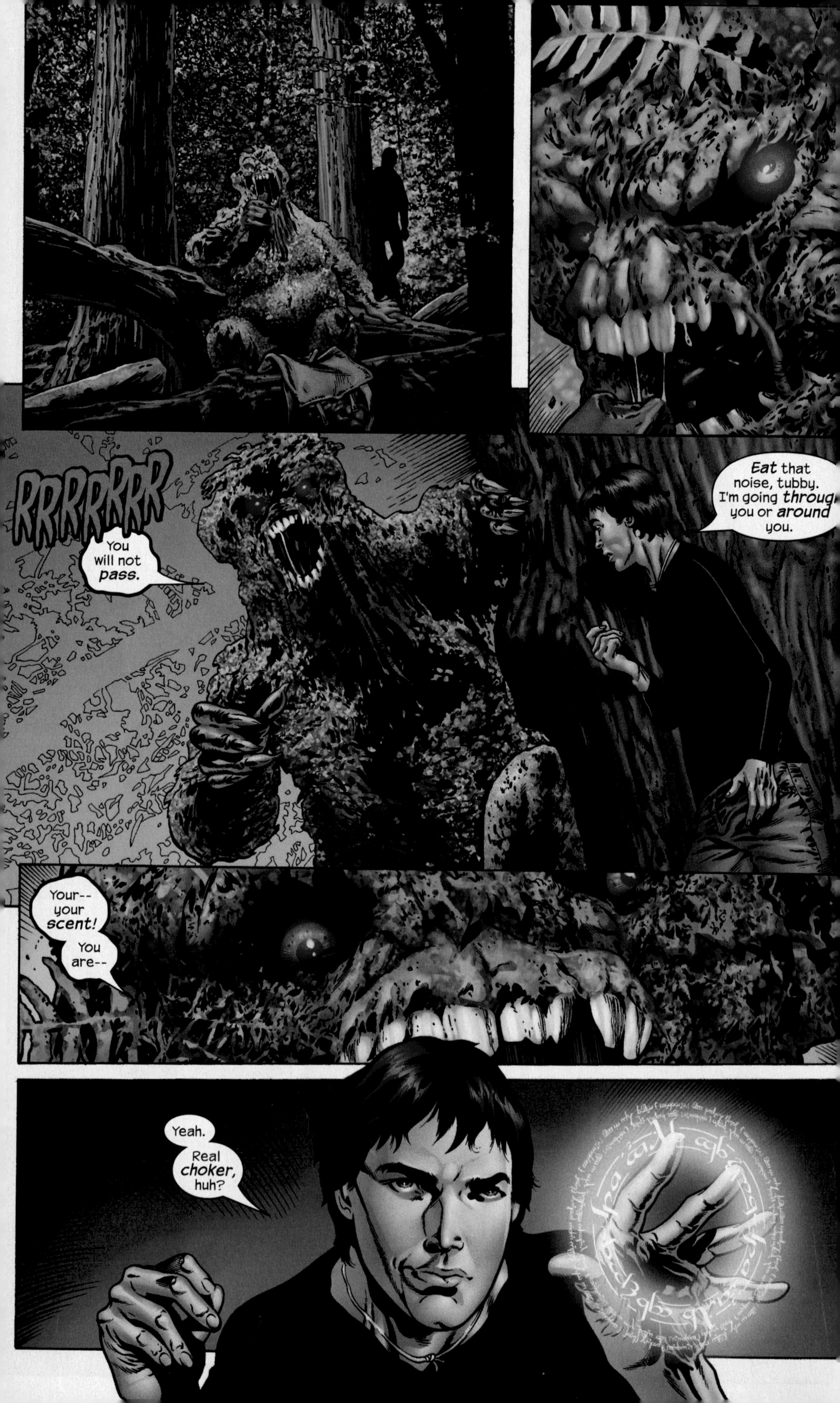
RRRRRRR
You will not pass.
Eat that noise, tubby. I'm going throug you or around you.
Your-- your scent!
You are--
Yeah.
Real choker, huh?

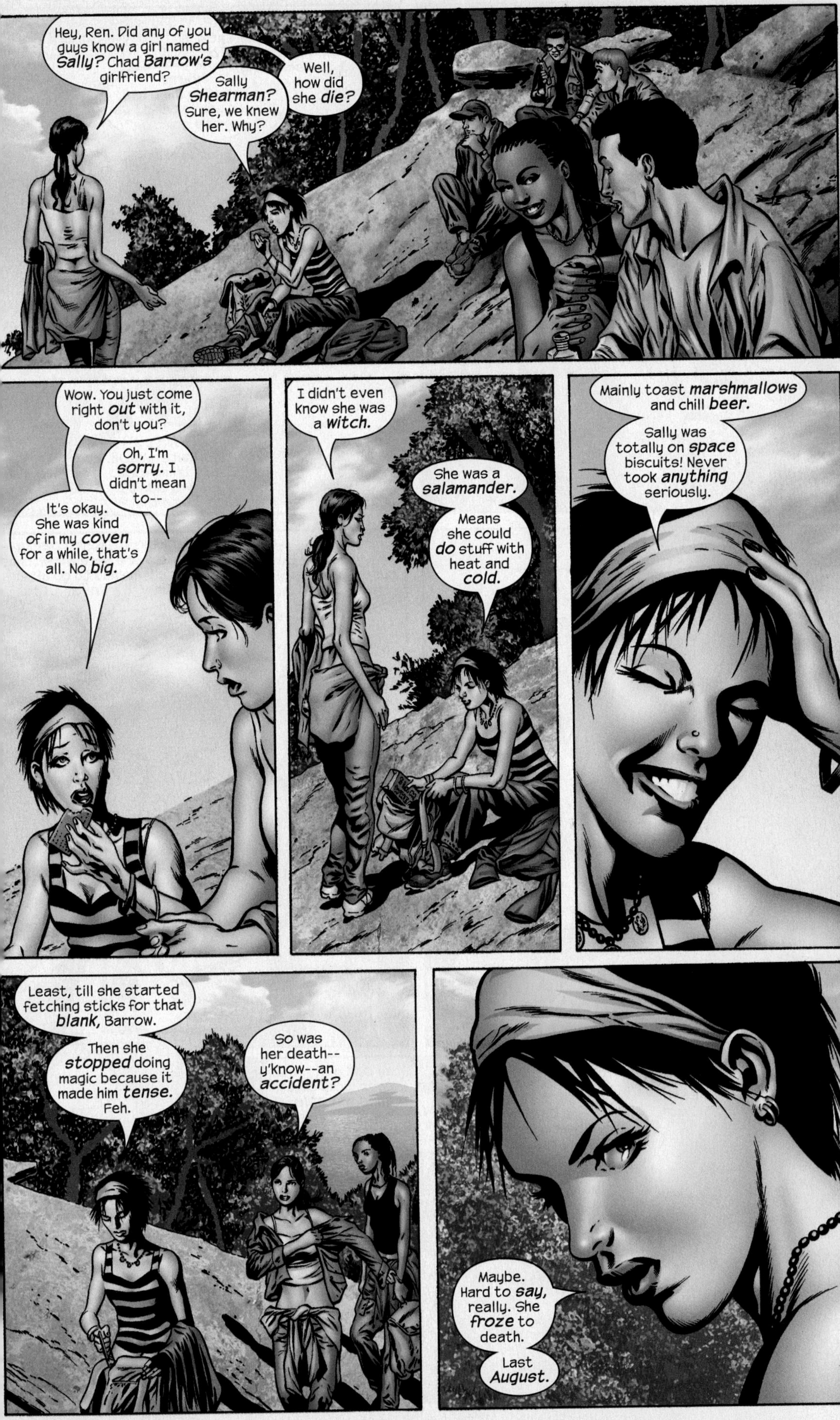
Hey, Ren. Did any of you guys know a girl named Sally? Chad Barrow's girlfriend?
Sally Shearman? Sure, we knew her. Why?
Well, how did she die?
Wow. You just come right out with it, don't you?
Oh, I'm sorry. I didn't mean to--
It's okay. She was kind of in my coven for a while, that's all. No big.
I didn't even know she was a witch.
She was a salamander.
Means she could do stuff with heat and cold.
Mainly toast marshmallows and chill beer.
Sally was totally on space biscuits! Never took anything seriously.
Least, till she started fetching sticks for that blank, Barrow.
Then she stopped doing magic because it made him tense. Feh.
So was her death-- y'know--an accident?
Maybe. Hard to say, really. She froze to death.
Last August.

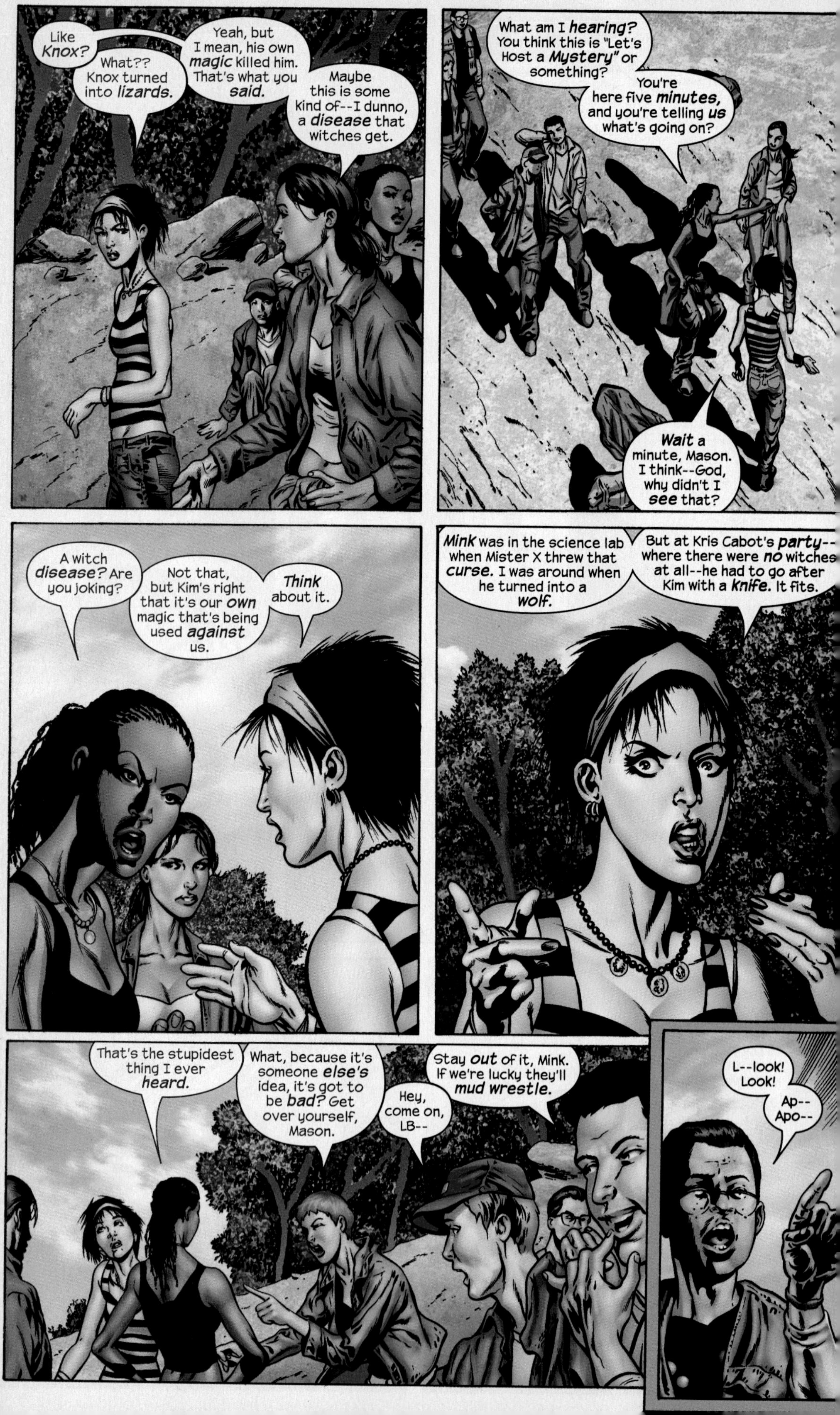
Like Knox?
Yeah, but I mean, his own magic killed him. That's what you said.
What?? Knox turned into lizards.
Maybe this is some kind of--I dunno, a disease that witches get.
What am I hearing? You think this is "Let's Host a Mystery" or something?
You're here five minutes, and you're telling us what's going on?
Wait a minute, Mason. I think--God, why didn't I see that?
A witch disease? Are you joking?
Not that, but Kim's right that it's our own magic that's being used against us.
Think about it.
Mink was in the science lab when Mister X threw that curse. I was around when he turned into a wolf.
But at Kris Cabot's party--where there were no witches at all--he had to go after Kim with a knife. It fits.
That's the stupidest thing I ever heard.
What, because it's someone else's idea, it's got to be bad? Get over yourself, Mason.
Hey, come on, LB--
Stay out of it, Mink. If we're lucky they'll mud wrestle.
L--look! Look!
Ap-- Apo--

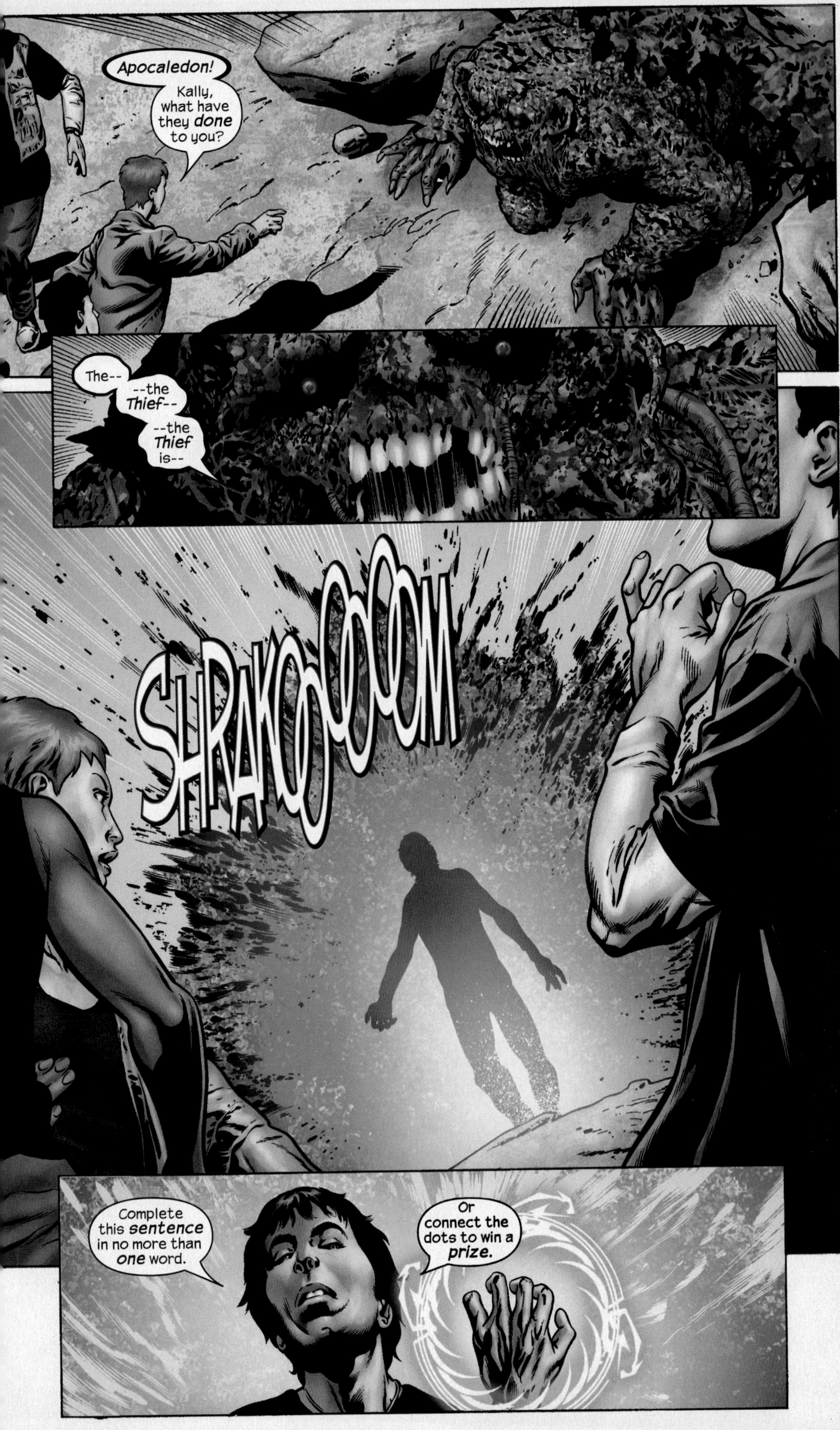
Apocaledon!
Kally, what have they done to you?
The--
--the Thief--
--the Thief is--
SHRAKOOOOOM
Complete this sentence in no more than one word.
Or connect the dots to win a prize.

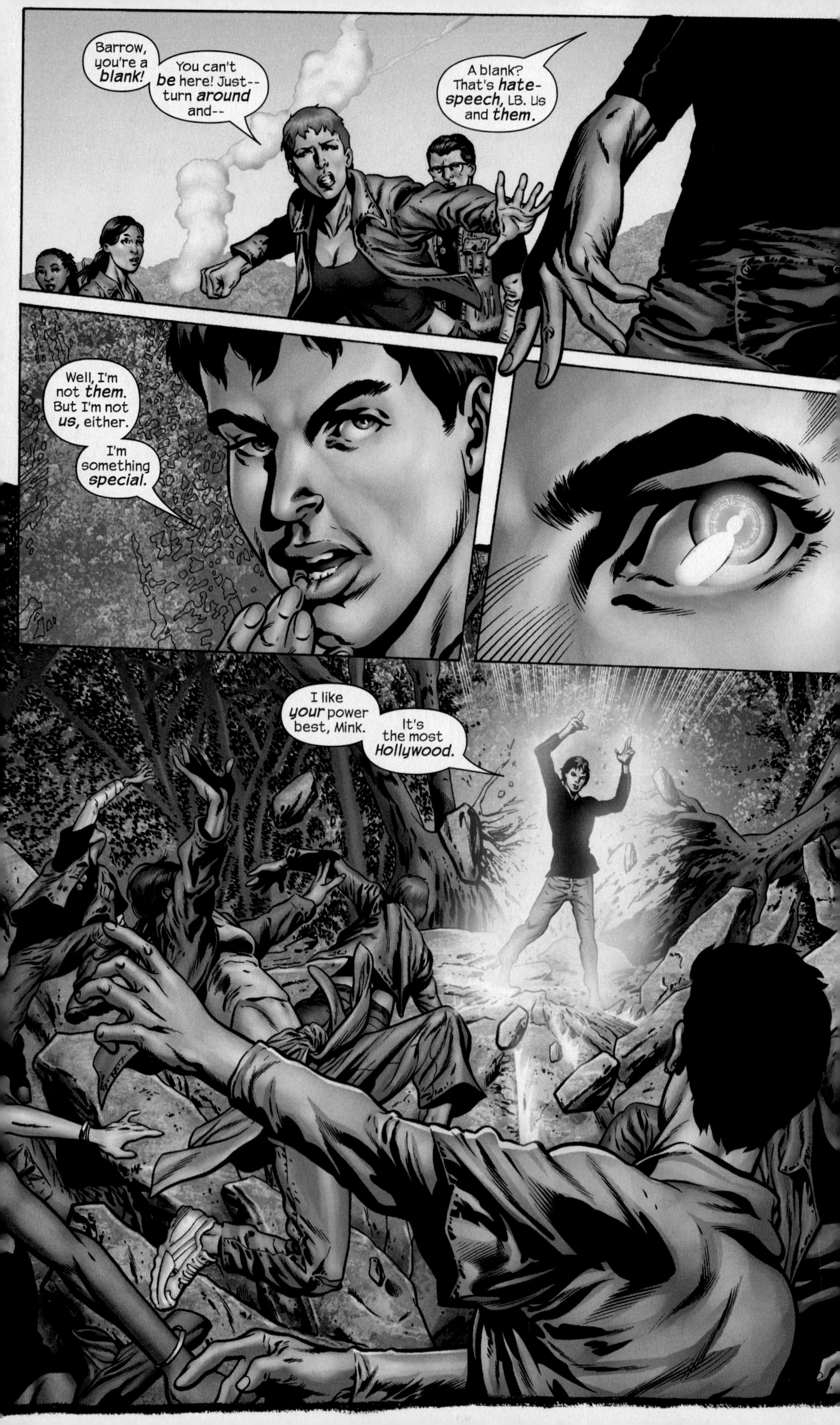
Barrow, you're a *blank!*
You can't *be* here! Just-- turn *around* and--
A blank? That's *hate-speech,* LB. Us and *them.*
Well, I'm not *them.* But I'm not *us,* either.
I'm something *special.*
I like *your* power best, Mink.
It's the most *Hollywood.*

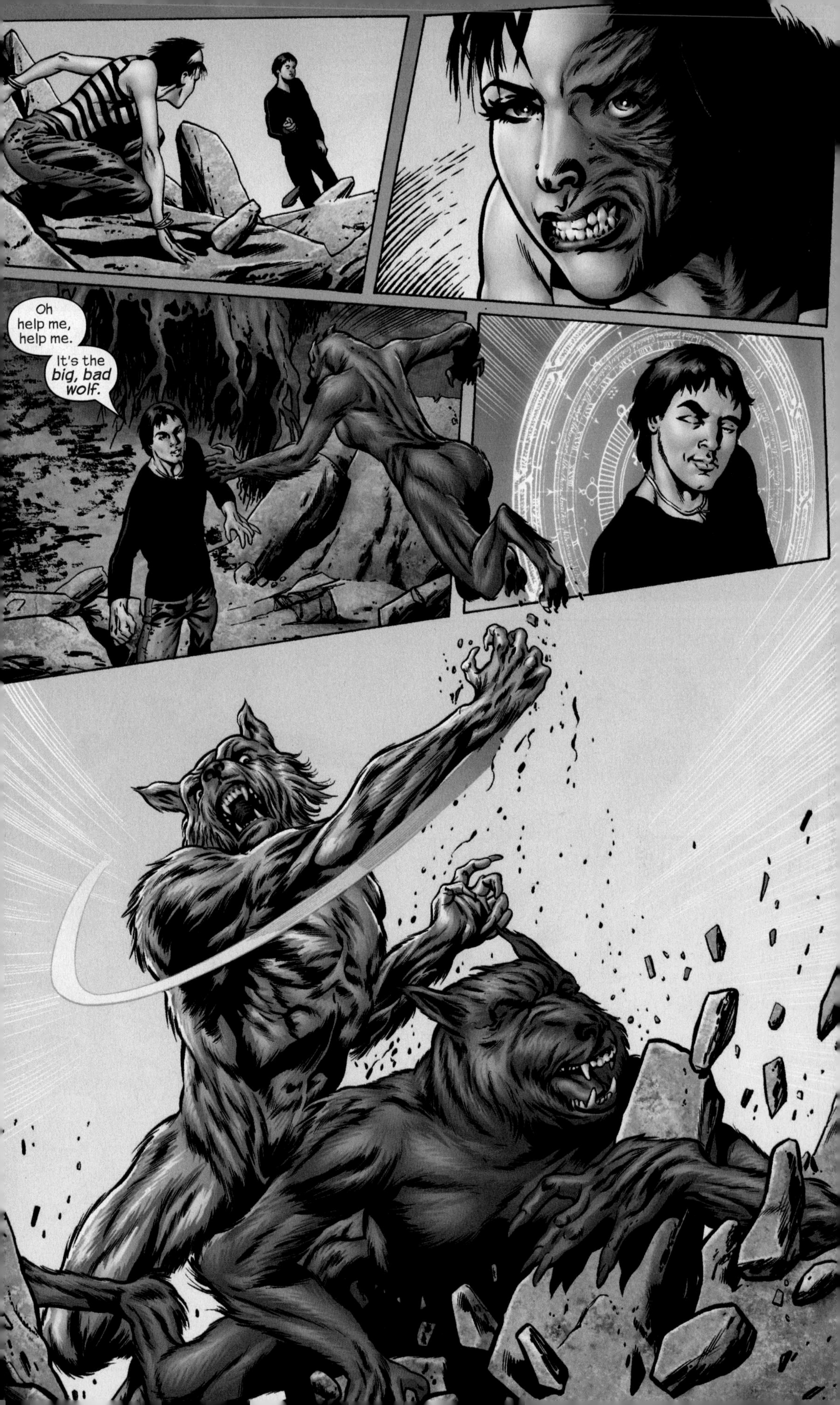

Oh help me, help me. It's the *big, bad wolf.*

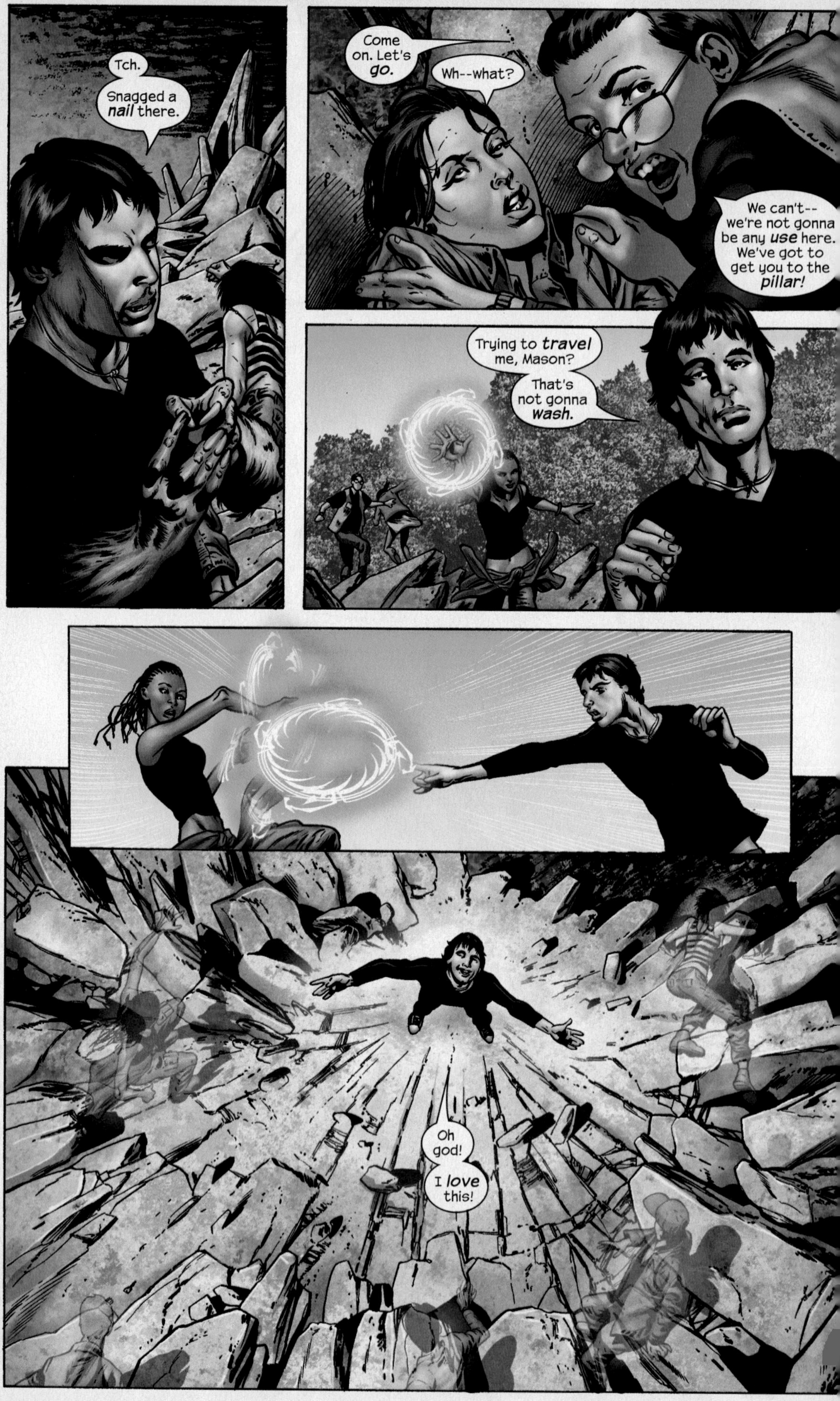

Tch.
Snagged a *nail* there.
Come on. Let's *go.*
Wh--what?
We can't-- we're not gonna be any *use* here. We've got to get you to the *pillar!*
Trying to *travel* me, Mason?
That's not gonna *wash.*
Oh god!
I *love* this!

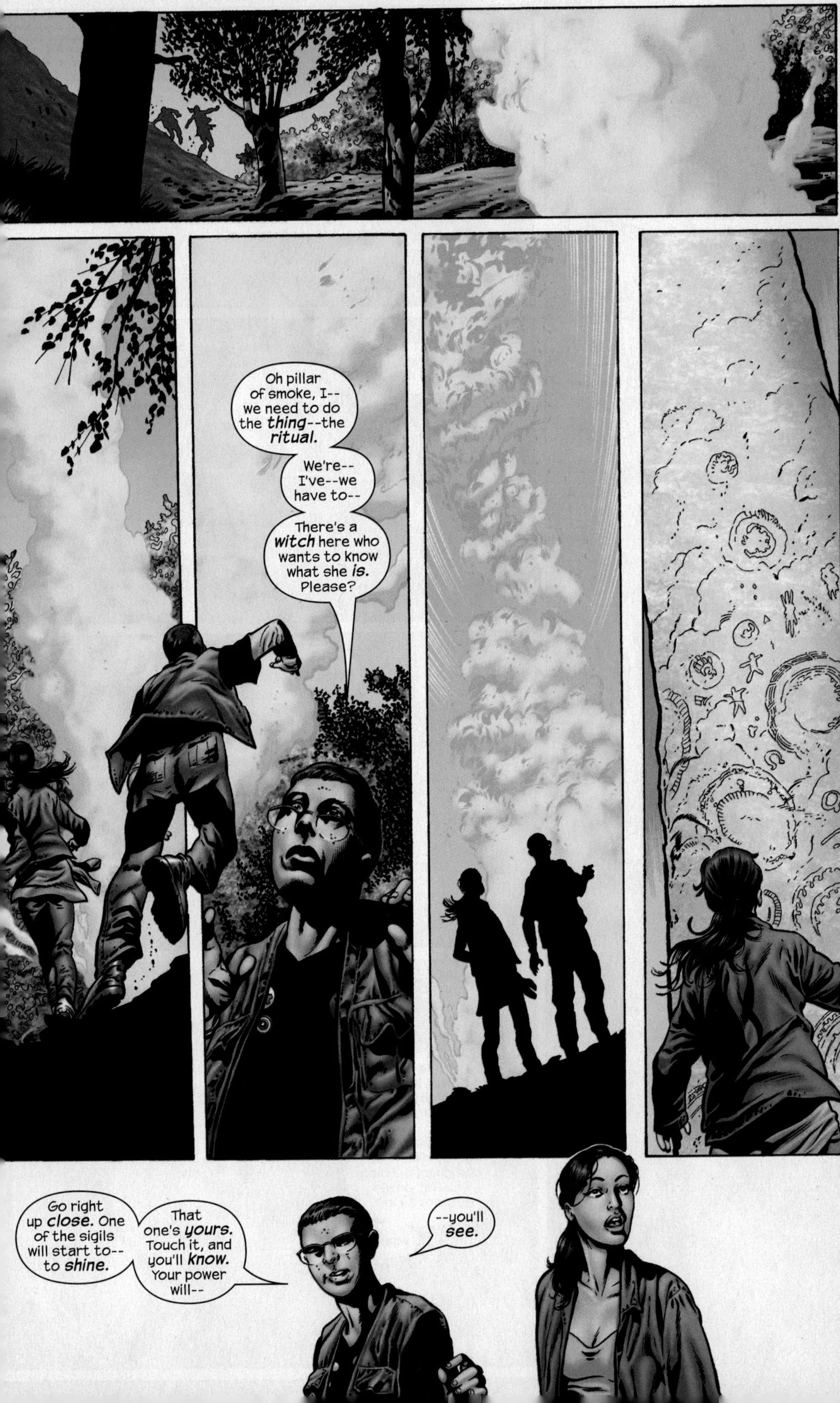

Oh pillar of smoke, I-- we need to do the *thing*--the *ritual.*
We're-- I've--we have to--
There's a *witch* here who wants to know what she *is.* Please?
Go right up *close.* One of the sigils will start to-- to *shine.*
That one's *yours.* Touch it, and you'll *know.* Your power will--
--you'll *see.*

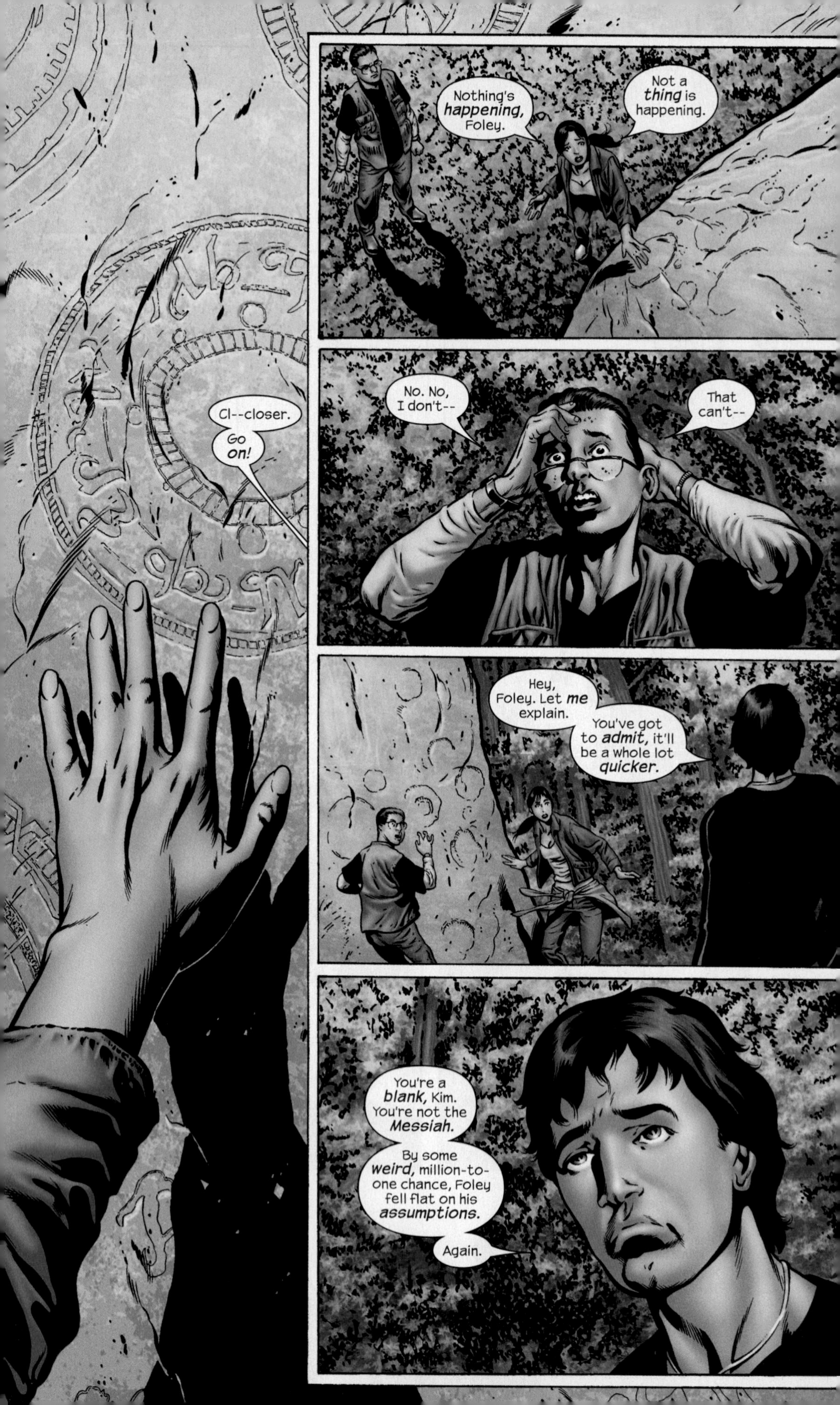

Nothing's *happening,* Foley.
Not a *thing* is happening.
Cl--closer.
Go *on!*
No. No, I don't--
That can't--
Hey, Foley. Let *me* explain.
You've got to *admit,* it'll be a whole lot *quicker.*
You're a *blank,* Kim. You're not the *Messiah.*
By some *weird,* million-to-one chance, Foley fell flat on his *assumptions.*
Again.

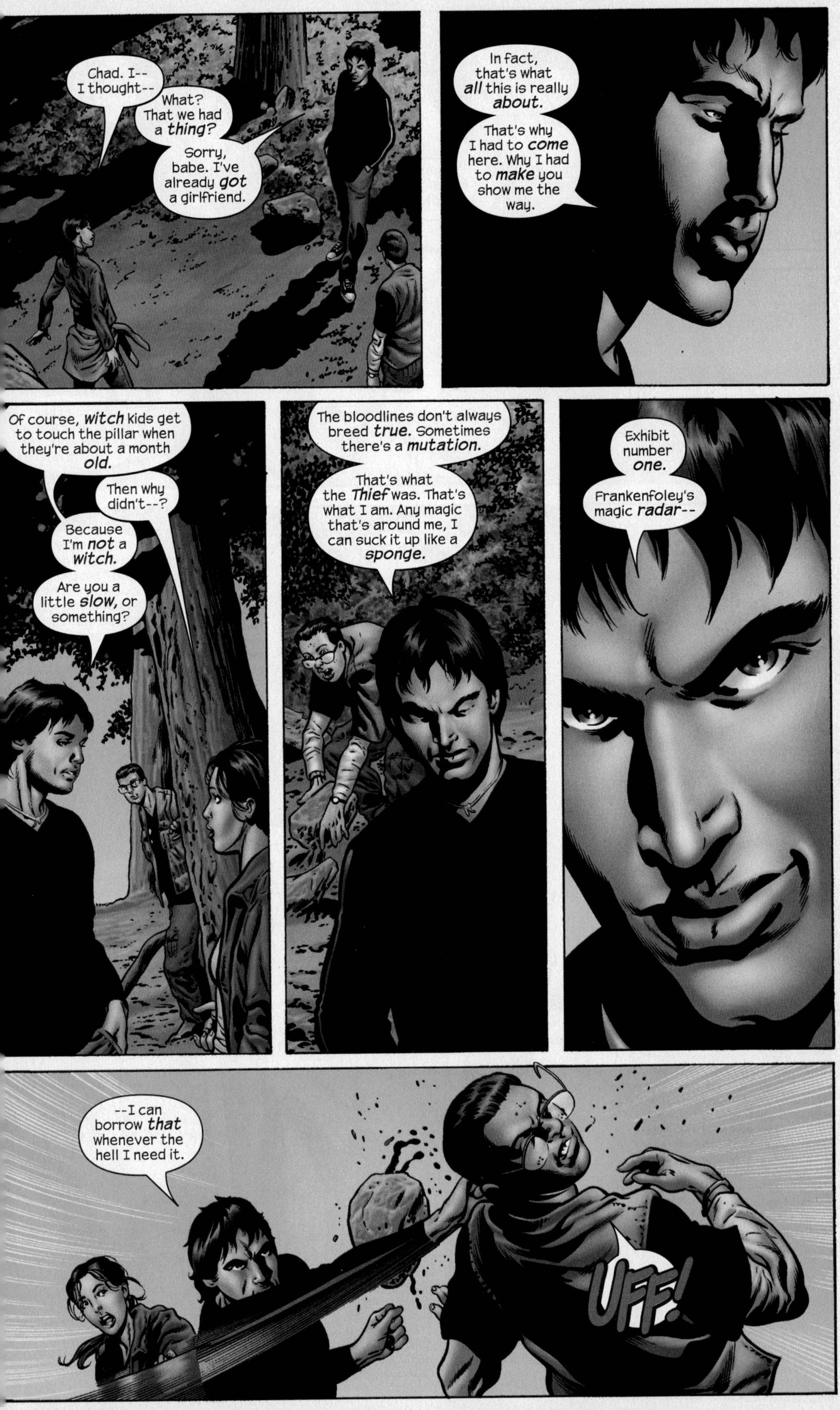

Chad. I-- I thought--
What? That we had a *thing*?
Sorry, babe. I've already *got* a girlfriend.
In fact, that's what *all* this is really *about*.
That's why I had to *come* here. Why I had to *make* you show me the way.
Of course, *witch* kids get to touch the pillar when they're about a month *old*.
Then why didn't--?
Because I'm *not* a *witch*.
Are you a little *slow*, or something?
The bloodlines don't always breed *true*. Sometimes there's a *mutation*.
That's what the *Thief* was. That's what I am. Any magic that's around me, I can suck it up like a *sponge*.
Exhibit number *one*.
Frankenfoley's magic *radar*--
--I can borrow *that* whenever the hell I need it.
UFF!

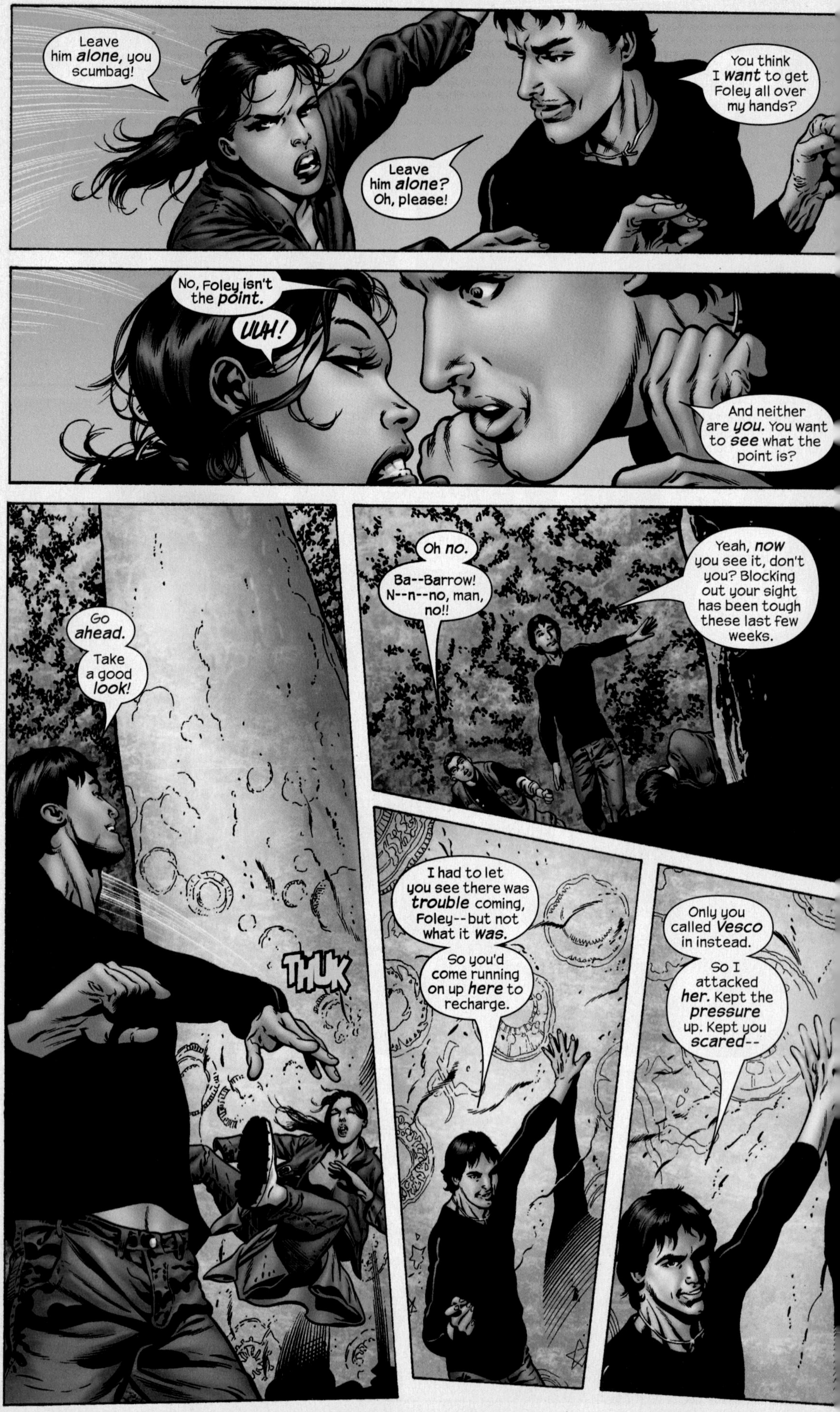

Leave him alone, you scumbag!
You think I want to get Foley all over my hands?
Leave him alone? Oh, please!
No, Foley isn't the point.
UUH!
And neither are you. You want to see what the point is?
Go ahead.
Take a good look!
THUK
Oh no.
Ba--Barrow! N--n--no, man, no!!
Yeah, now you see it, don't you? Blocking out your sight has been tough these last few weeks.
I had to let you see there was trouble coming, Foley--but not what it was.
So you'd come running on up here to recharge.
Only you called Vesco in instead.
So I attacked her. Kept the pressure up. Kept you scared--

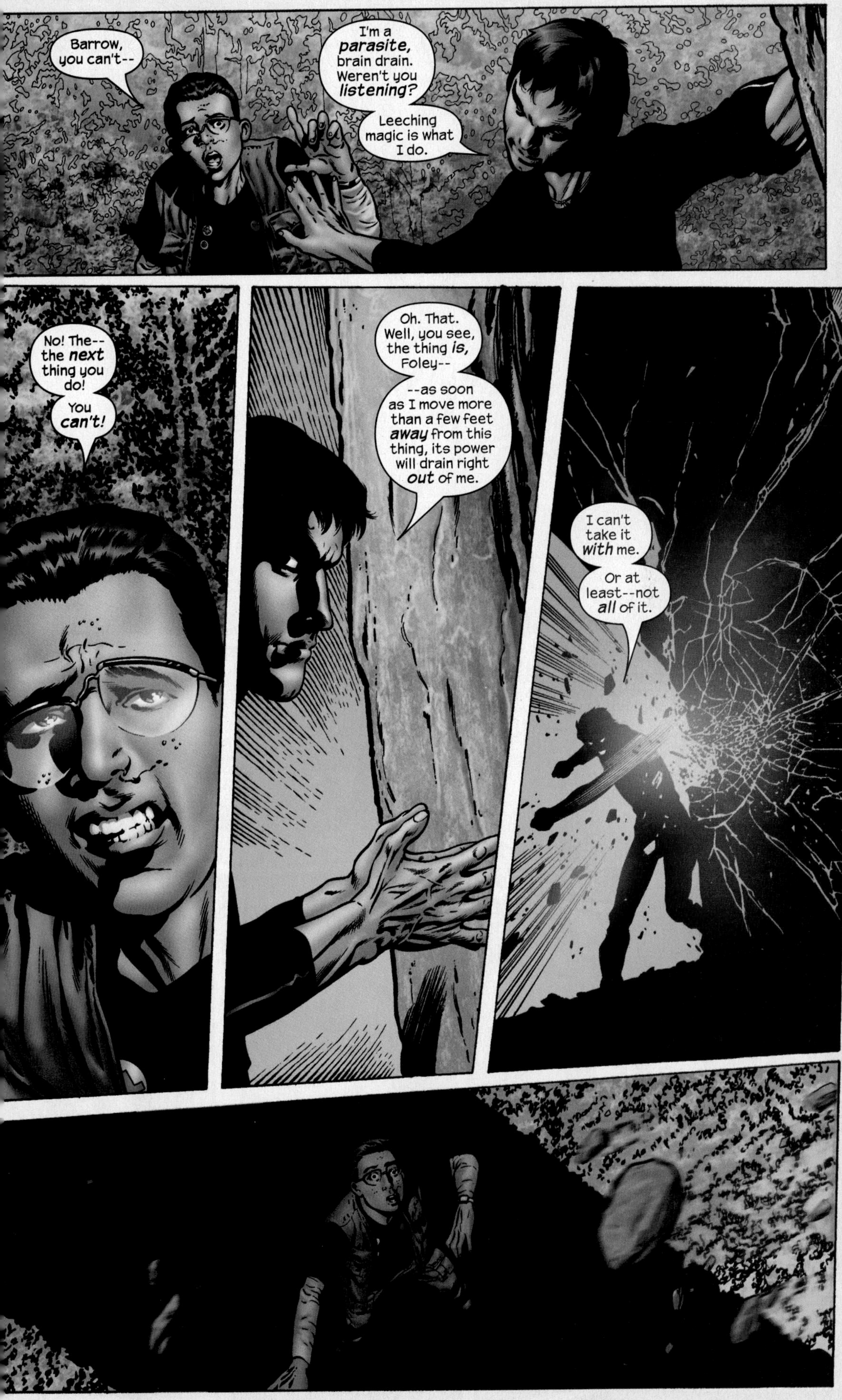
Barrow, you can't--
I'm a *parasite,* brain drain. Weren't you *listening?*
Leeching magic is what I do.
No! The-- the *next* thing you do!
You *can't!*
Oh. That. Well, you see, the thing *is,* Foley--
--as soon as I move more than a few feet *away* from this thing, its power will drain right *out* of me.
I can't take it *with* me.
Or at least--not *all* of it.

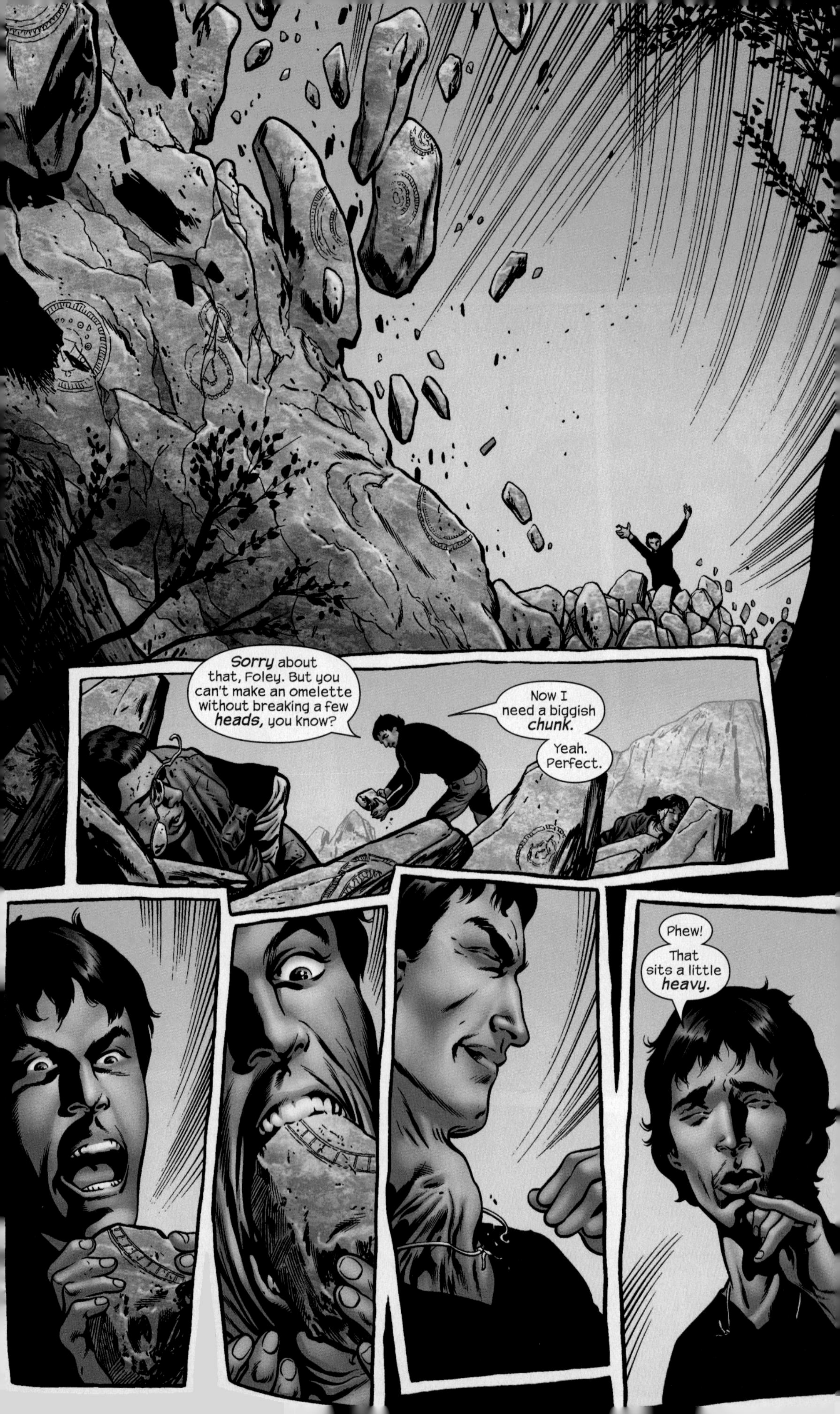
Sorry about that, Foley. But you can't make an omelette without breaking a few heads, you know?
Now I need a biggish chunk.
Yeah. Perfect.
Phew!
That sits a little heavy.

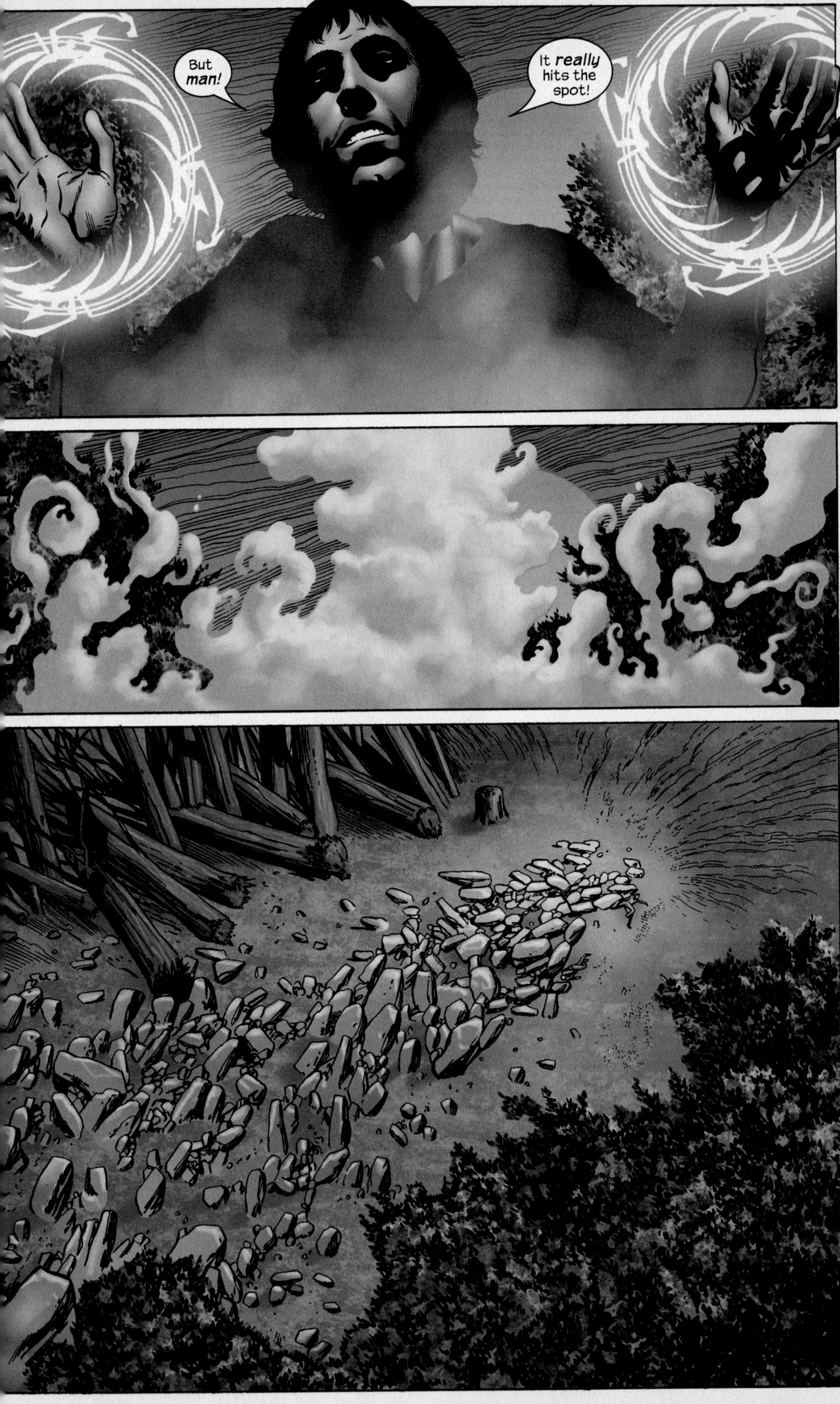
But *man!*
It *really* hits the spot!

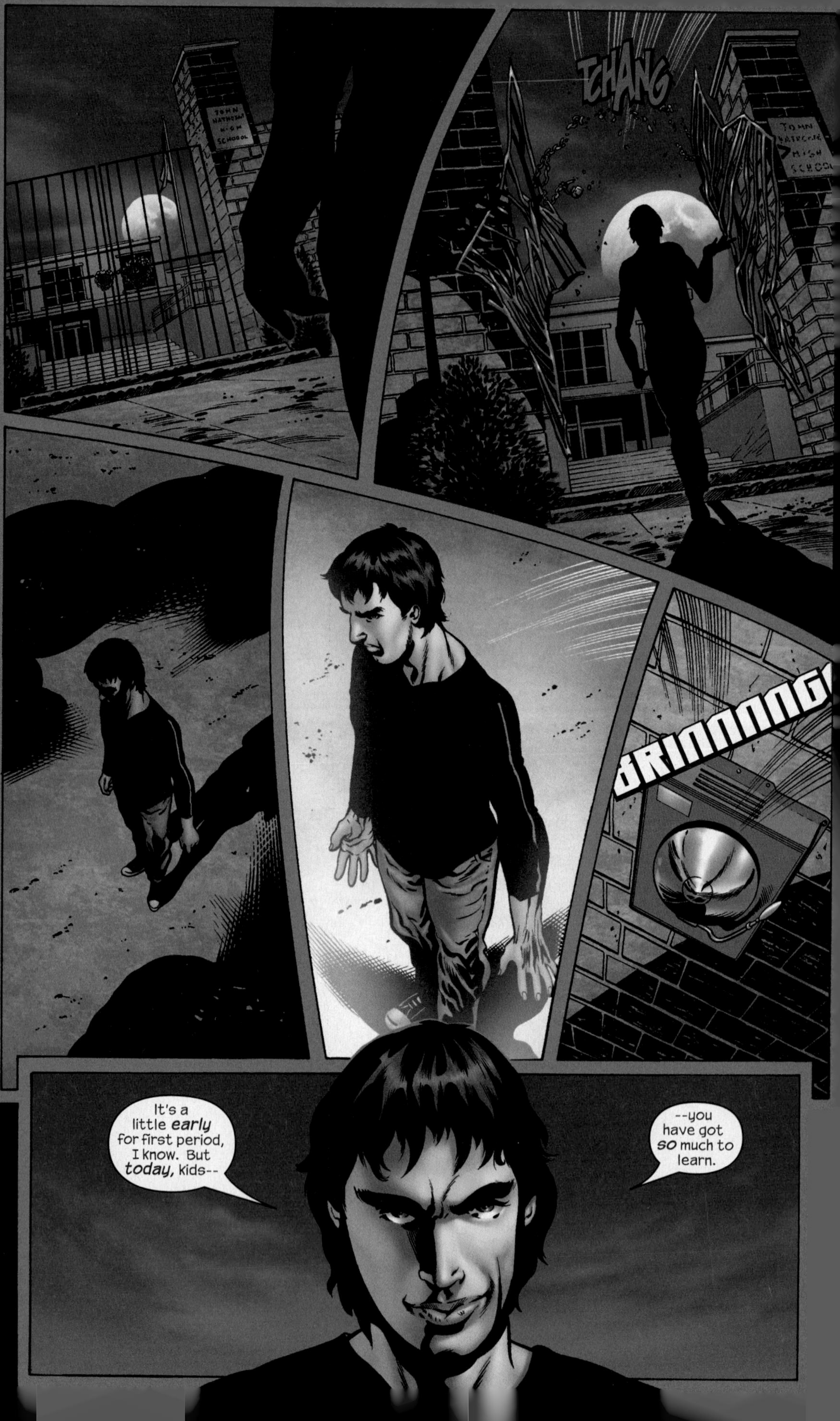
JOHN NATHOSIAN HIGH SCHOOL
TCHANG
BRINNNNNG
It's a little *early* for first period, I know. But *today,* kids--
--you have got *so* much to learn.

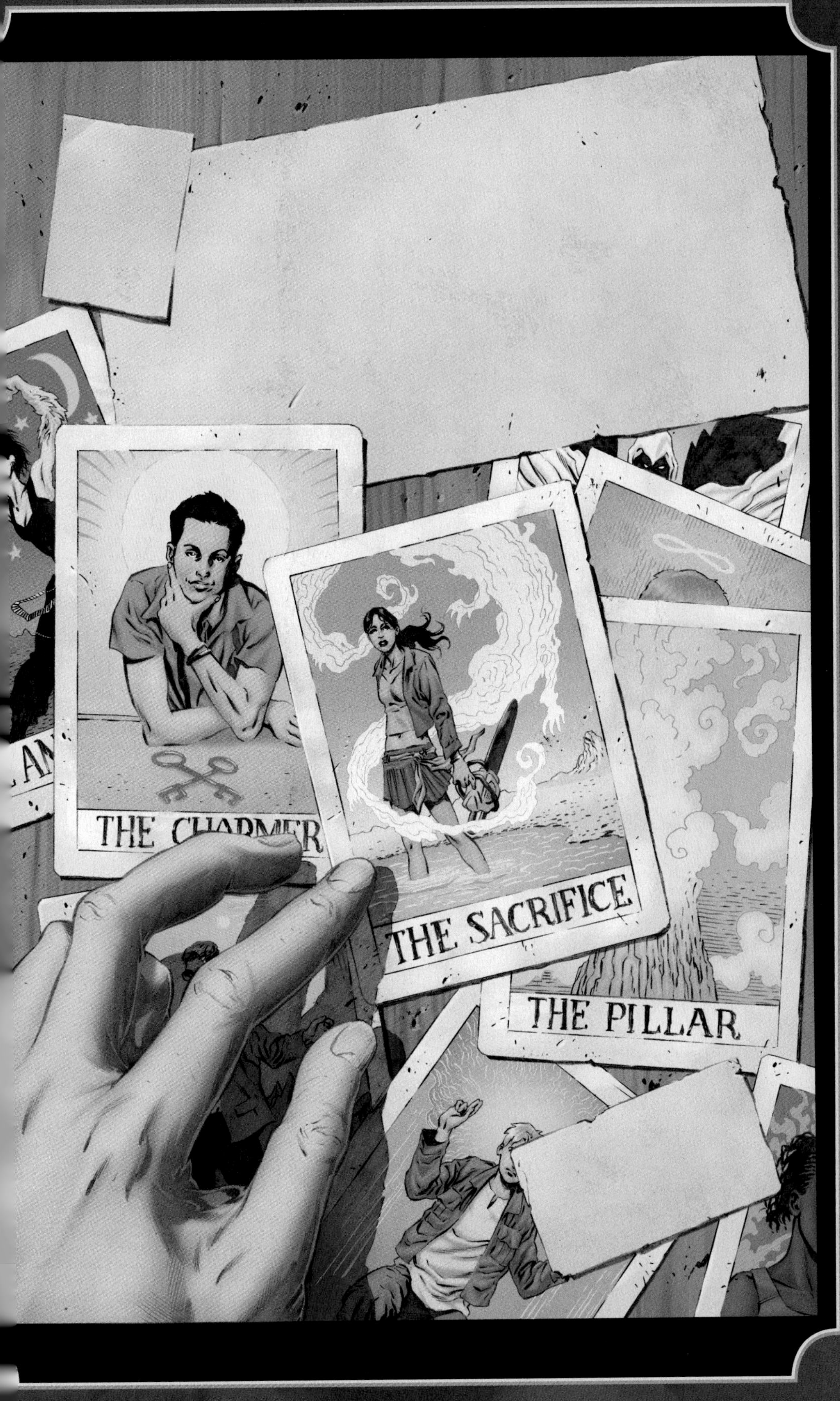
THE CHARMER
THE SACRIFICE
THE PILLAR

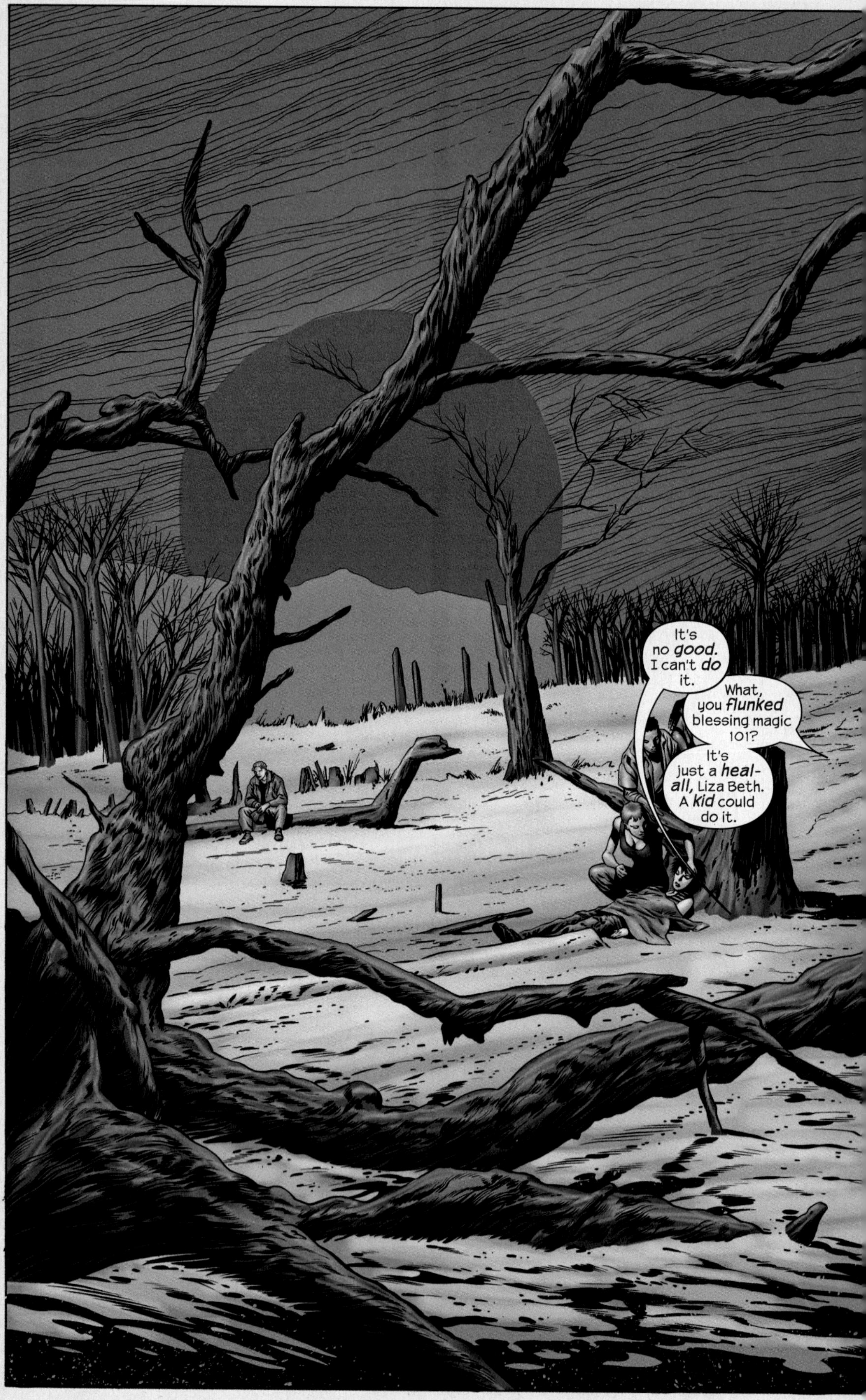
It's no good. I can't do it.
What, you flunked blessing magic 101?
It's just a heal-all, Liza Beth. A kid could do it.

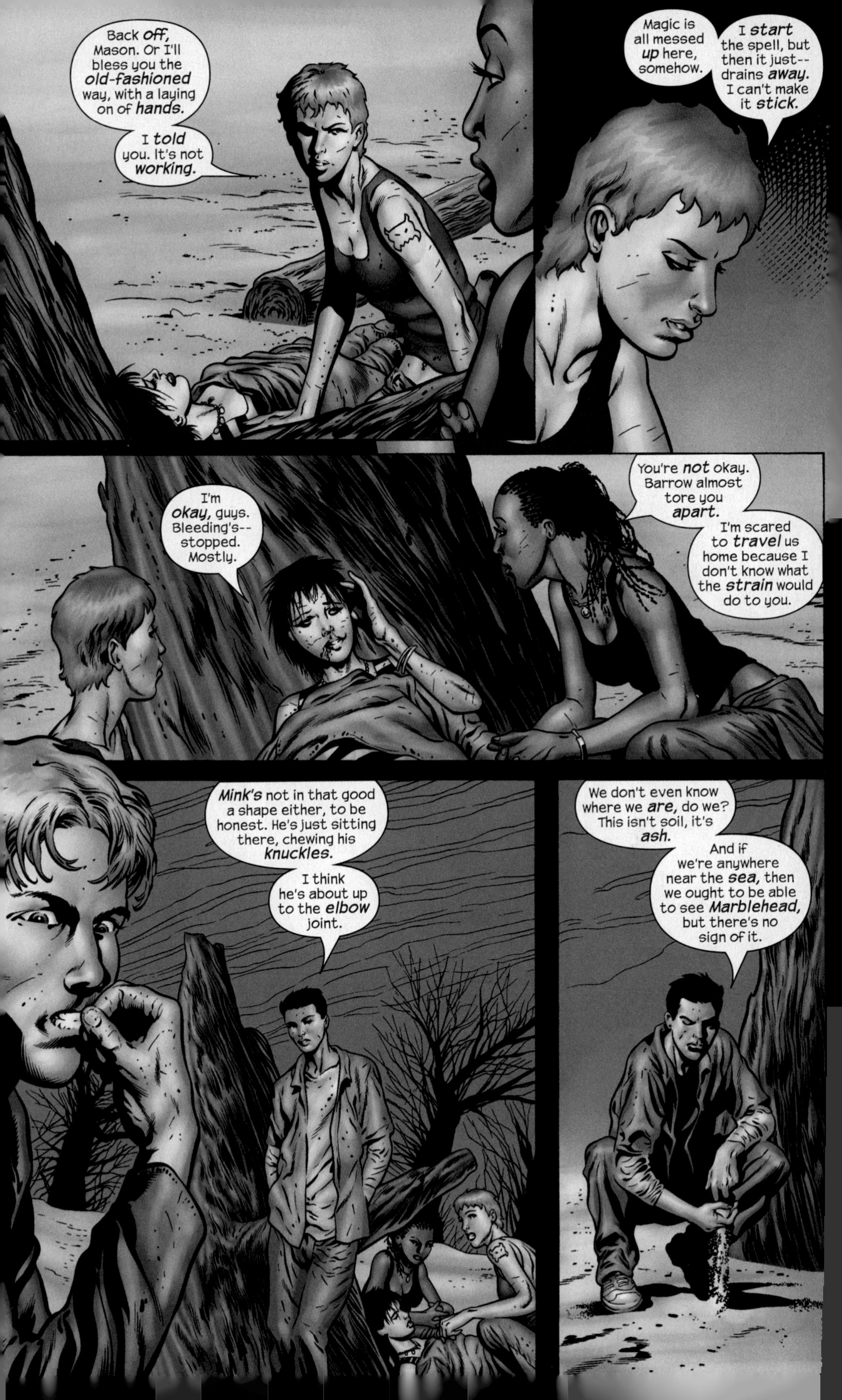

Back off, Mason. Or I'll bless you the old-fashioned way, with a laying on of hands.
I told you. It's not working.
Magic is all messed up here, somehow.
I start the spell, but then it just--drains away. I can't make it stick.
I'm okay, guys. Bleeding's--stopped. Mostly.
You're not okay. Barrow almost tore you apart.
I'm scared to travel us home because I don't know what the strain would do to you.
Mink's not in that good a shape either, to be honest. He's just sitting there, chewing his knuckles.
I think he's about up to the elbow joint.
We don't even know where we are, do we? This isn't soil, it's ash.
And if we're anywhere near the sea, then we ought to be able to see Marblehead, but there's no sign of it.

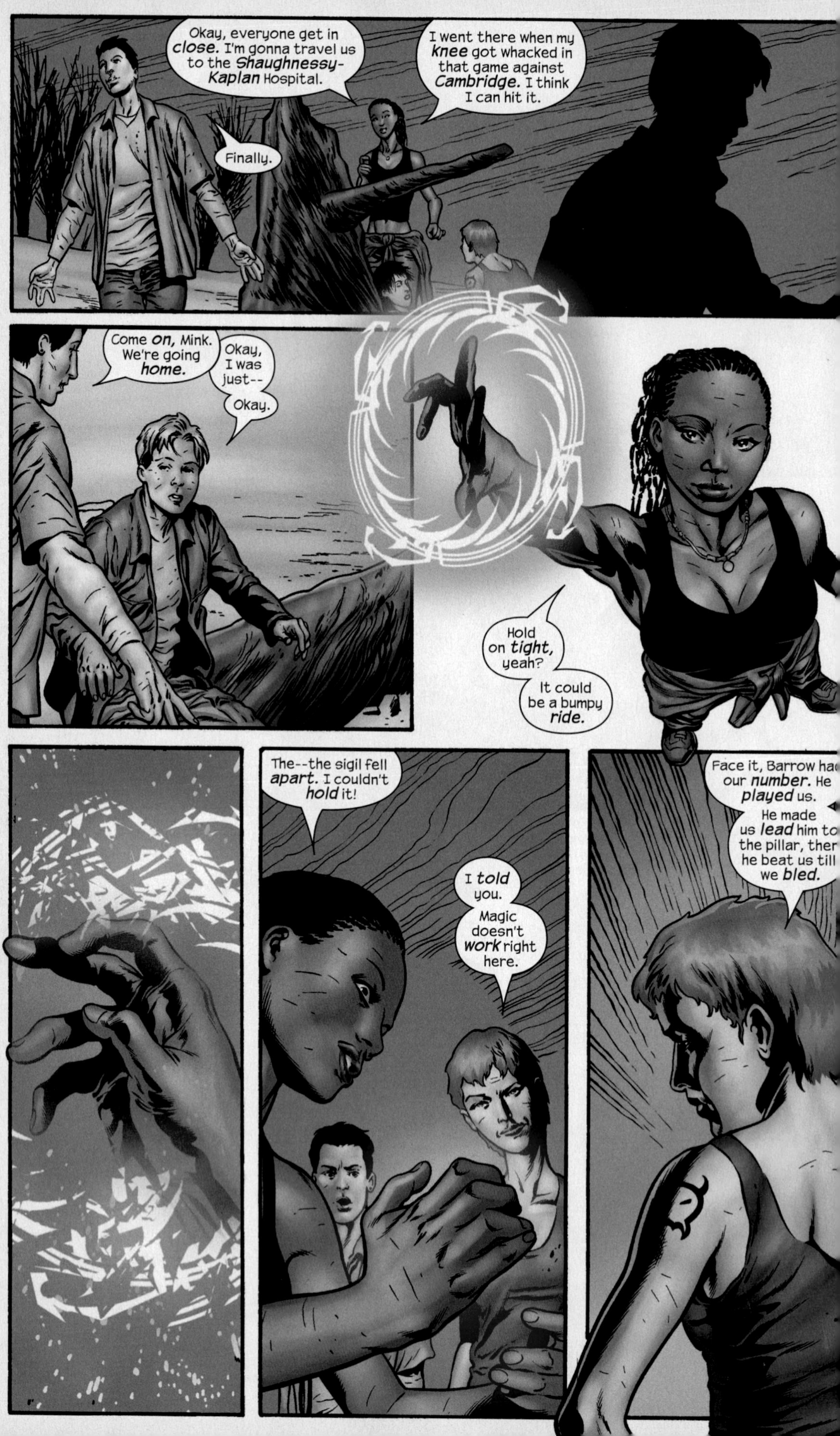
Okay, everyone get in close. I'm gonna travel us to the Shaughnessy-Kaplan Hospital.
I went there when my knee got whacked in that game against Cambridge. I think I can hit it.
Finally.
Come on, Mink. We're going home.
Okay, I was just--
Okay.
Hold on tight, yeah?
It could be a bumpy ride.
The--the sigil fell apart. I couldn't hold it!
I told you.
Magic doesn't work right here.
Face it, Barrow ha
our number. He played us.
He made us lead him to the pillar, ther he beat us till we bled.

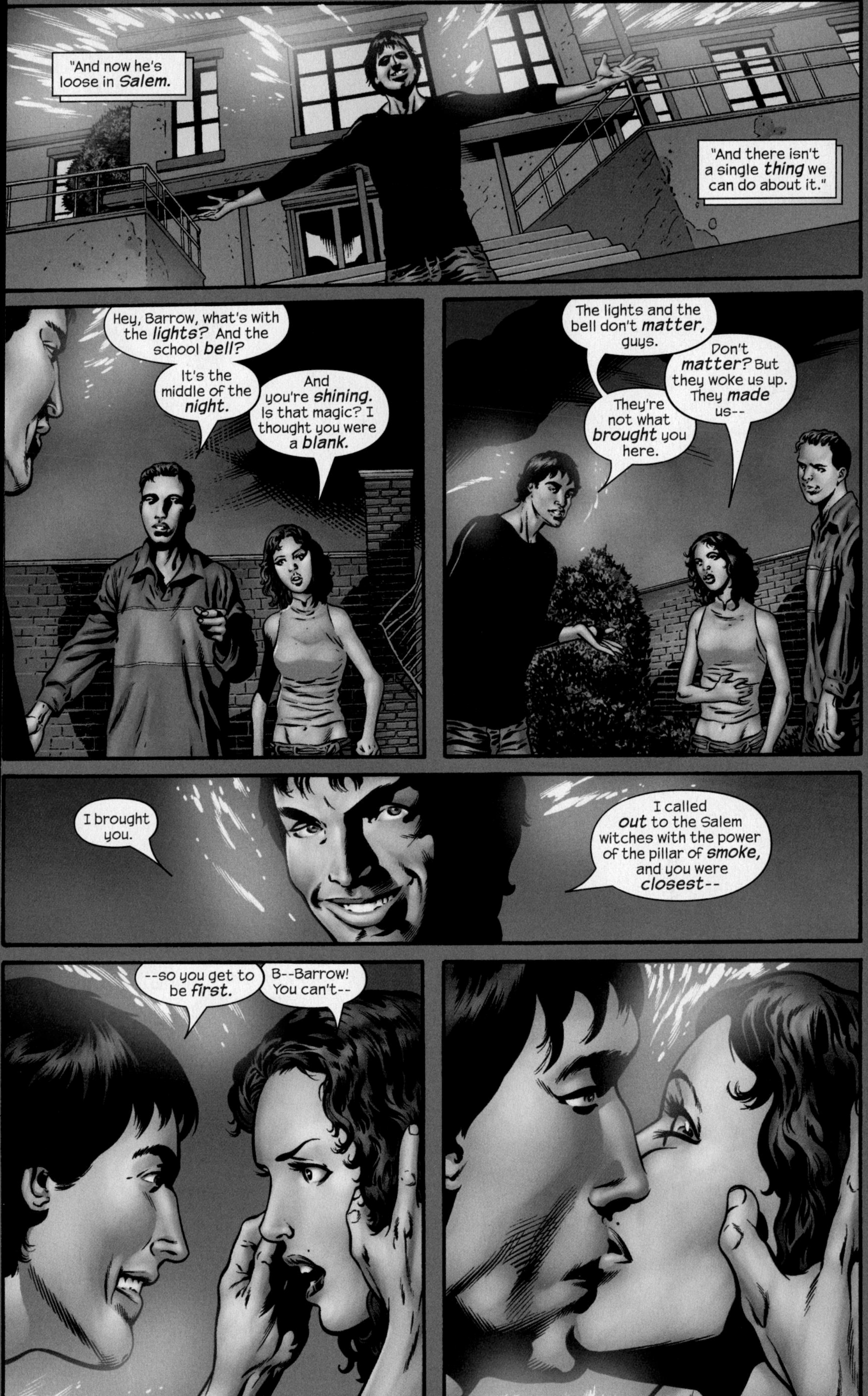

"And now he's loose in Salem.
"And there isn't a single thing we can do about it."
Hey, Barrow, what's with the lights? And the school bell?
It's the middle of the night.
And you're shining. Is that magic? I thought you were a blank.
The lights and the bell don't matter, guys.
They're not what brought you here.
Don't matter? But they woke us up. They made us--
I brought you.
I called out to the Salem witches with the power of the pillar of smoke, and you were closest--
--so you get to be first.
B--Barrow! You can't--

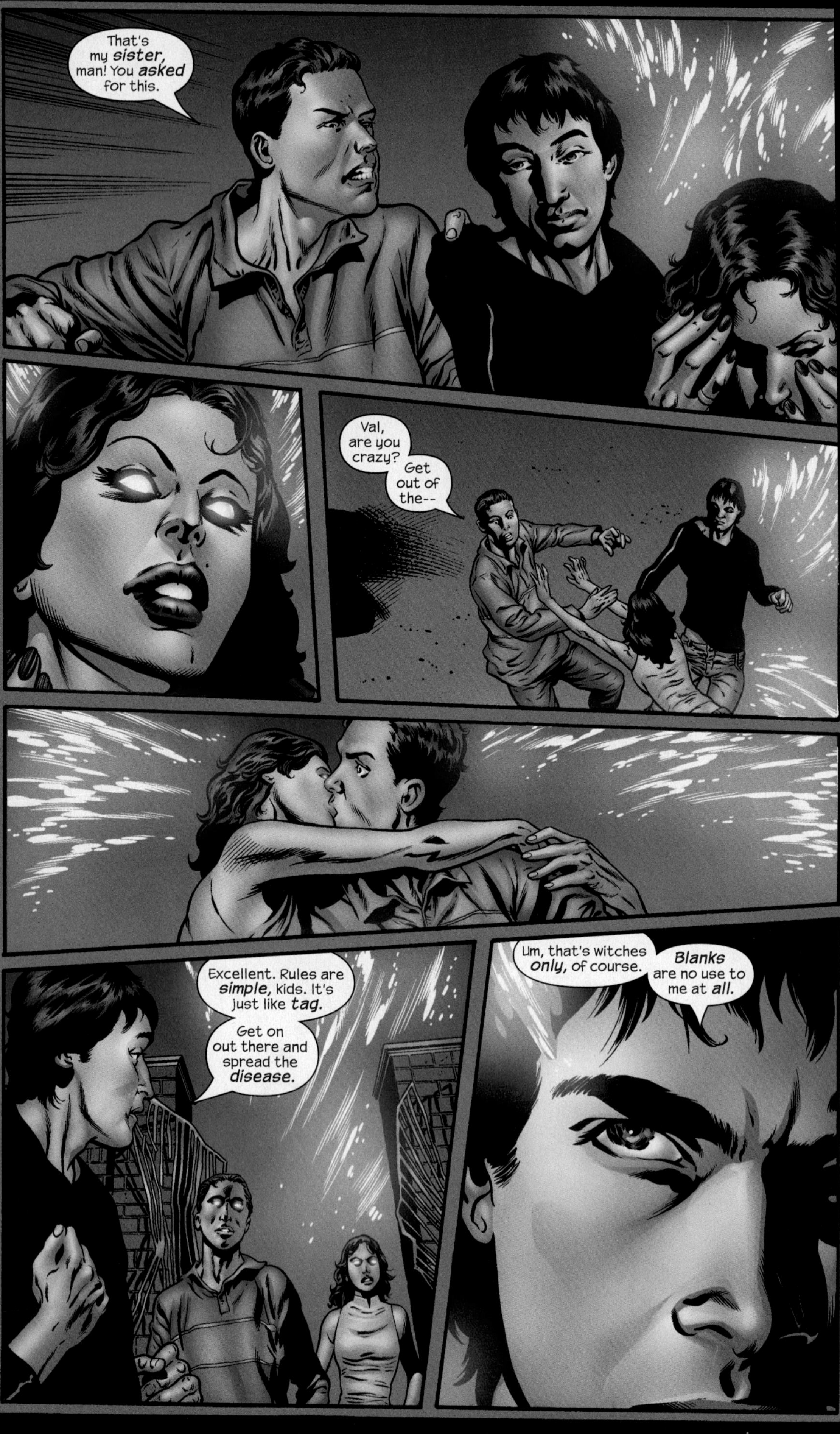
That's my *sister,* man! You *asked* for this.
Val, are you crazy?
Get out of the--
Excellent. Rules are *simple,* kids. It's just like *tag.*
Get on out there and spread the *disease.*
Um, that's witches *only,* of course.
Blanks are no use to me at *all.*

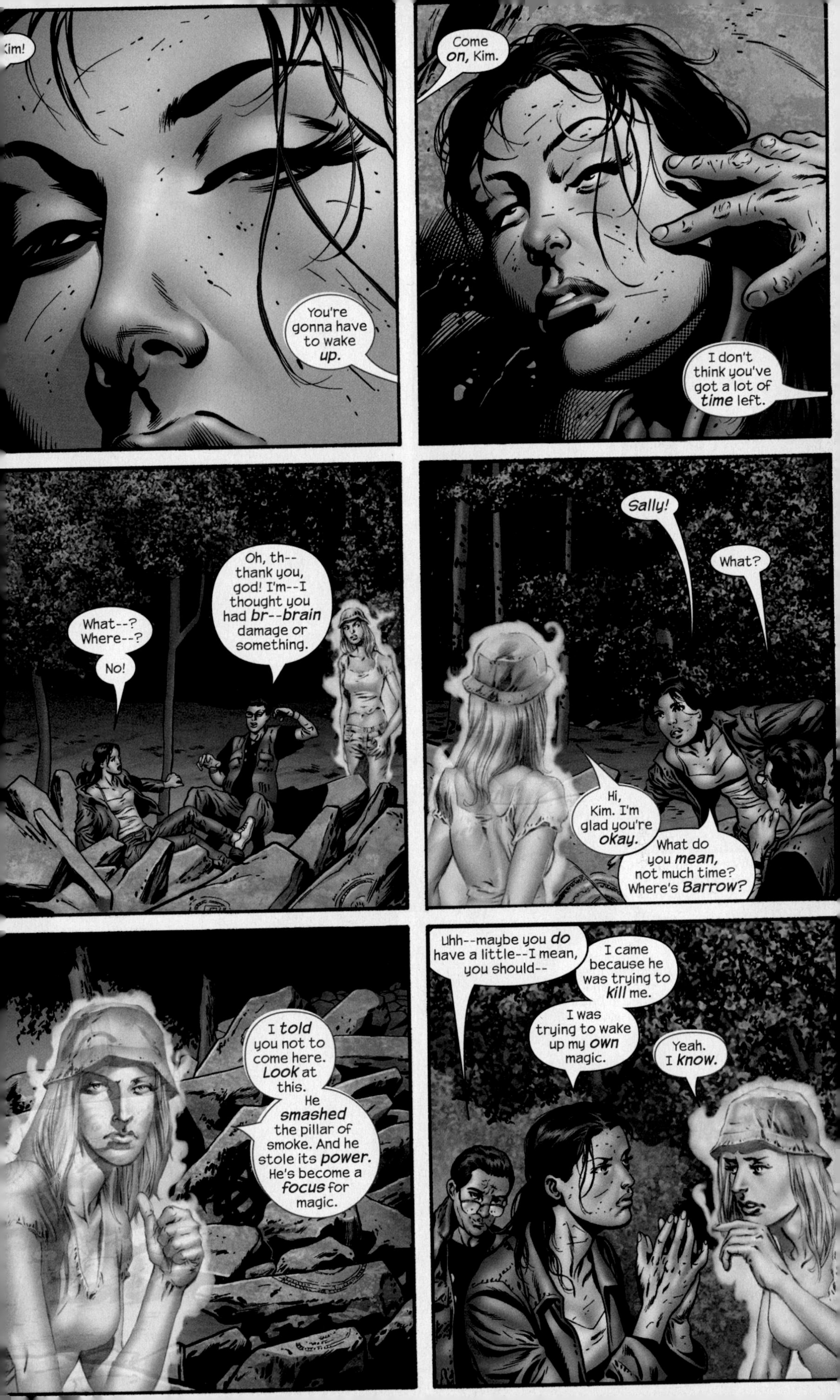

Kim!
You're gonna have to wake up.
Come on, Kim.
I don't think you've got a lot of time left.
What--? Where--?
No!
Oh, th-- thank you, god! I'm--I thought you had br--brain damage or something.
Sally!
What?
Hi, Kim. I'm glad you're okay.
What do you mean, not much time? Where's Barrow?
I told you not to come here. Look at this.
He smashed the pillar of smoke. And he stole its power. He's become a focus for magic.
Uhh--maybe you do have a little--I mean, you should--
I came because he was trying to kill me.
I was trying to wake up my own magic.
Yeah. I know.

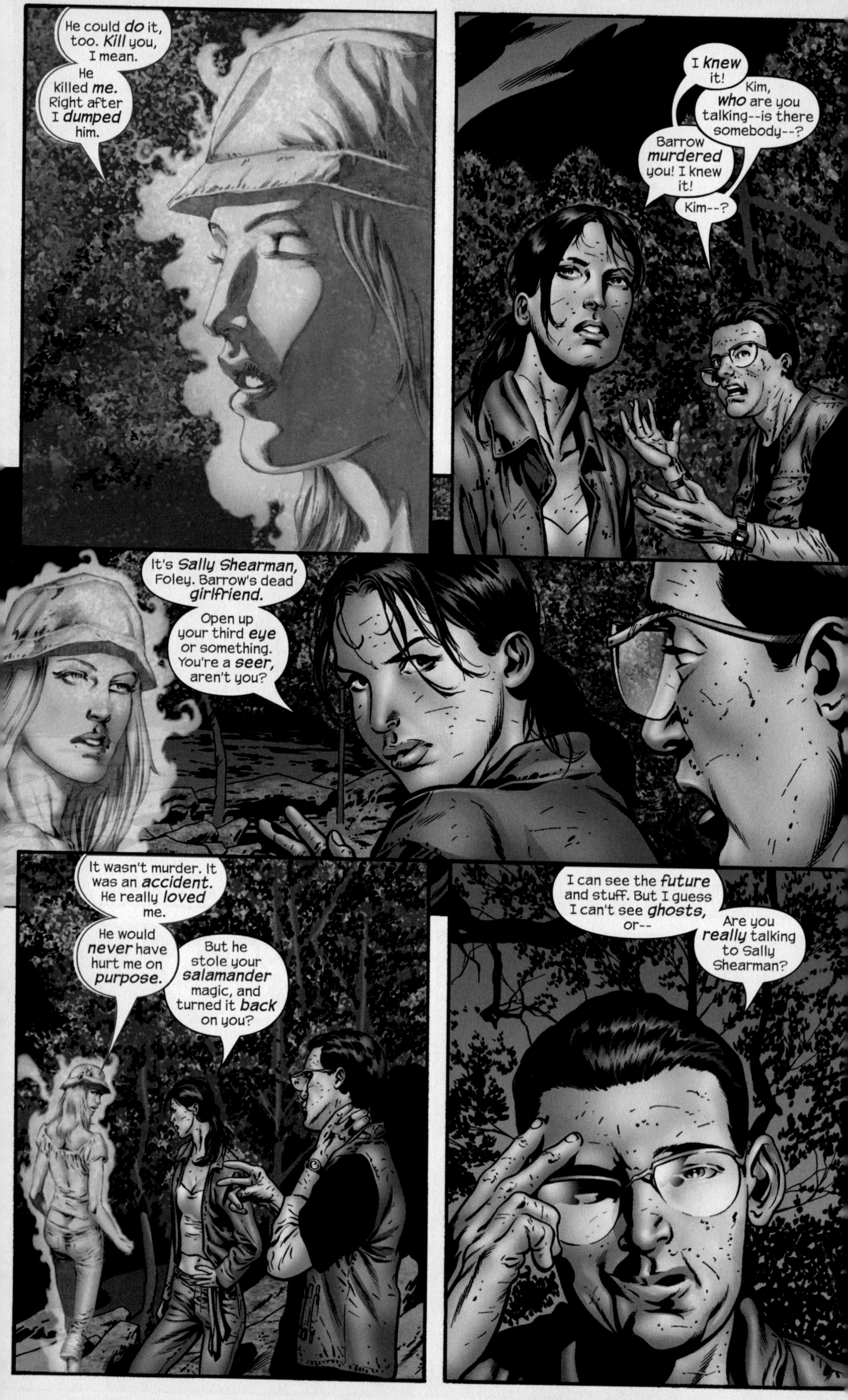
He could do it, too. Kill you, I mean.
He killed me. Right after I dumped him.
I knew it!
Kim, who are you talking--is there somebody--?
Barrow murdered you! I knew it!
Kim--?
It's Sally Shearman, Foley. Barrow's dead girlfriend.
Open up your third eye or something. You're a seer, aren't you?
It wasn't murder. It was an accident. He really loved me.
He would never have hurt me on purpose.
But he stole your salamander magic, and turned it back on you?
I can see the future and stuff. But I guess I can't see ghosts, or--
Are you really talking to Sally Shearman?

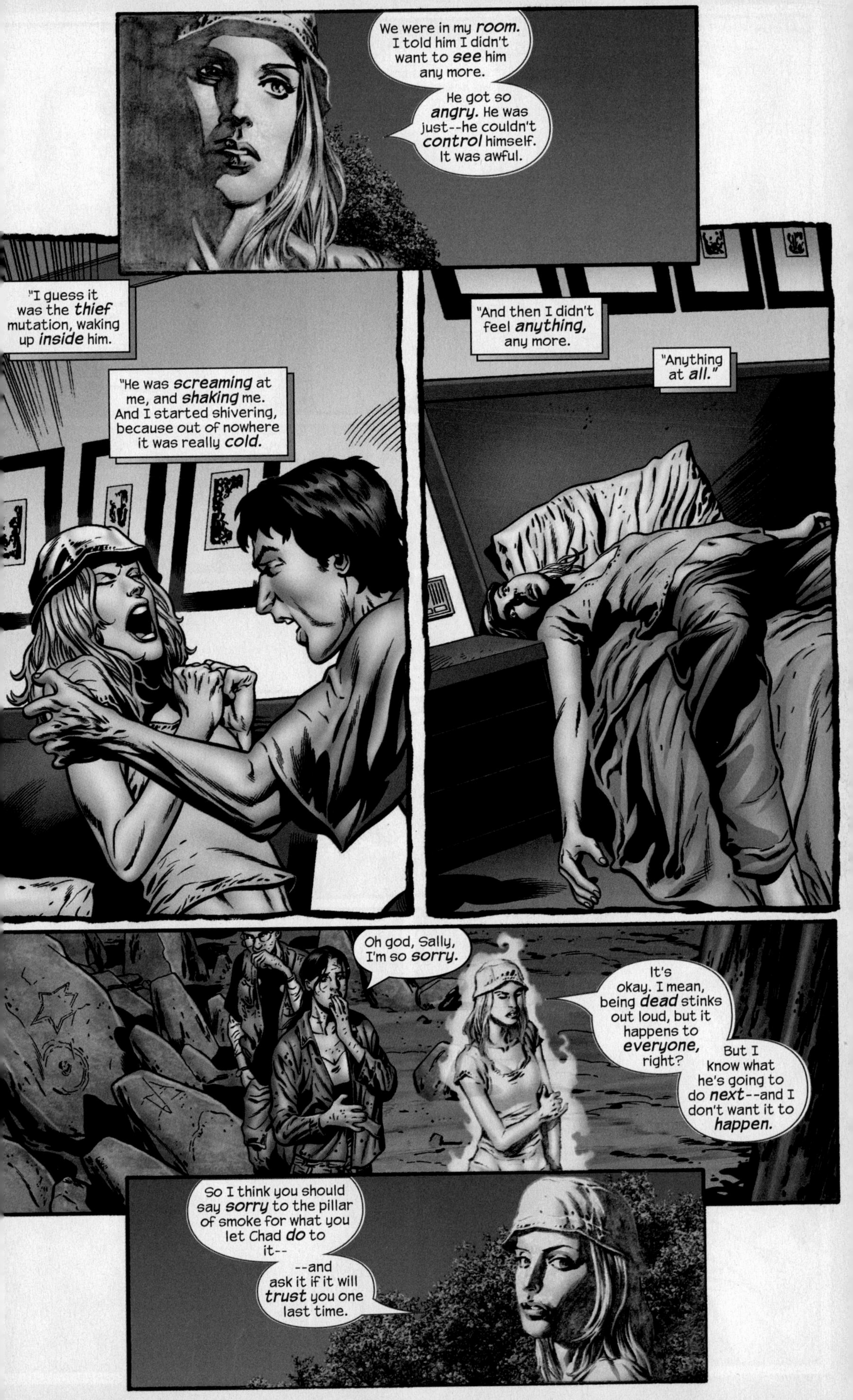

We were in my room. I told him I didn't want to see him any more.
He got so angry. He was just--he couldn't control himself. It was awful.
"I guess it was the thief mutation, waking up inside him.
"He was screaming at me, and shaking me. And I started shivering, because out of nowhere it was really cold.
"And then I didn't feel anything, any more.
"Anything at all."
Oh god, Sally, I'm so sorry.
It's okay. I mean, being dead stinks out loud, but it happens to everyone, right?
But I know what he's going to do next--and I don't want it to happen.
So I think you should say sorry to the pillar of smoke for what you let Chad do to it--
--and ask it if it will trust you one last time.

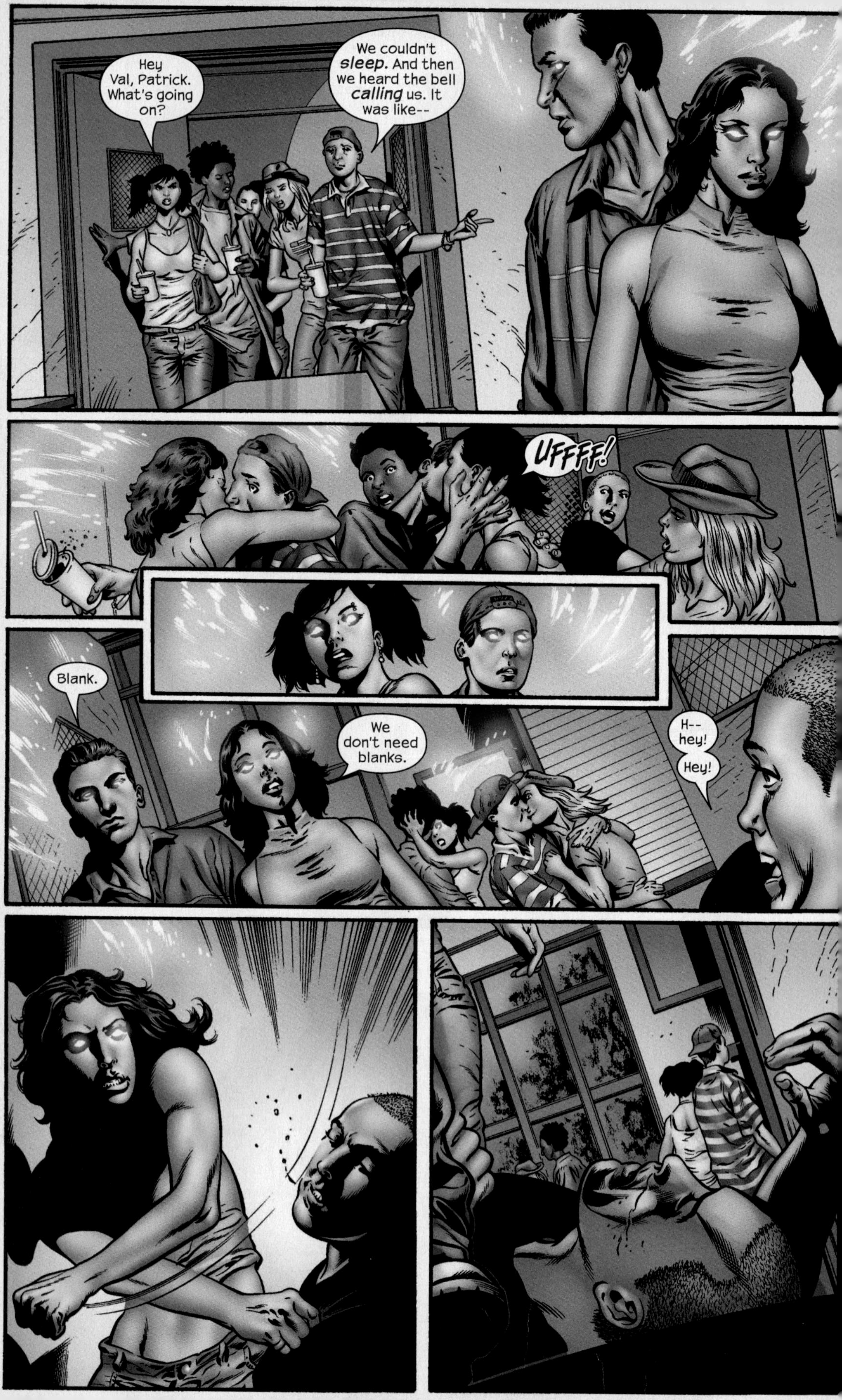
Hey
Val, Patrick.
What's going
on?
We couldn't
sleep. And then
we heard the bell
calling us. It
was like--
UFFFF!
Blank.
We
don't need
blanks.
H--
hey!
Hey!

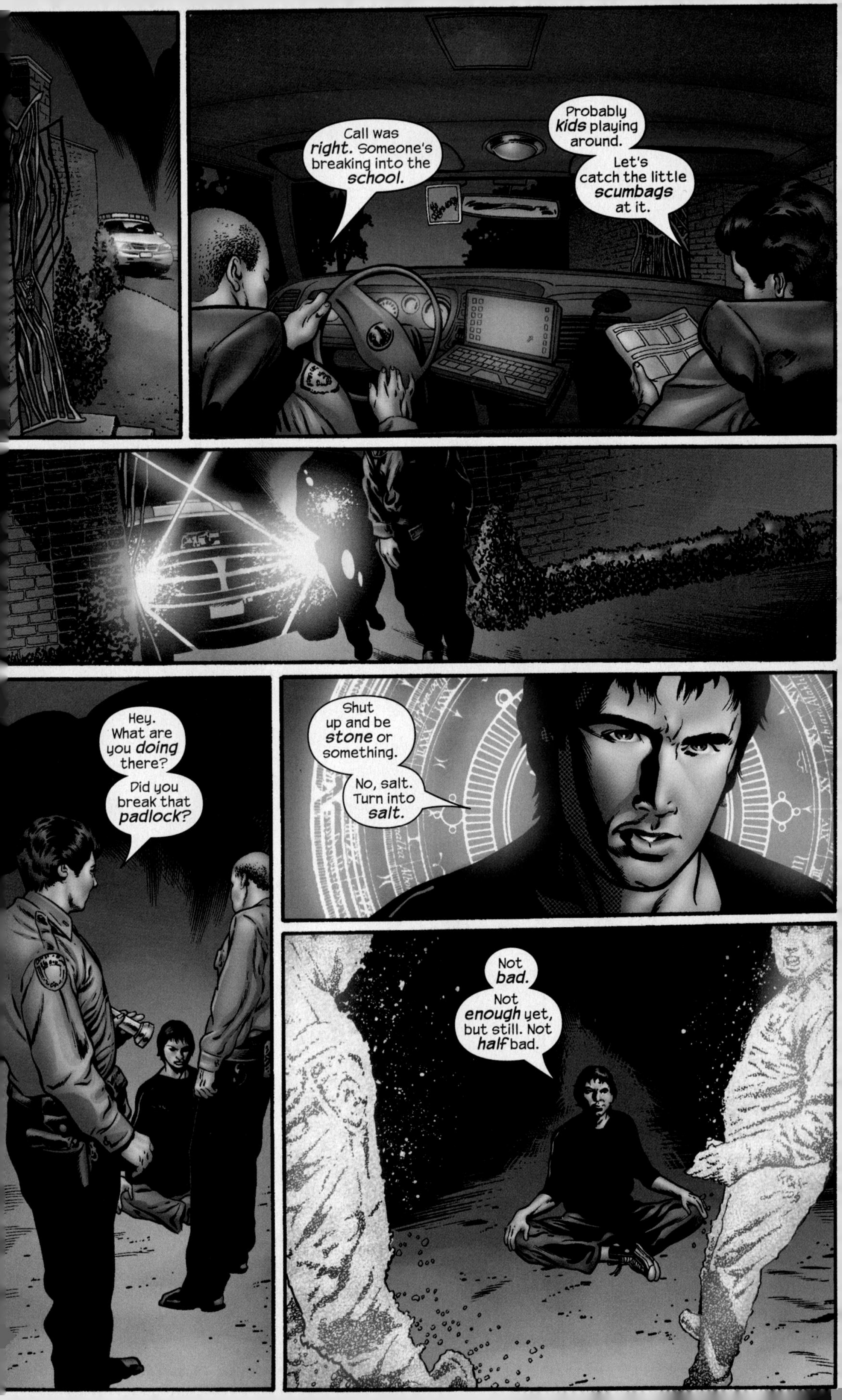
Call was right. Someone's breaking into the school.
Probably kids playing around.
Let's catch the little scumbags at it.
Hey. What are you doing there?
Did you break that padlock?
Shut up and be stone or something.
No, salt. Turn into salt.
Not bad.
Not enough yet, but still. Not half bad.

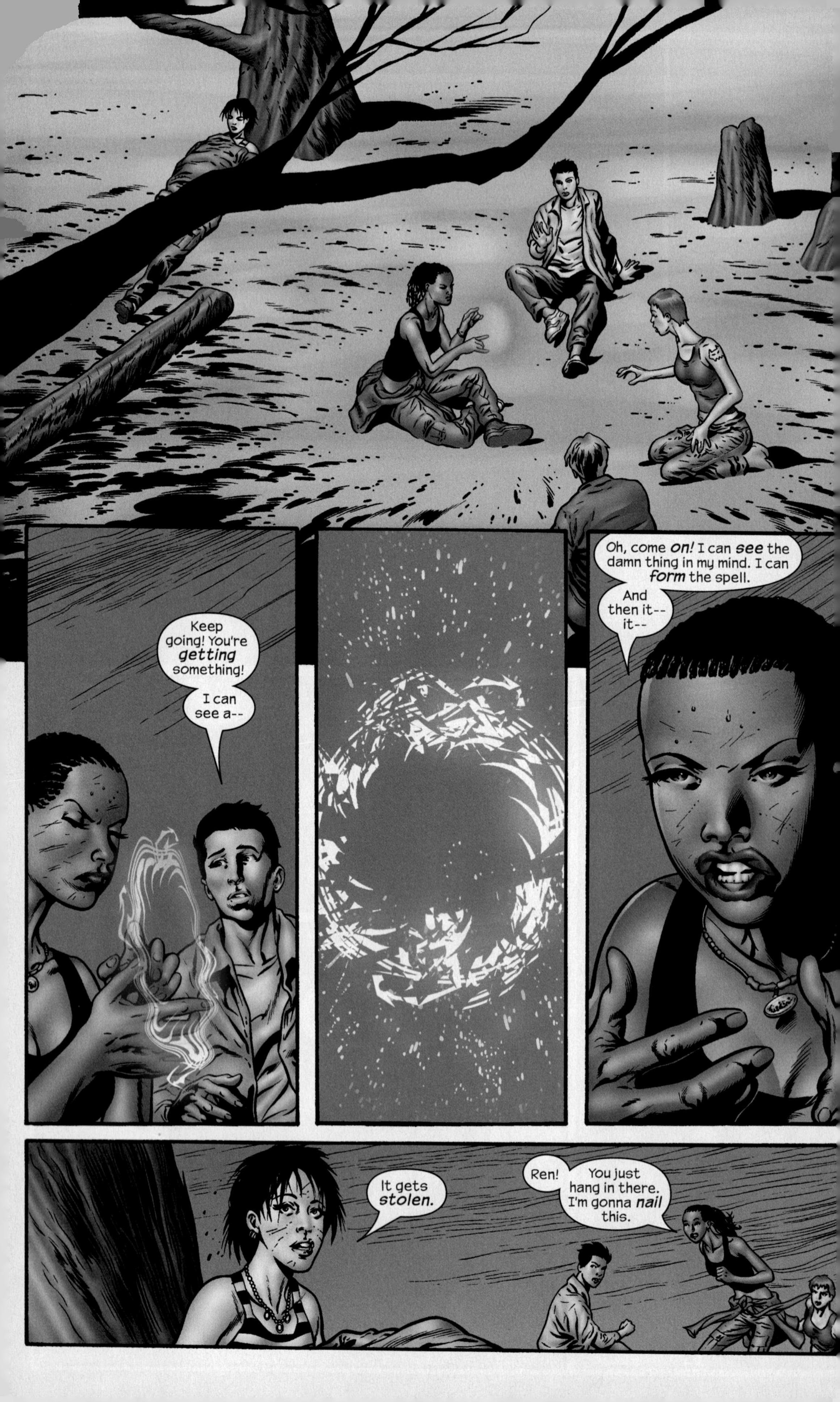
Keep going! You're getting something!
I can see a--
Oh, come on! I can see the damn thing in my mind. I can form the spell.
And then it-- it--
It gets stolen.
Ren!
You just hang in there. I'm gonna nail this.

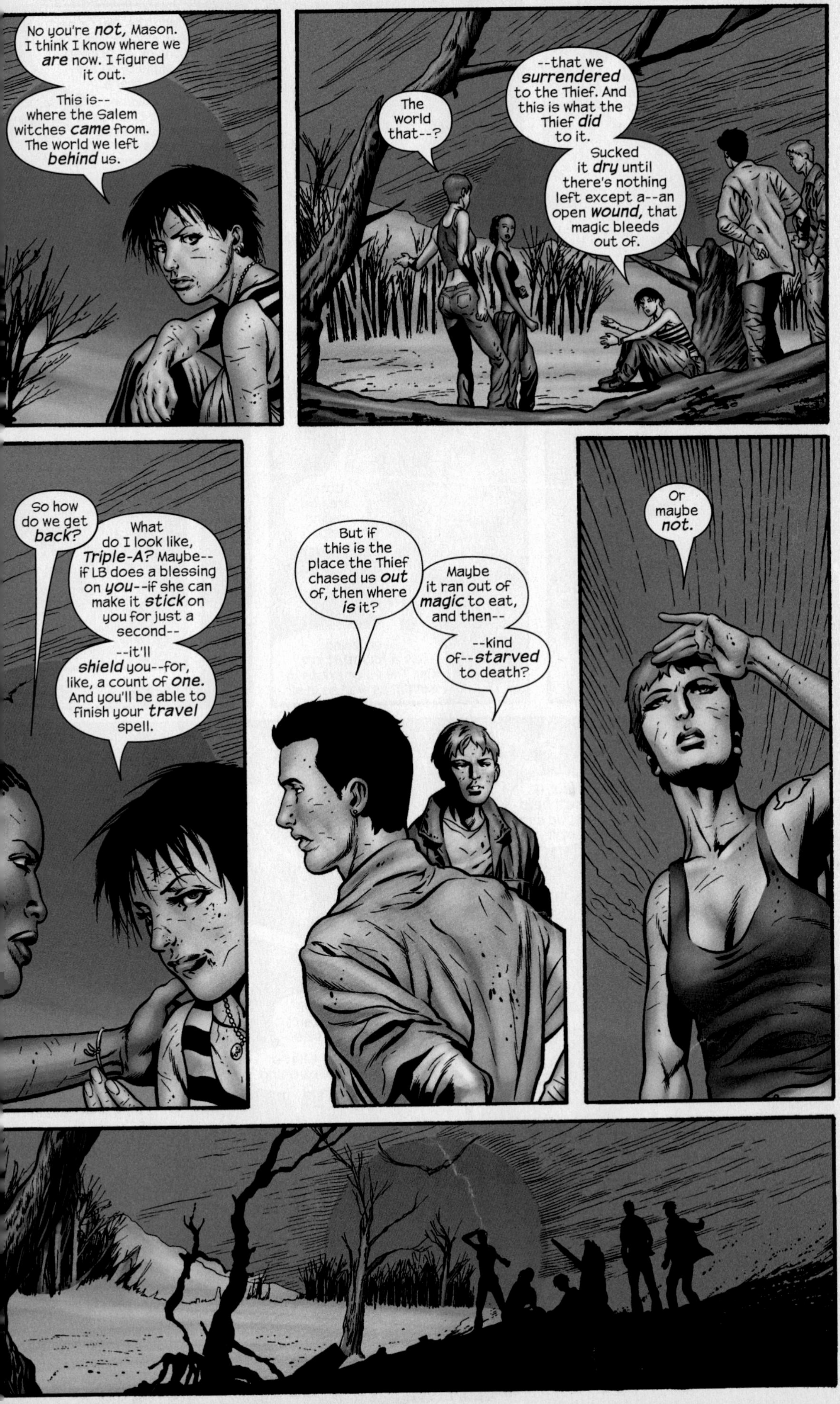

No you're not, Mason. I think I know where we are now. I figured it out.
This is-- where the Salem witches came from. The world we left behind us.
The world that--?
--that we surrendered to the Thief. And this is what the Thief did to it.
Sucked it dry until there's nothing left except a--an open wound, that magic bleeds out of.
So how do we get back?
What do I look like, Triple-A? Maybe--if LB does a blessing on you--if she can make it stick on you for just a second--
--it'll shield you--for, like, a count of one. And you'll be able to finish your travel spell.
But if this is the place the Thief chased us out of, then where is it?
Maybe it ran out of magic to eat, and then--
--kind of--starved to death?
Or maybe not.

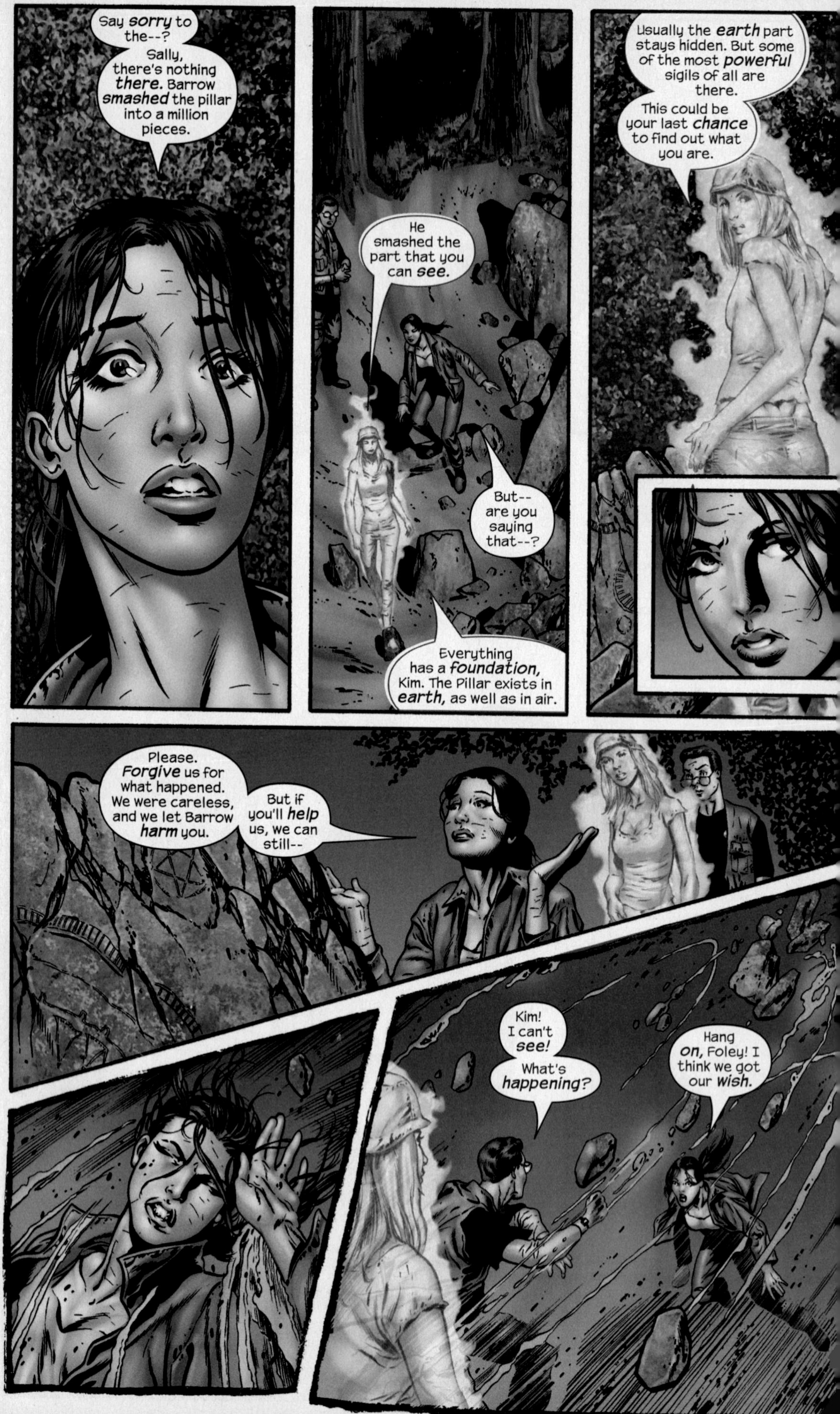

Say sorry to the--?
Sally, there's nothing there. Barrow smashed the pillar into a million pieces.
He smashed the part that you can see.
But-- are you saying that--?
Everything has a foundation, Kim. The Pillar exists in earth, as well as in air.
Usually the earth part stays hidden. But some of the most powerful sigils of all are there.
This could be your last chance to find out what you are.
Please. Forgive us for what happened. We were careless, and we let Barrow harm you.
But if you'll help us, we can still--
Kim! I can't see!
What's happening?
Hang on, Foley! I think we got our wish.

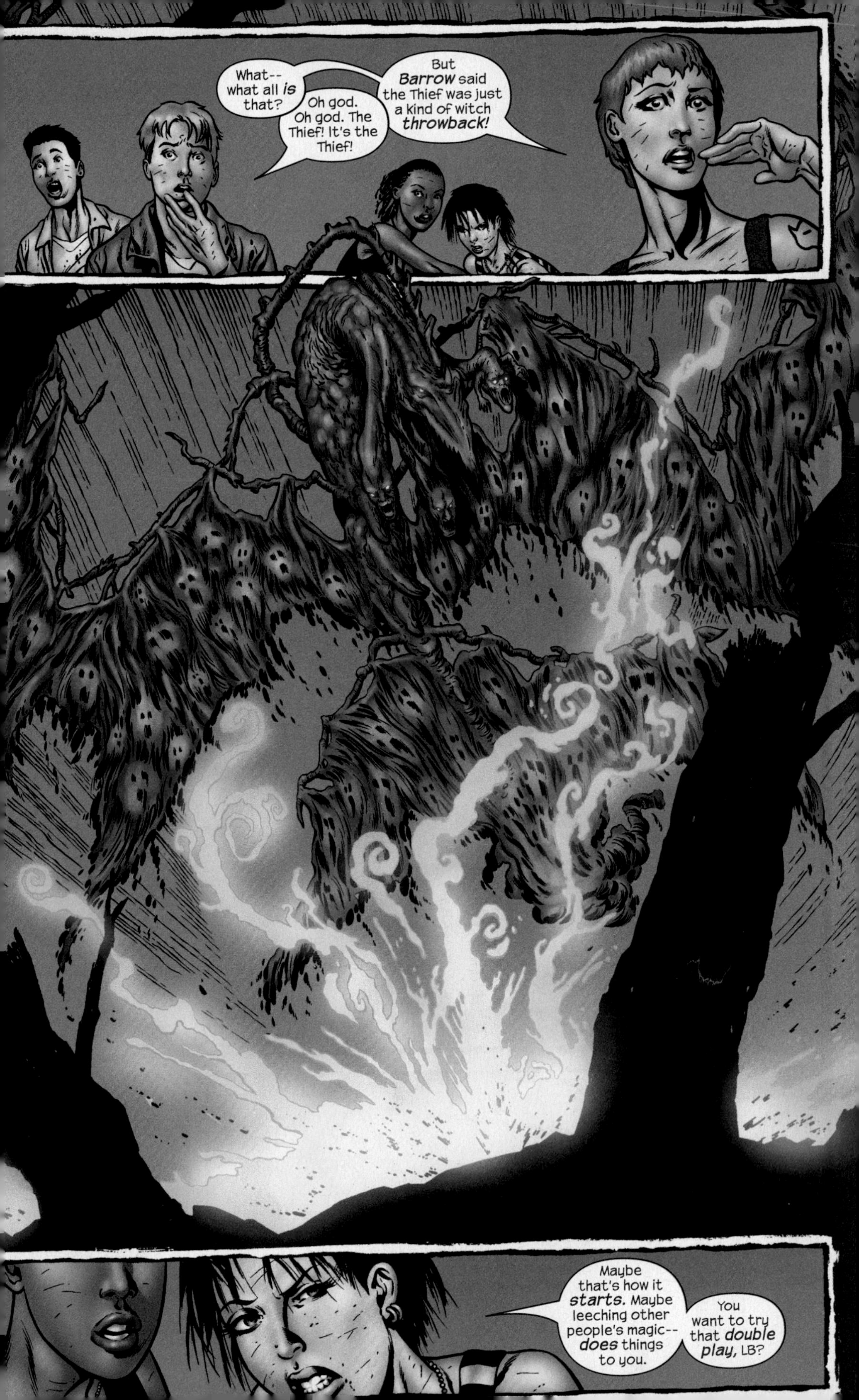
What-- what all is that?
Oh god. Oh god. The Thief! It's the Thief!
But Barrow said the Thief was just a kind of witch throwback!
Maybe that's how it starts. Maybe leeching other people's magic-- does things to you.
You want to try that double play, LB?

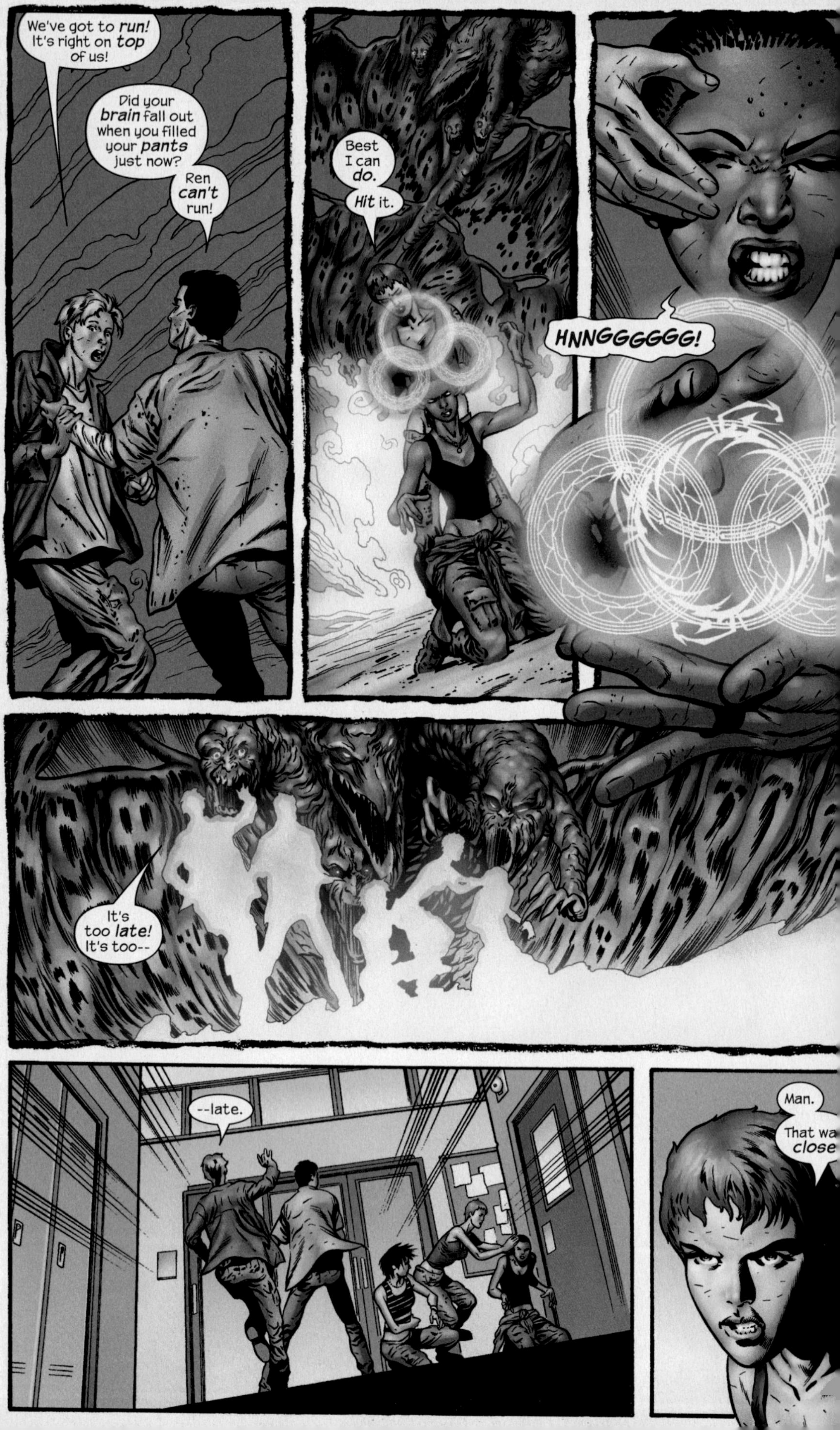

We've got to run! It's right on top of us!
Did your brain fall out when you filled your pants just now?
Ren can't run!
Best I can do.
Hit it.
HNNGGGGGG!
It's too late! It's too--
--late.
Man.
That wa
close

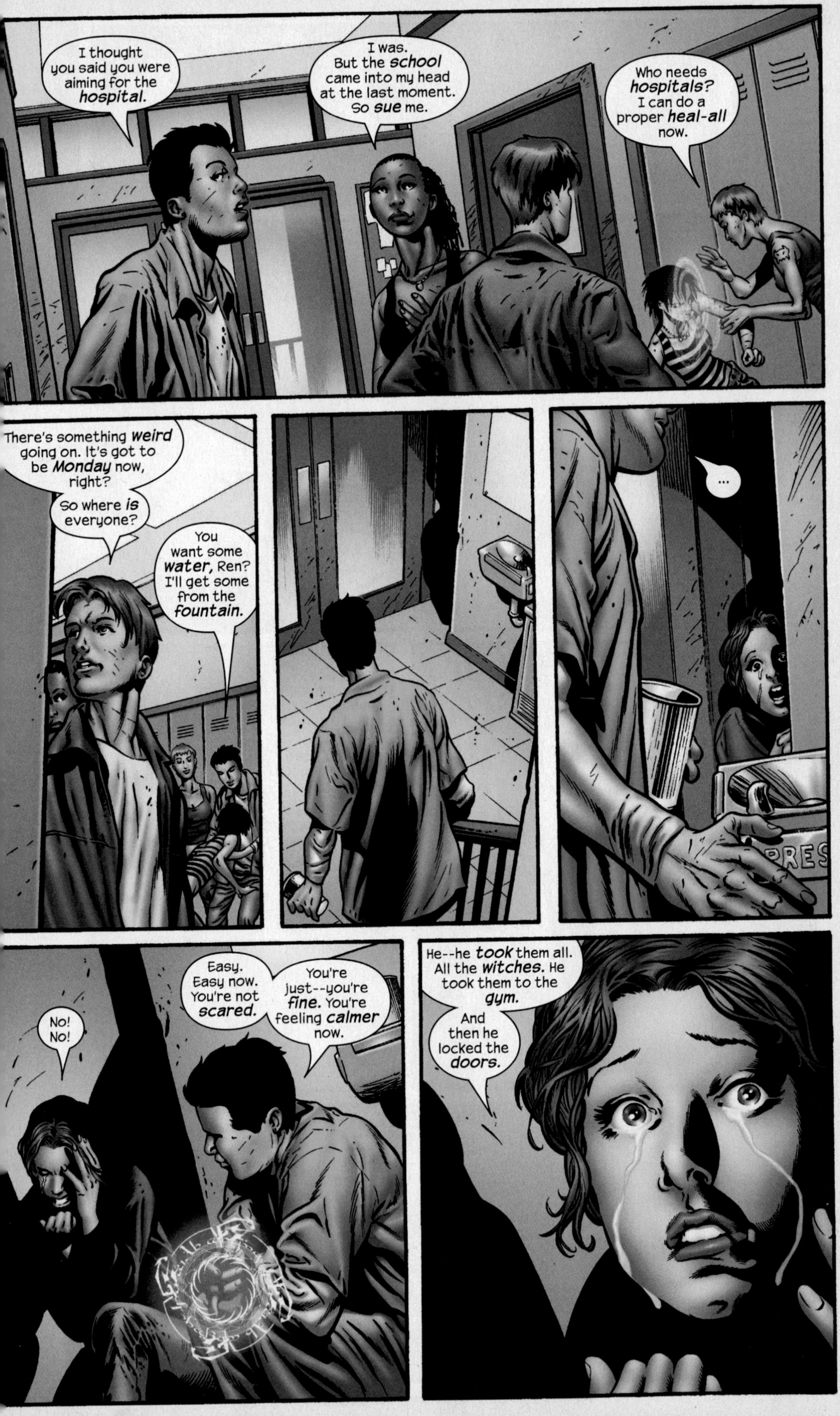
I thought you said you were aiming for the hospital.
I was. But the school came into my head at the last moment. So sue me.
Who needs hospitals? I can do a proper heal-all now.
There's something weird going on. It's got to be Monday now, right?
So where is everyone?
You want some water, Ren? I'll get some from the fountain.
...
PRES
No! No!
Easy. Easy now. You're not scared.
You're just--you're fine. You're feeling calmer now.
He--he took them all. All the witches. He took them to the gym.
And then he locked the doors.

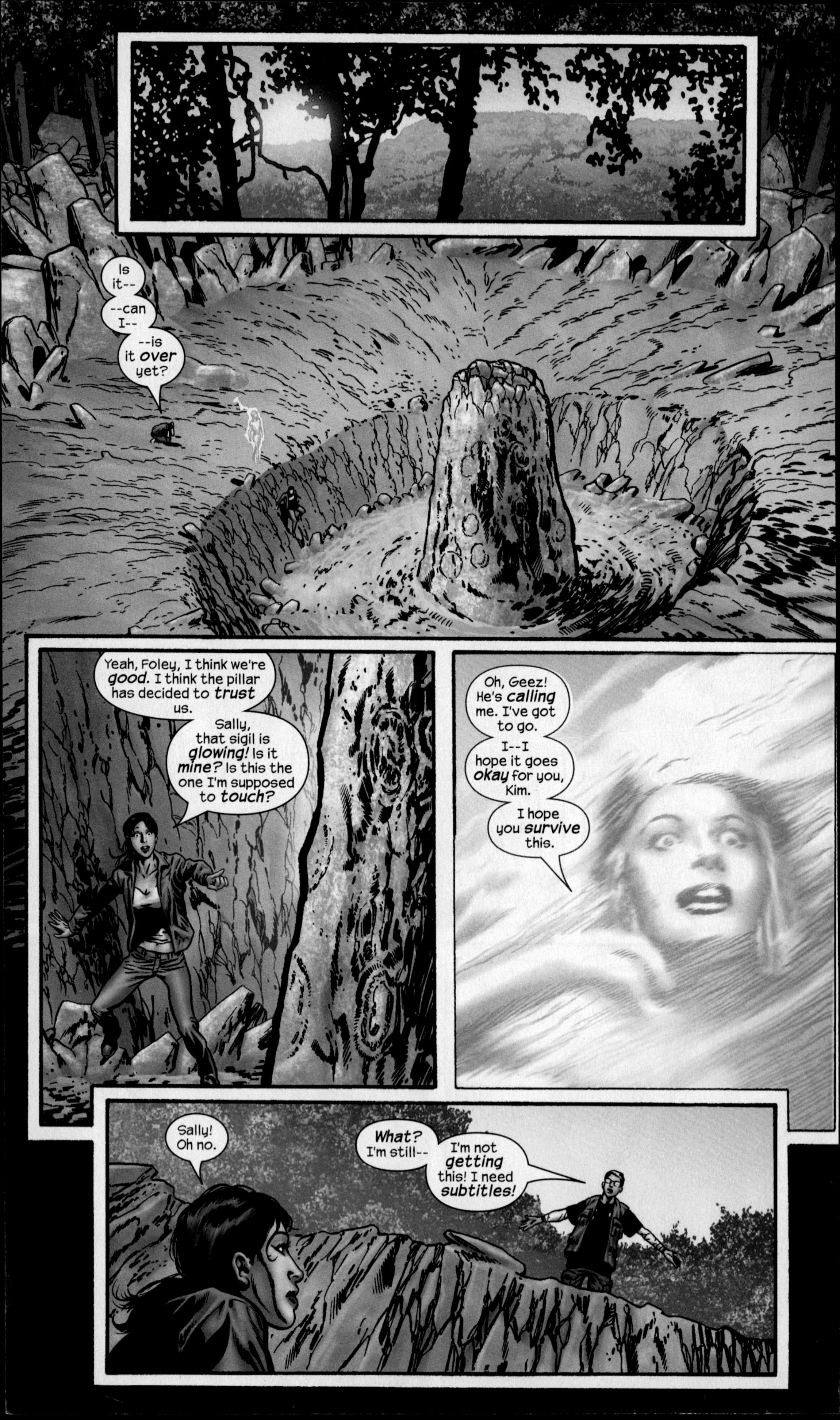
Is it--
--can I--
--is it *over* yet?
Yeah, Foley, I think we're *good*. I think the pillar has decided to *trust* us.
Sally, that sigil is *glowing!* Is it *mine?* Is this the one I'm supposed to *touch?*
Oh, Geez! He's *calling* me. I've got to go.
I--I hope it goes *okay* for you, Kim.
I hope you *survive* this.
Sally! Oh no.
What? I'm still--
I'm not *getting* this! I need *subtitles!*

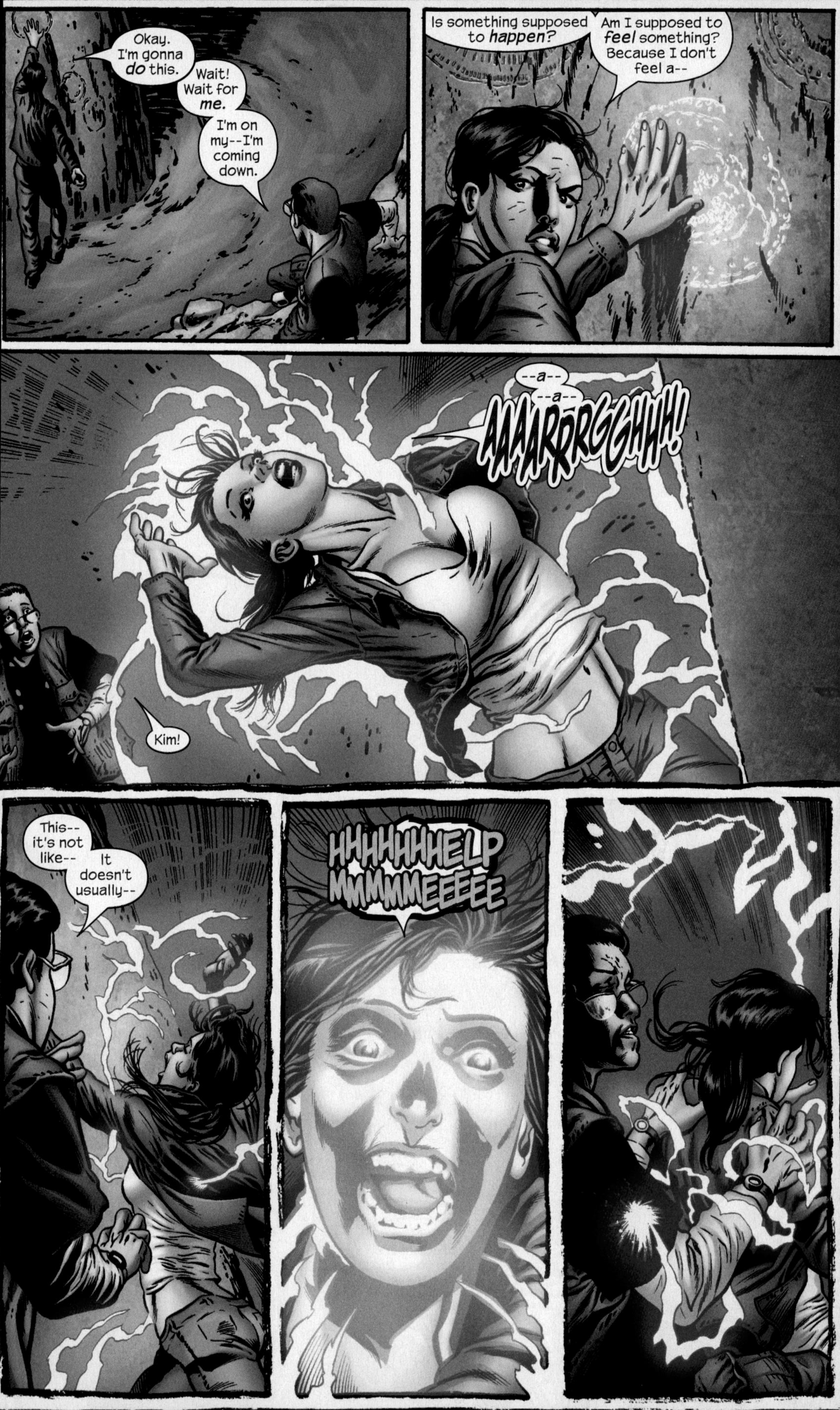

Okay. I'm gonna *do* this.
Wait! Wait for *me.*
I'm on my--I'm coming down.
Is something supposed to *happen*?
Am I supposed to *feel* something? Because I don't feel a--
--a--
--a--
AAAARRRGGHHH!
Kim!
This-- it's not like--
It doesn't usually--
HHHHHHHELP MMMMMEEEEE

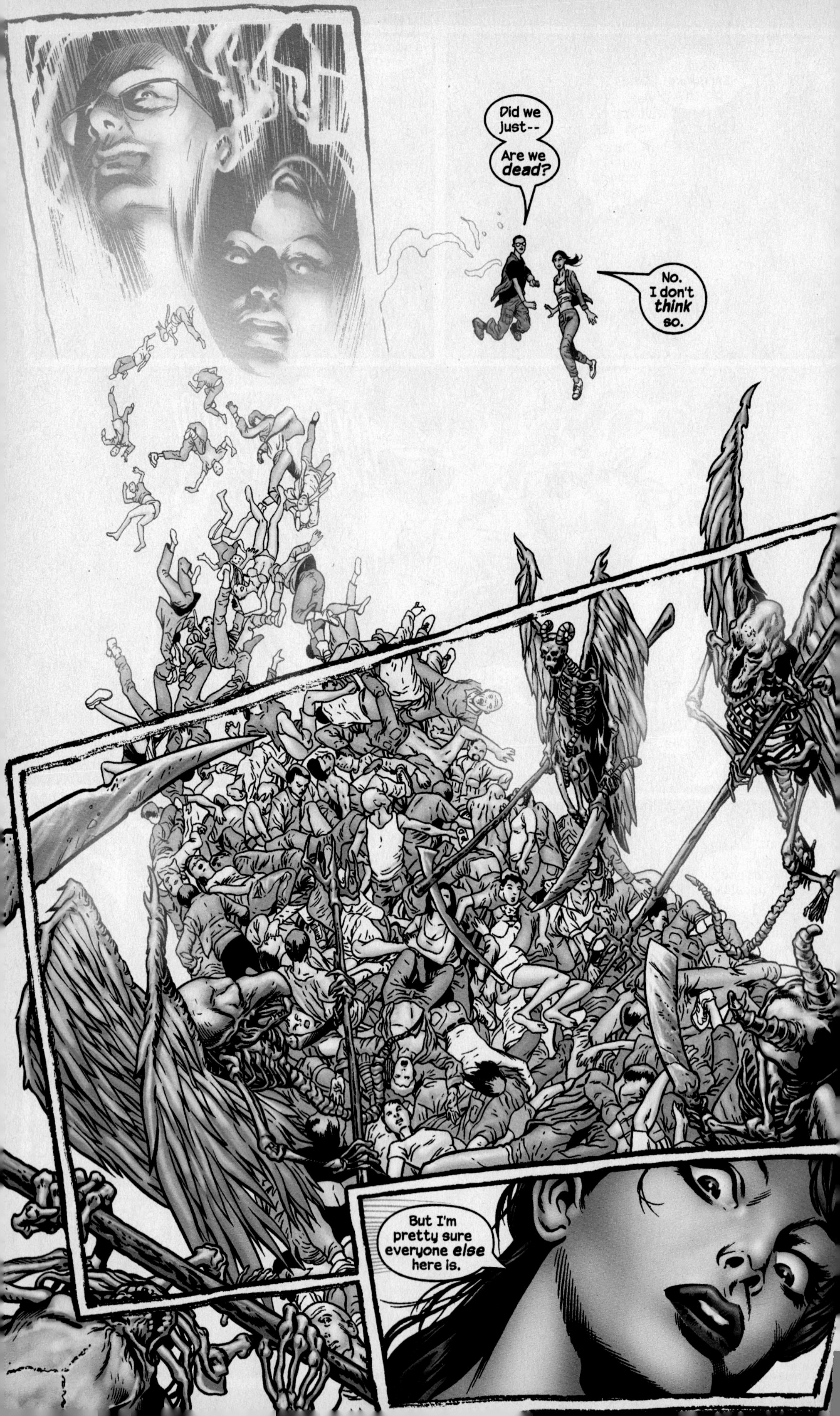
Did we just--
Are we *dead?*
No. I don't *think* so.
But I'm pretty sure everyone *else* here is.

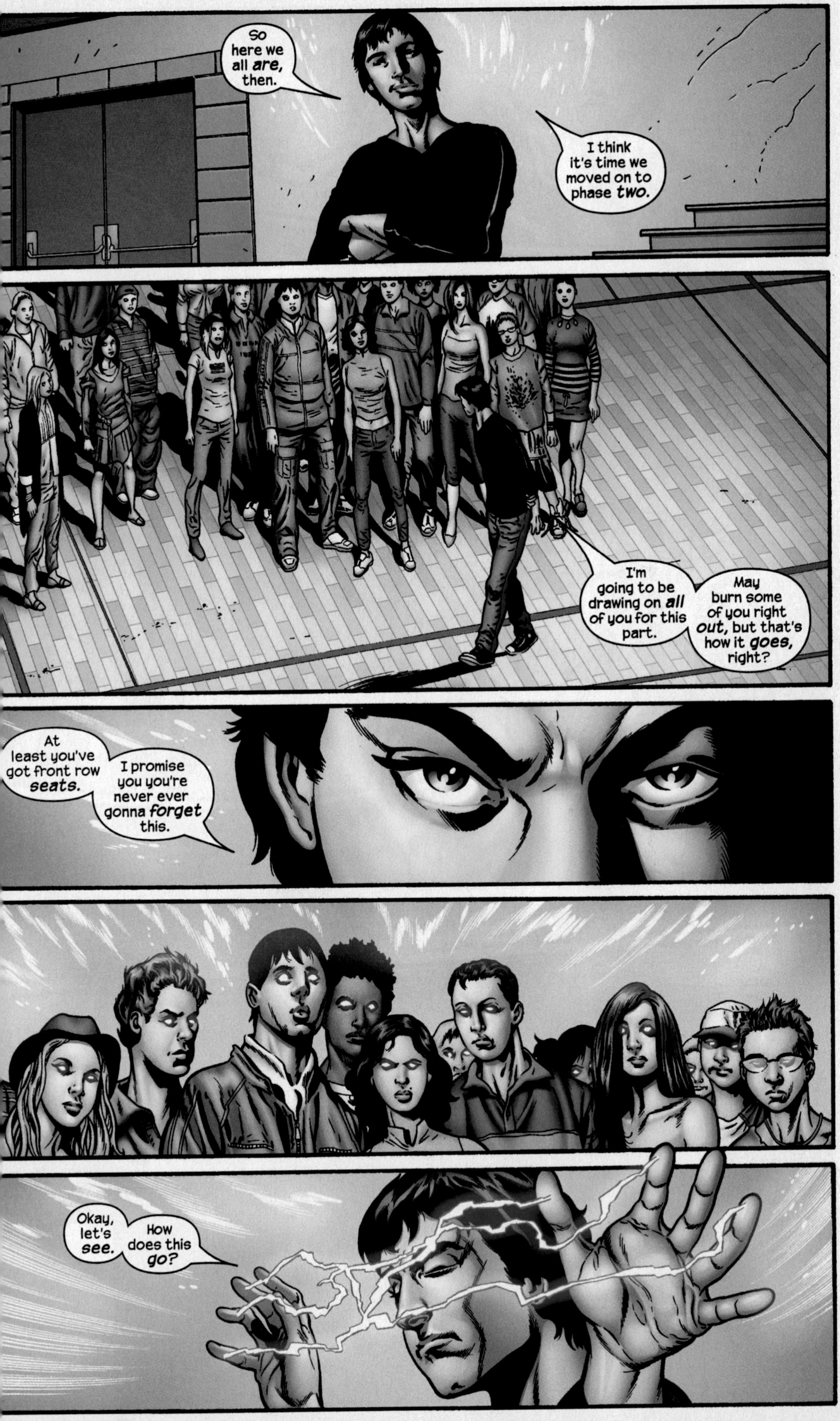
So here we all *are*, then.
I think it's time we moved on to phase *two*.
I'm going to be drawing on *all* of you for this part.
May burn some of you right *out*, but that's how it *goes*, right?
At least you've got front row *seats*.
I promise you you're never ever gonna *forget* this.
Okay, let's *see*.
How does this *go?*

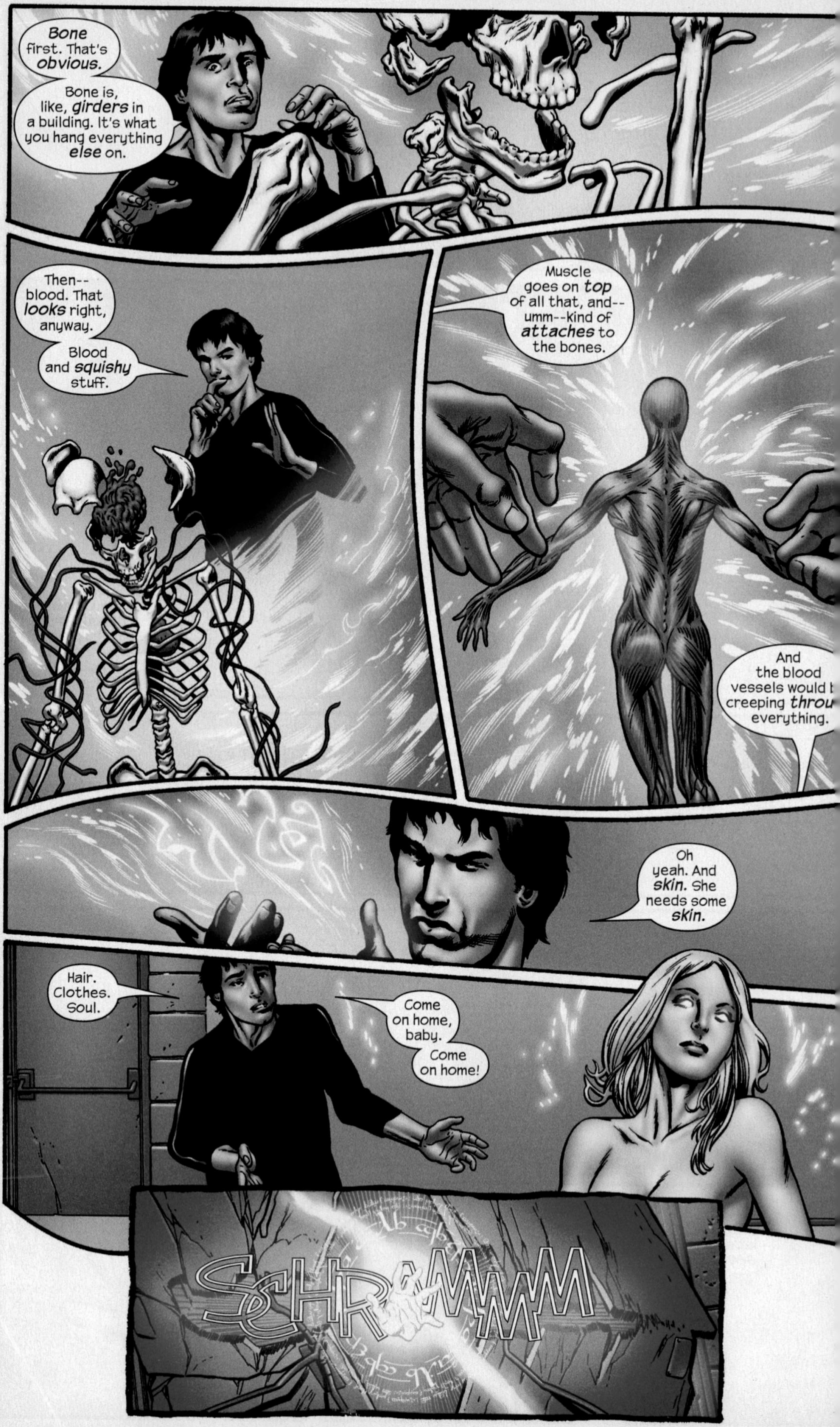
Bone first. That's obvious.
Bone is, like, girders in a building. It's what you hang everything else on.
Then--blood. That looks right, anyway.
Blood and squishy stuff.
Muscle goes on top of all that, and--umm--kind of attaches to the bones.
And the blood vessels would b creeping throu everything.
Oh yeah. And skin. She needs some skin.
Hair. Clothes. Soul.
Come on home, baby.
Come on home!
SCHRAMMMM

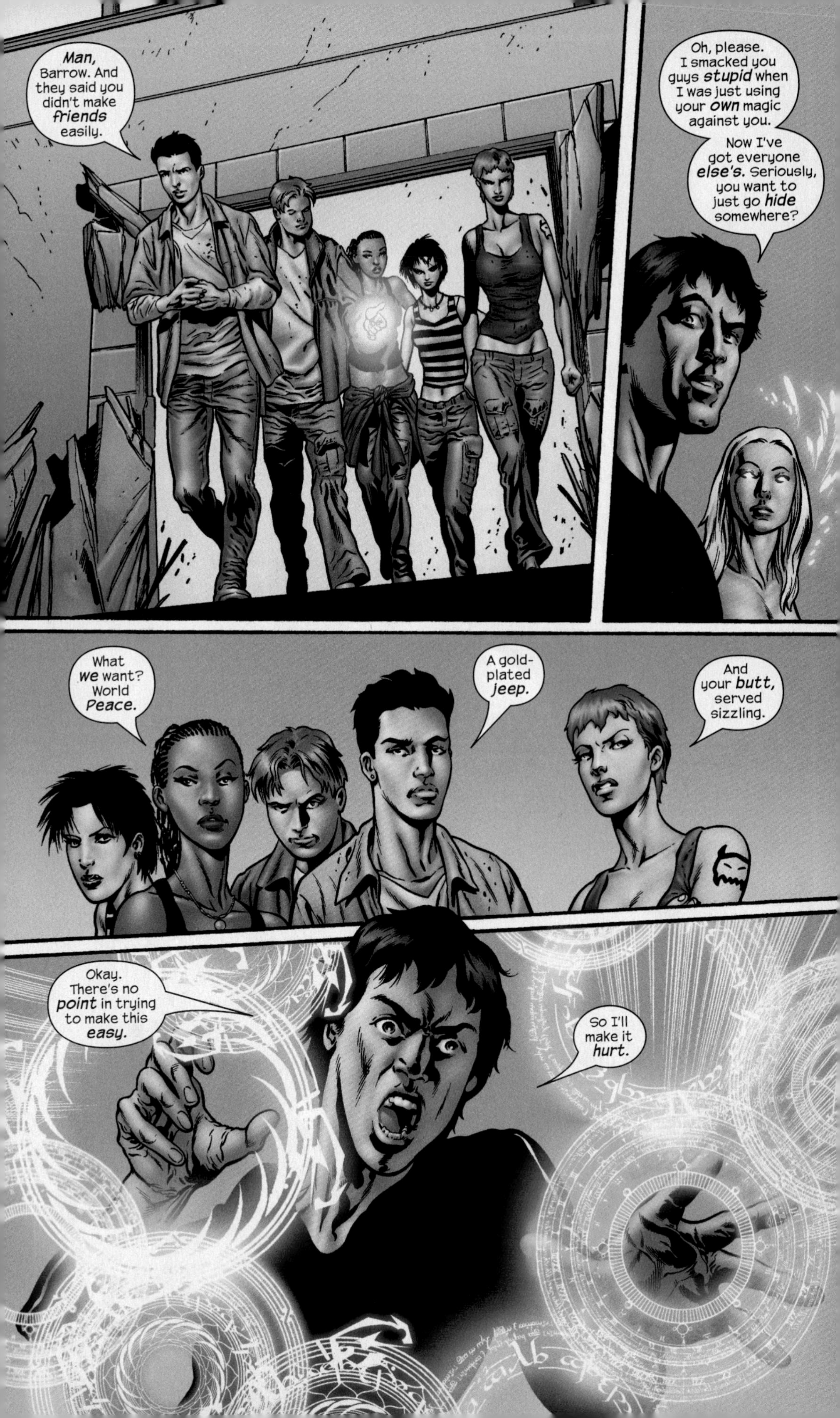

Man, Barrow. And they said you didn't make friends easily.
Oh, please. I smacked you guys stupid when I was just using your own magic against you.
Now I've got everyone else's. Seriously, you want to just go hide somewhere?
What we want? World Peace.
A gold-plated jeep.
And your butt, served sizzling.
Okay. There's no point in trying to make this easy.
So I'll make it hurt.

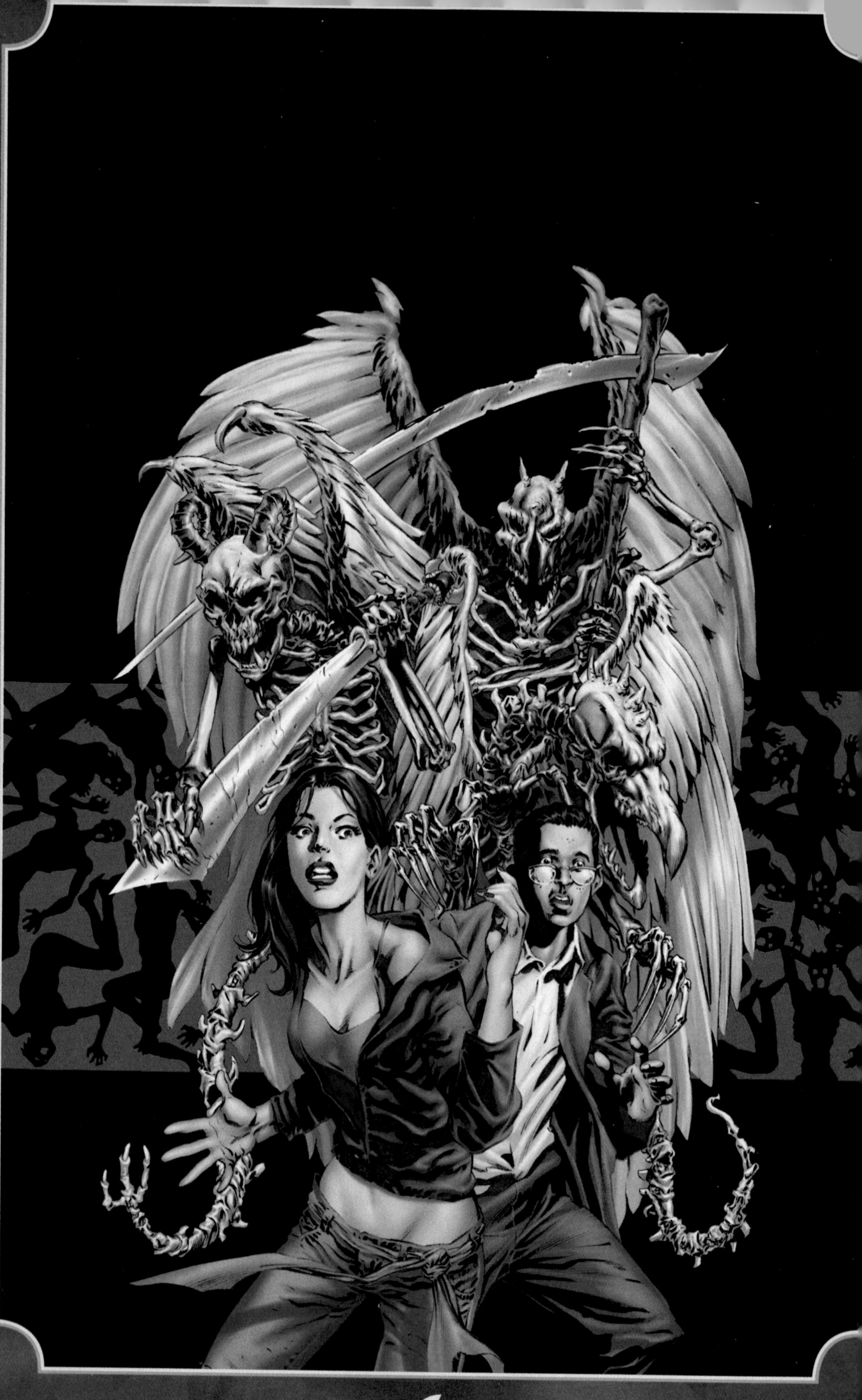

6

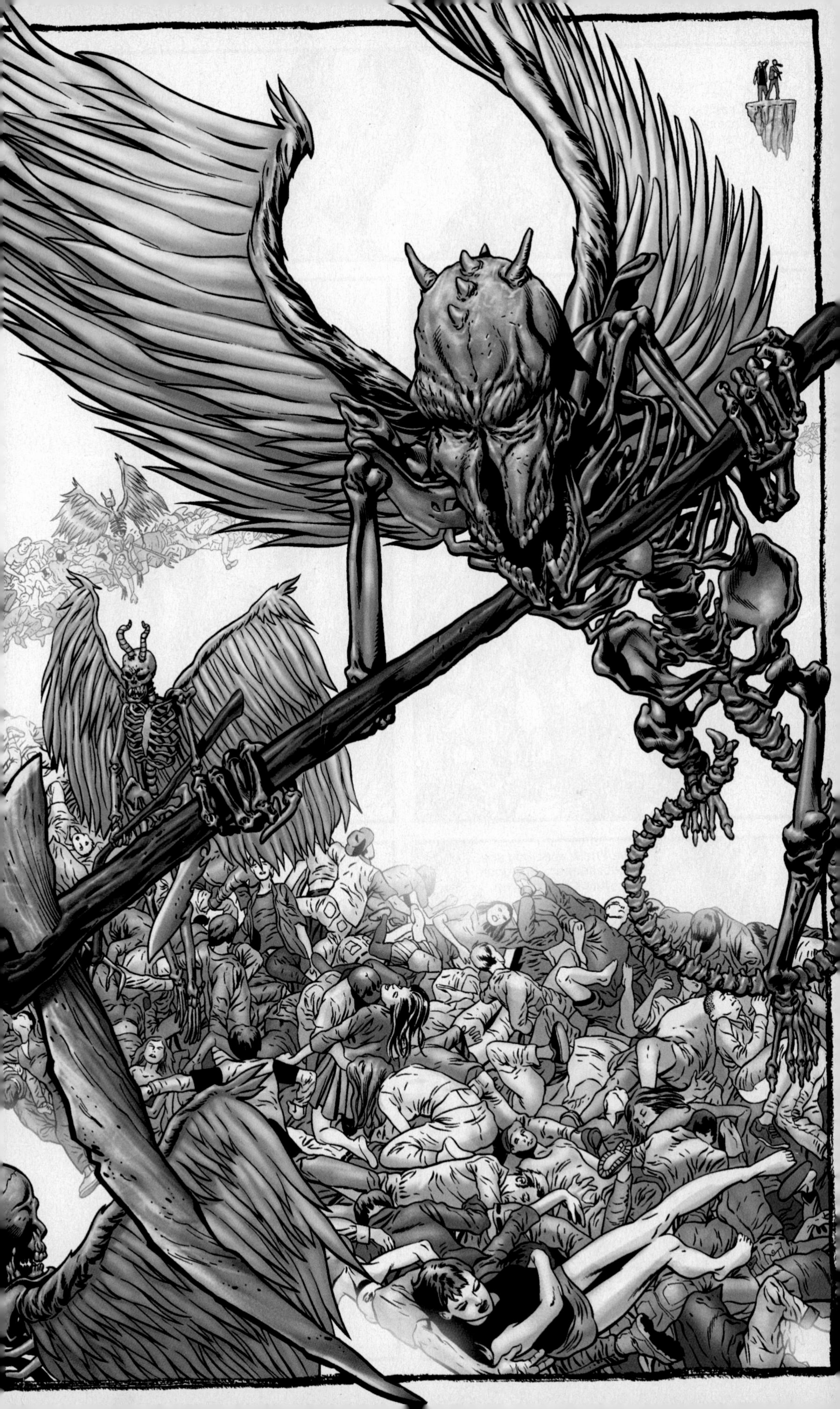

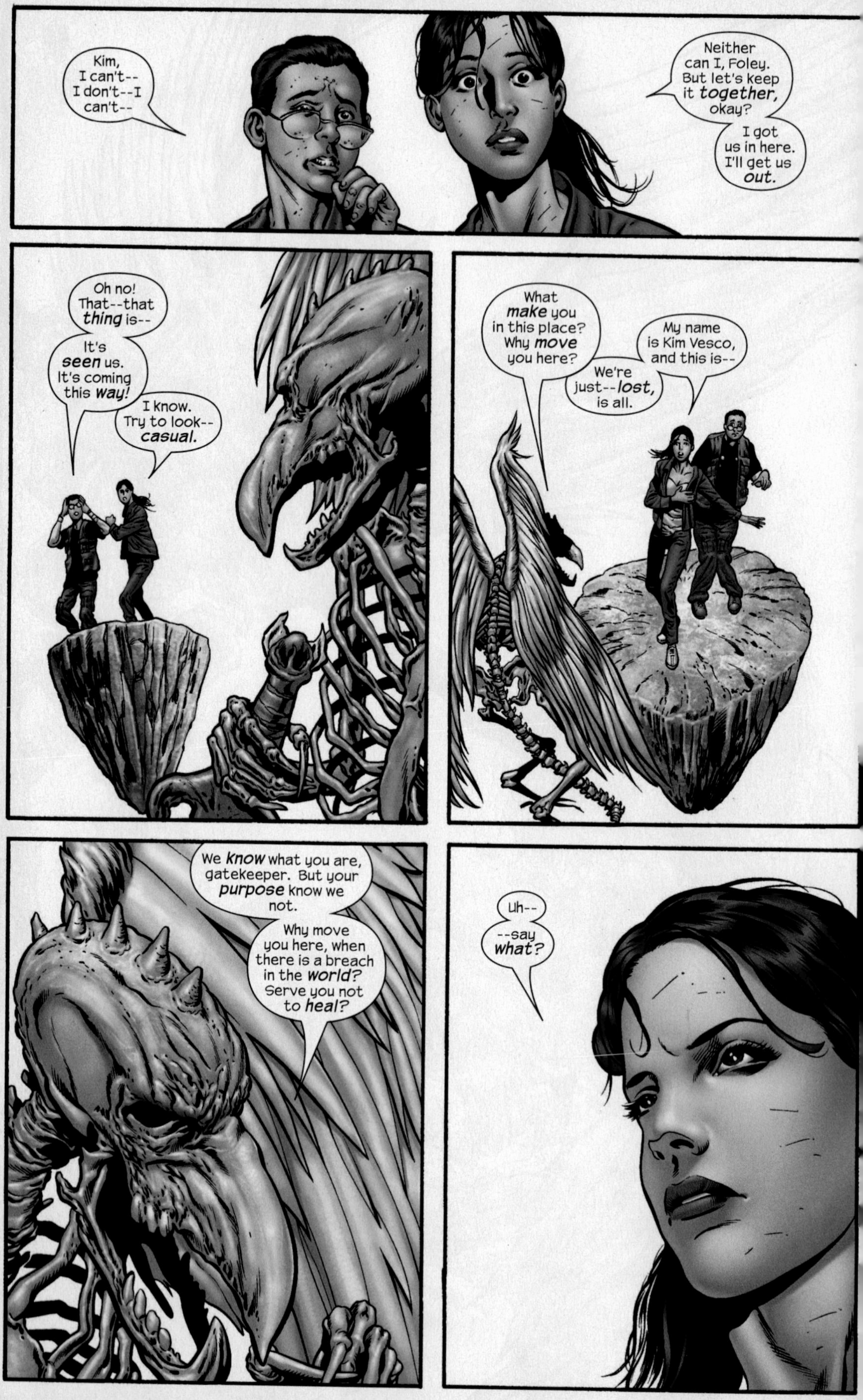

Kim, I can't-- I don't--I can't--
Neither can I, Foley. But let's keep it together, okay?
I got us in here. I'll get us out.
Oh no! That--that thing is--
It's seen us. It's coming this way!
I know. Try to look--casual.
What make you in this place? Why move you here?
My name is Kim Vesco, and this is--
We're just--lost, is all.
We know what you are, gatekeeper. But your purpose know we not.
Why move you here, when there is a breach in the world? Serve you not to heal?
Uh--
--say what?

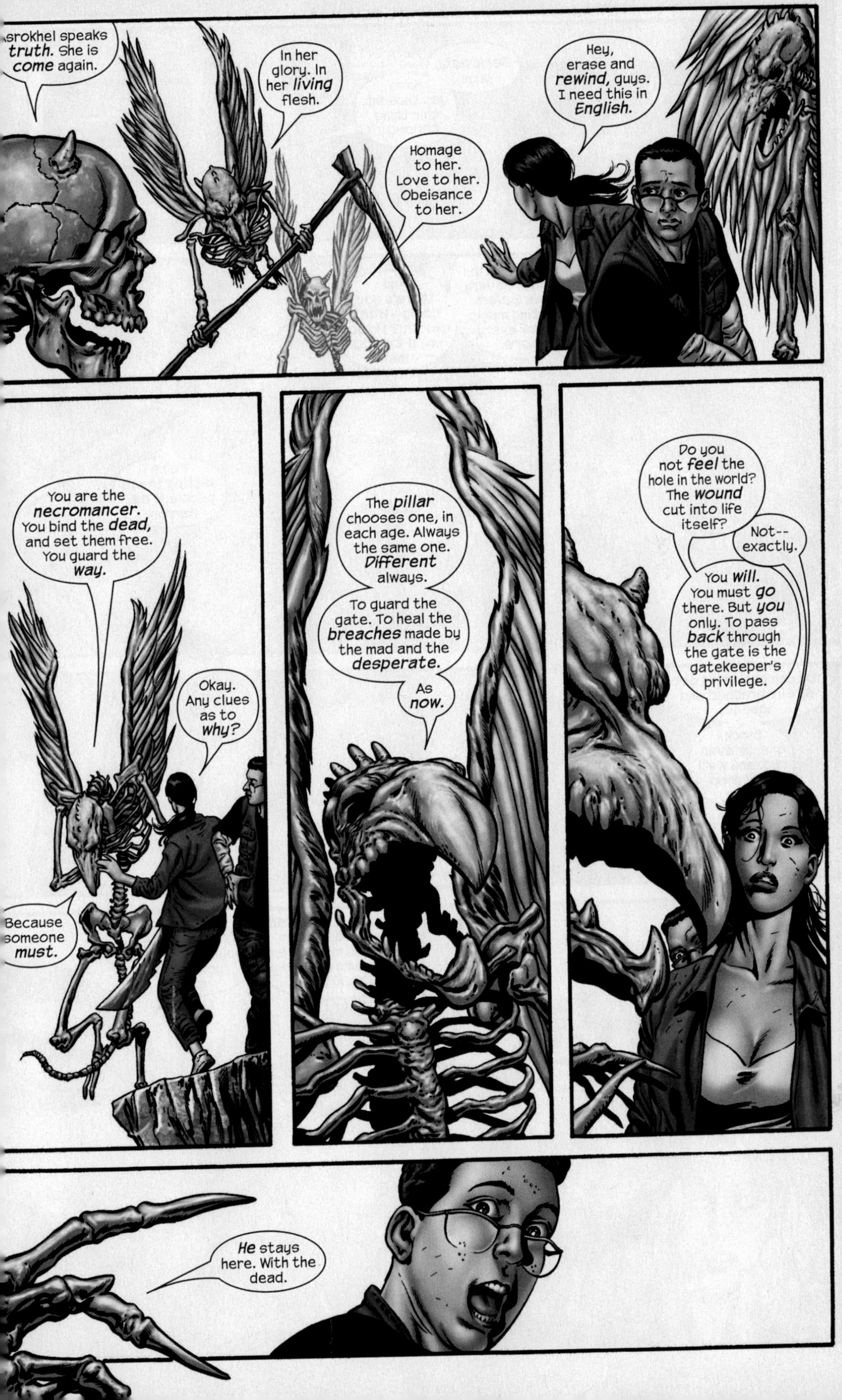

...srokhel speaks truth. She is come again.
In her glory. In her living flesh.
Homage to her. Love to her. Obeisance to her.
Hey, erase and rewind, guys. I need this in English.
You are the necromancer. You bind the dead, and set them free. You guard the way.
Okay. Any clues as to why?
Because someone must.
The pillar chooses one, in each age. Always the same one. Different always.
To guard the gate. To heal the breaches made by the mad and the desperate.
As now.
Do you not feel the hole in the world? The wound cut into life itself?
Not--exactly.
You will. You must go there. But you only. To pass back through the gate is the gatekeeper's privilege.
He stays here. With the dead.

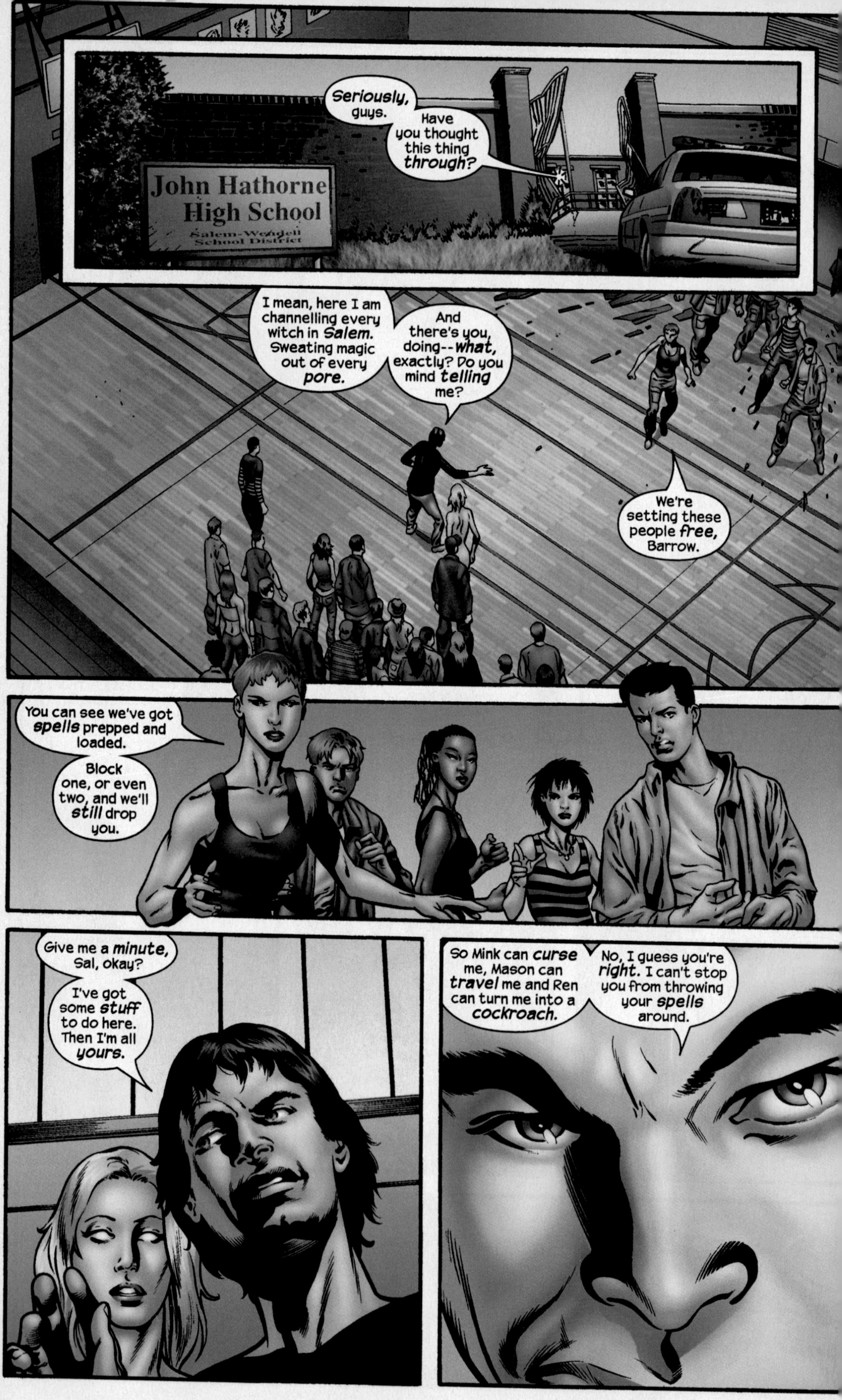
Seriously, guys.
Have you thought this thing through?
John Hathorne High School
Salem-Wenden School District
I mean, here I am channelling every witch in Salem. Sweating magic out of every pore.
And there's you, doing--what, exactly? Do you mind telling me?
We're setting these people free, Barrow.
You can see we've got spells prepped and loaded.
Block one, or even two, and we'll still drop you.
Give me a minute, Sal, okay?
I've got some stuff to do here. Then I'm all yours.
No, I guess you're right. I can't stop you from throwing your spells around.
So Mink can curse me, Mason can travel me and Ren can turn me into a cockroach.

But I can sure make you *wish* you hadn't.

AAAAAA!

Curse. Transform. Travel.

Hey, let's make a *daisy* chain.

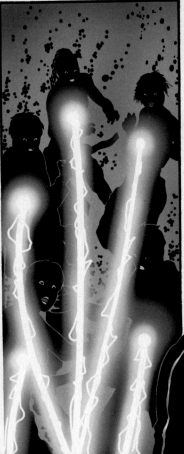

Man! Is there *anything* I can't do?

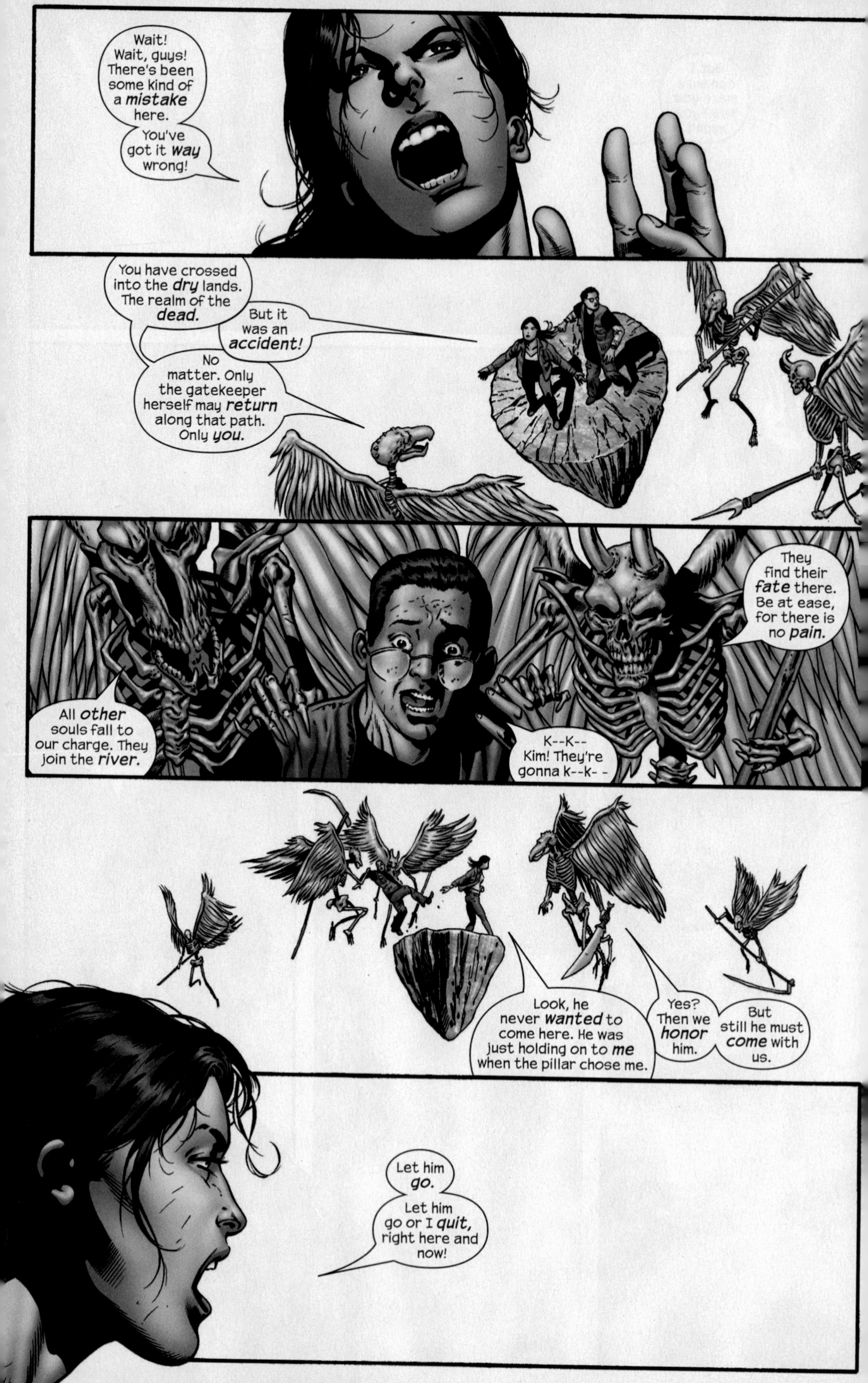

Wait! Wait, guys! There's been some kind of a *mistake* here.
You've got it *way* wrong!
You have crossed into the *dry* lands. The realm of the *dead.*
But it was an *accident!*
No matter. Only the gatekeeper herself may *return* along that path. Only *you.*
All *other* souls fall to our charge. They join the *river.*
They find their *fate* there. Be at ease, for there is no *pain.*
K--K-- Kim! They're gonna k--k- -
Look, he never *wanted* to come here. He was just holding on to *me* when the pillar chose me.
Yes? Then we *honor* him.
But still he must *come* with us.
Let him *go.*
Let him go or I *quit,* right here and now!

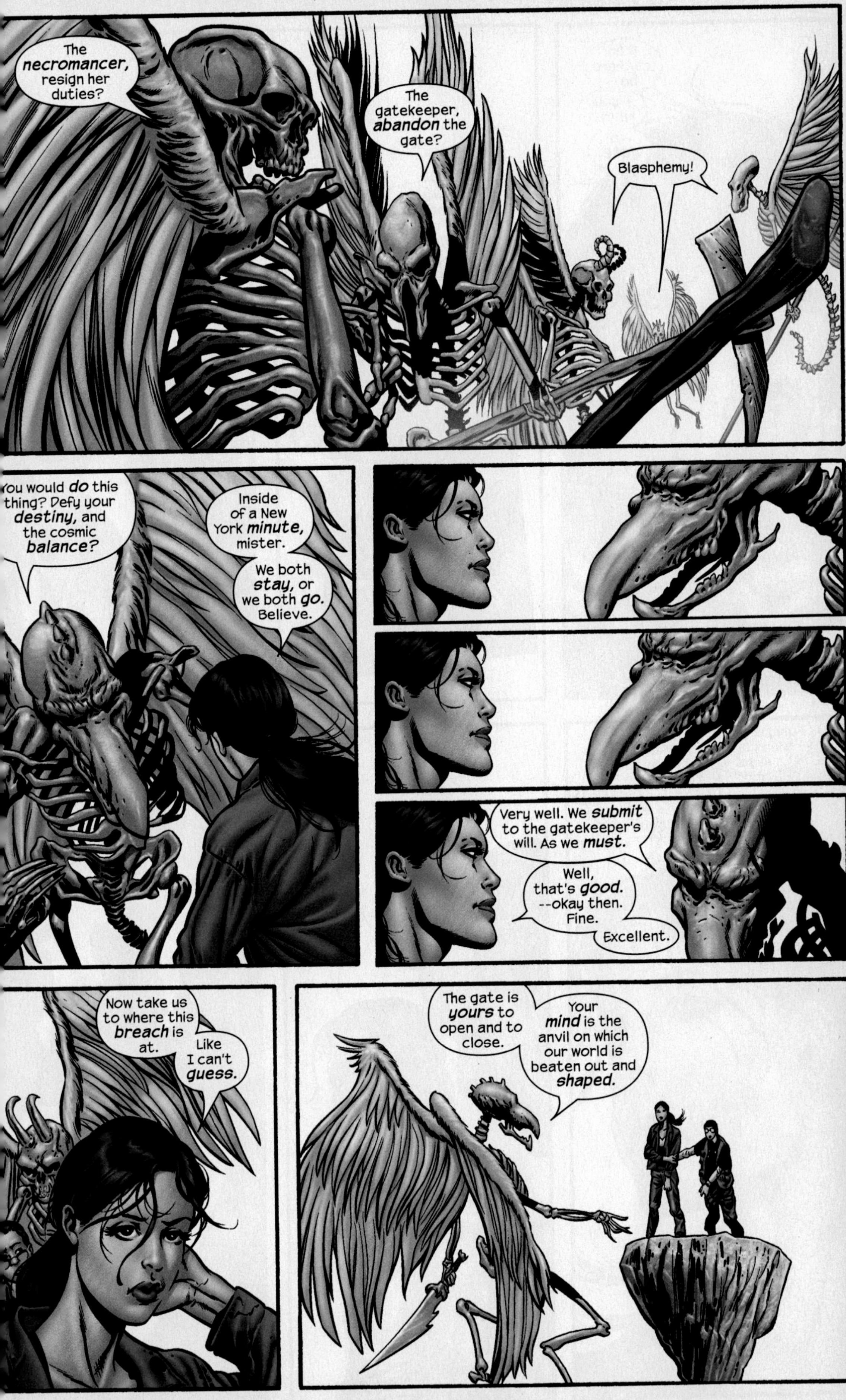
The necromancer, resign her duties?
The gatekeeper, abandon the gate?
Blasphemy!
You would do this thing? Defy your destiny, and the cosmic balance?
Inside of a New York minute, mister.
We both stay, or we both go. Believe.
Very well. We submit to the gatekeeper's will. As we must.
Well, that's good. --okay then. Fine.
Excellent.
Now take us to where this breach is at.
Like I can't guess.
The gate is yours to open and to close.
Your mind is the anvil on which our world is beaten out and shaped.

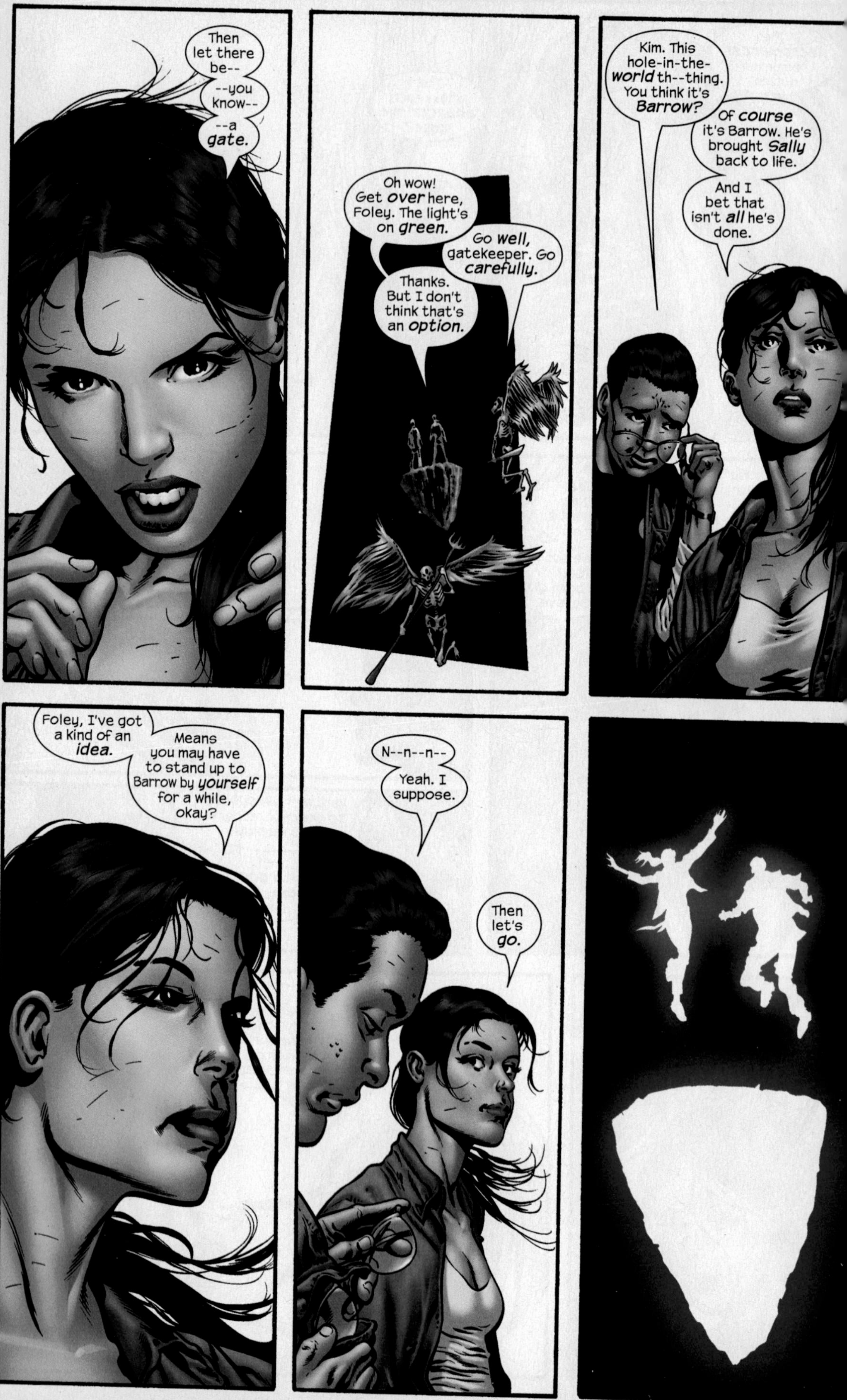
Then let there be--
--you know--
--a gate.
Oh wow! Get over here, Foley. The light's on green.
Go well, gatekeeper. Go carefully.
Thanks. But I don't think that's an option.
Kim. This hole-in-the-world th--thing. You think it's Barrow?
Of course it's Barrow. He's brought Sally back to life.
And I bet that isn't all he's done.
Foley, I've got a kind of an idea.
Means you may have to stand up to Barrow by yourself for a while, okay?
N--n--n--
Yeah. I suppose.
Then let's go.

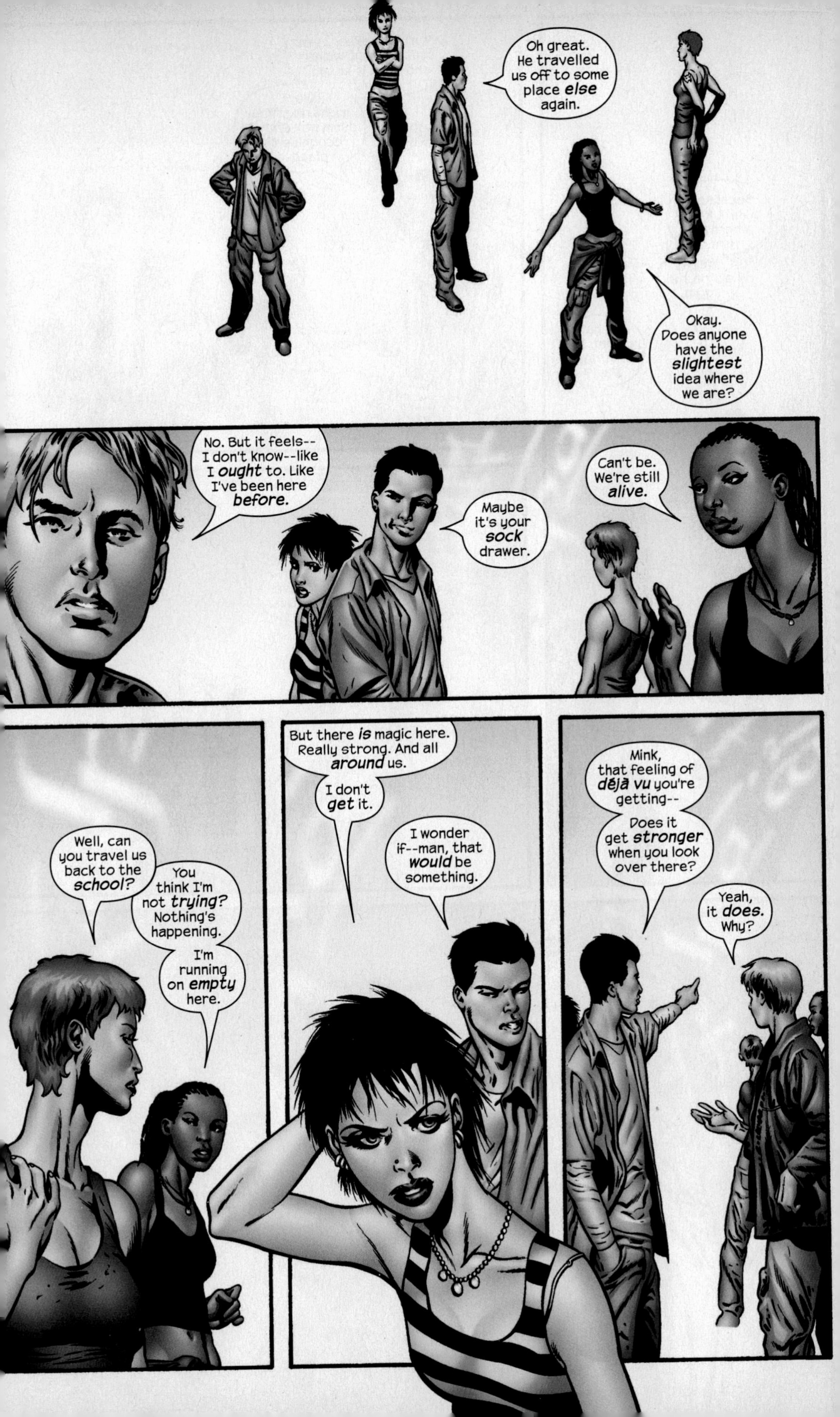
Oh great. He travelled us off to some place else again.
Okay. Does anyone have the slightest idea where we are?
No. But it feels--I don't know--like I ought to. Like I've been here before.
Maybe it's your sock drawer.
Can't be. We're still alive.
Well, can you travel us back to the school?
You think I'm not trying? Nothing's happening.
I'm running on empty here.
But there is magic here. Really strong. And all around us.
I don't get it.
I wonder if--man, that would be something.
Mink, that feeling of déjà vu you're getting--
Does it get stronger when you look over there?
Yeah, it does. Why?

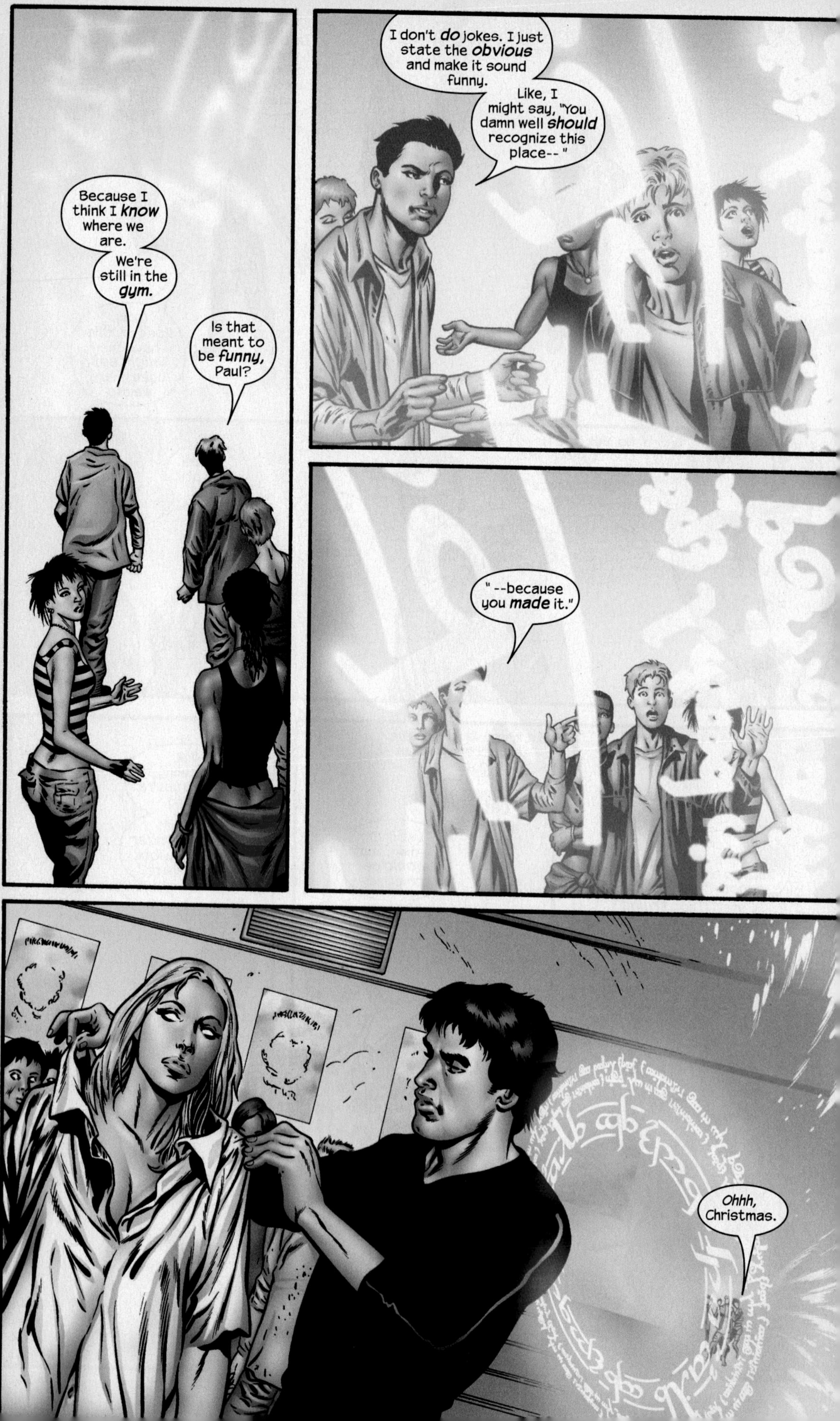
Because I think I *know* where we are.
We're still in the *gym.*
Is that meant to be *funny,* Paul?
I don't *do* jokes. I just state the *obvious* and make it sound funny.
Like, I might say, "You damn well *should* recognize this place-- "
" --because you *made* it."
Ohhh, Christmas.

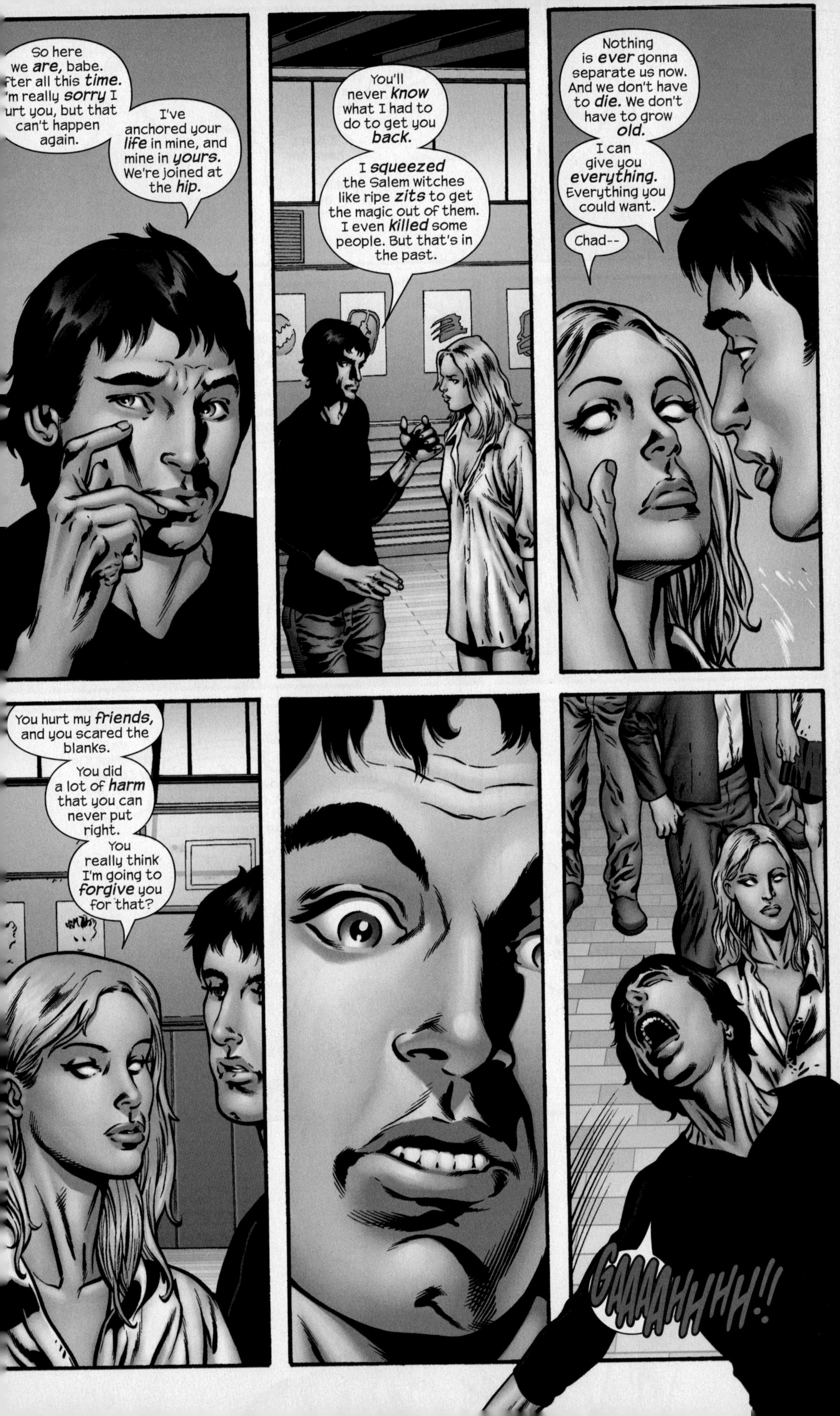

So here we are, babe. fter all this time. 'm really sorry I urt you, but that can't happen again.
I've anchored your life in mine, and mine in yours. We're joined at the hip.
You'll never know what I had to do to get you back.
I squeezed the Salem witches like ripe zits to get the magic out of them. I even killed some people. But that's in the past.
Nothing is ever gonna separate us now. And we don't have to die. We don't have to grow old.
I can give you everything. Everything you could want.
Chad--
You hurt my friends, and you scared the blanks.
You did a lot of harm that you can never put right.
You really think I'm going to forgive you for that?
GAAAAHHHH!!

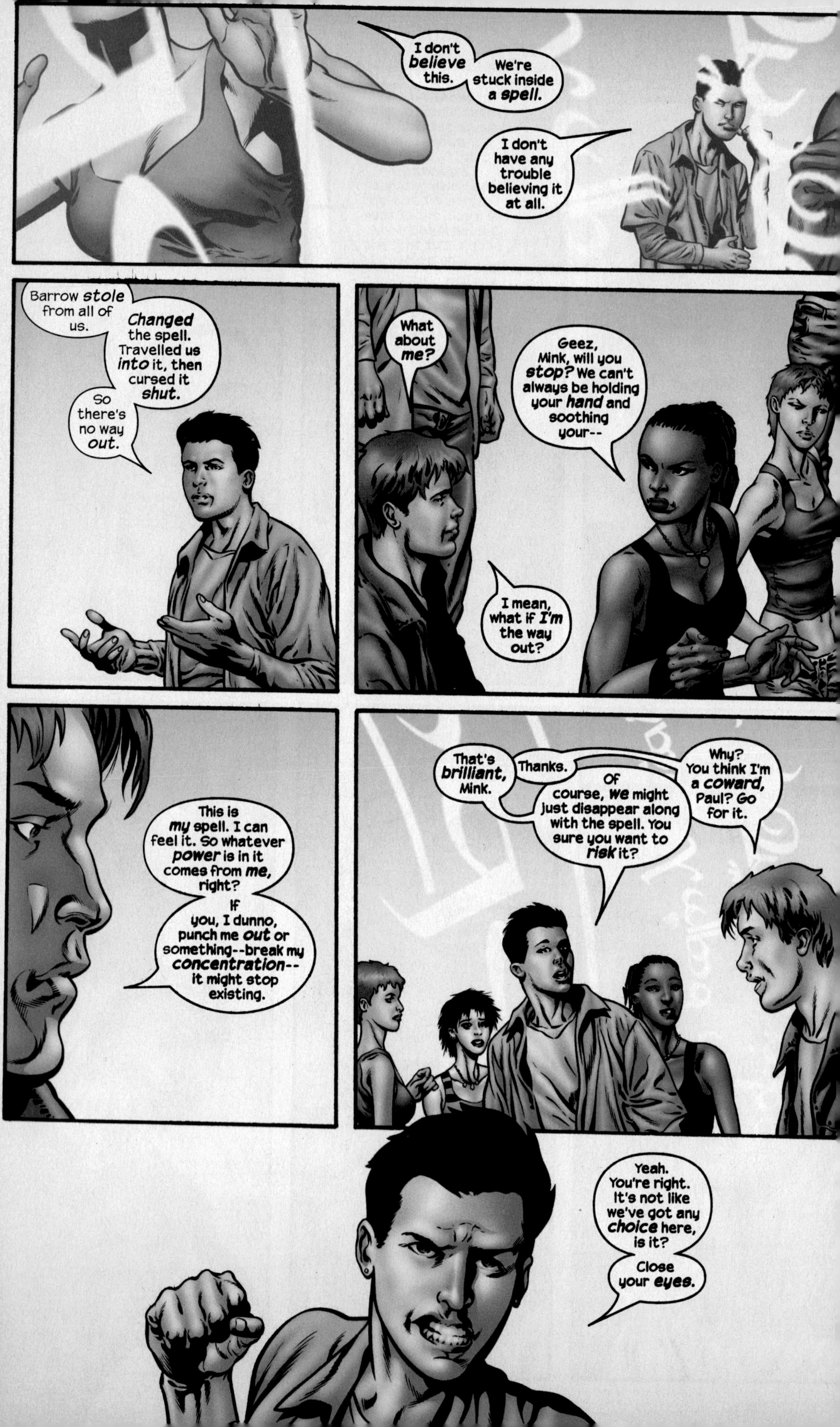

I don't believe this.
We're stuck inside a spell.
I don't have any trouble believing it at all.
Barrow stole from all of us.
Changed the spell. Travelled us into it, then cursed it shut.
So there's no way out.
What about me?
Geez, Mink, will you stop? We can't always be holding your hand and soothing your--
I mean, what if I'm the way out?
This is my spell. I can feel it. So whatever power is in it comes from me, right?
If you, I dunno, punch me out or something--break my concentration--it might stop existing.
That's brilliant, Mink.
Thanks.
Of course, we might just disappear along with the spell. You sure you want to risk it?
Why? You think I'm a coward, Paul? Go for it.
Yeah. You're right. It's not like we've got any choice here, is it?
Close your eyes.

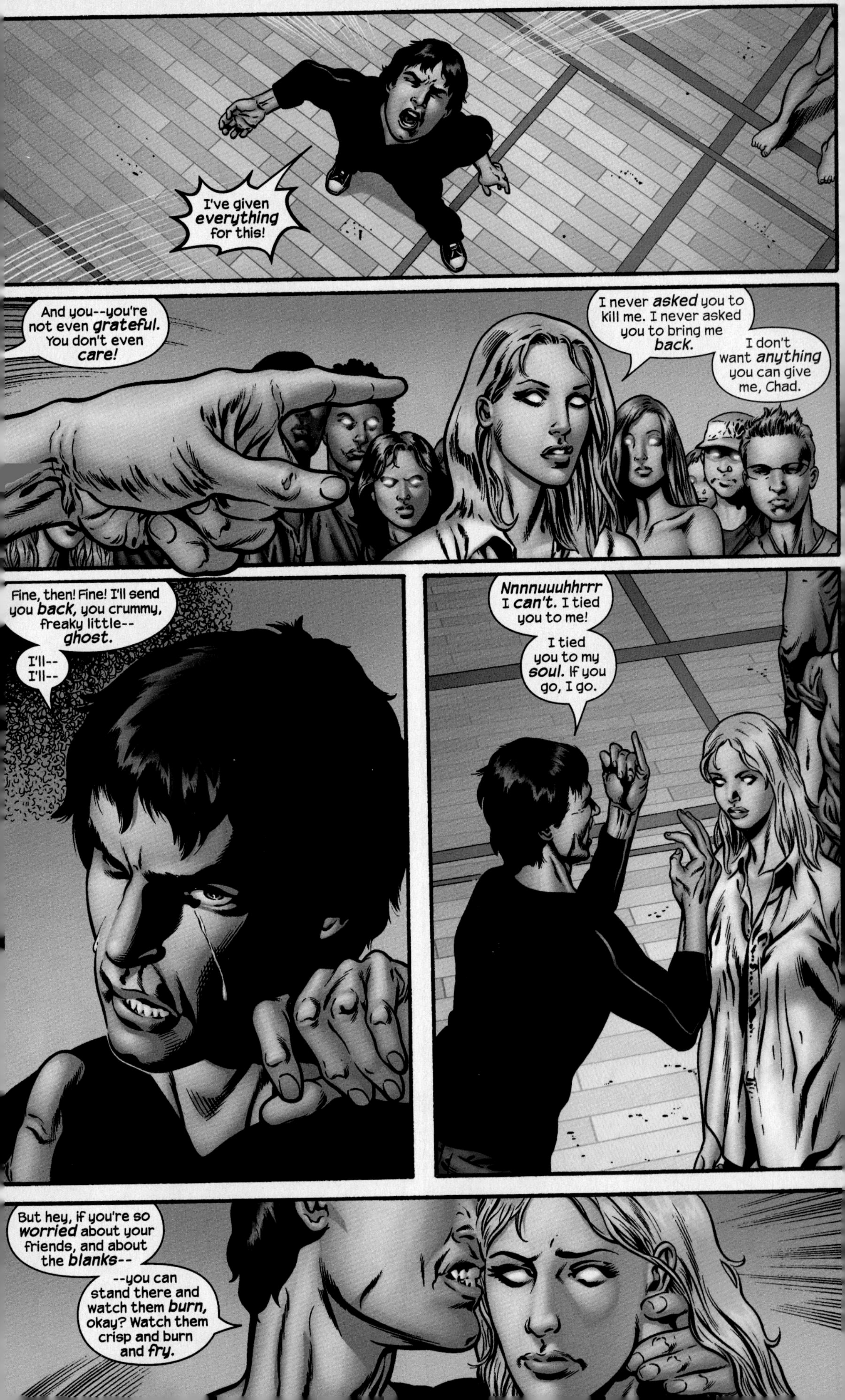

I've given everything for this!
And you--you're not even grateful. You don't even care!
I never asked you to kill me. I never asked you to bring me back.
I don't want anything you can give me, Chad.
Fine, then! Fine! I'll send you back, you crummy, freaky little-- ghost.
I'll-- I'll--
Nnnnuuuhhrrr I can't. I tied you to me!
I tied you to my soul. If you go, I go.
But hey, if you're so worried about your friends, and about the blanks--
--you can stand there and watch them burn, okay? Watch them crisp and burn and fry.

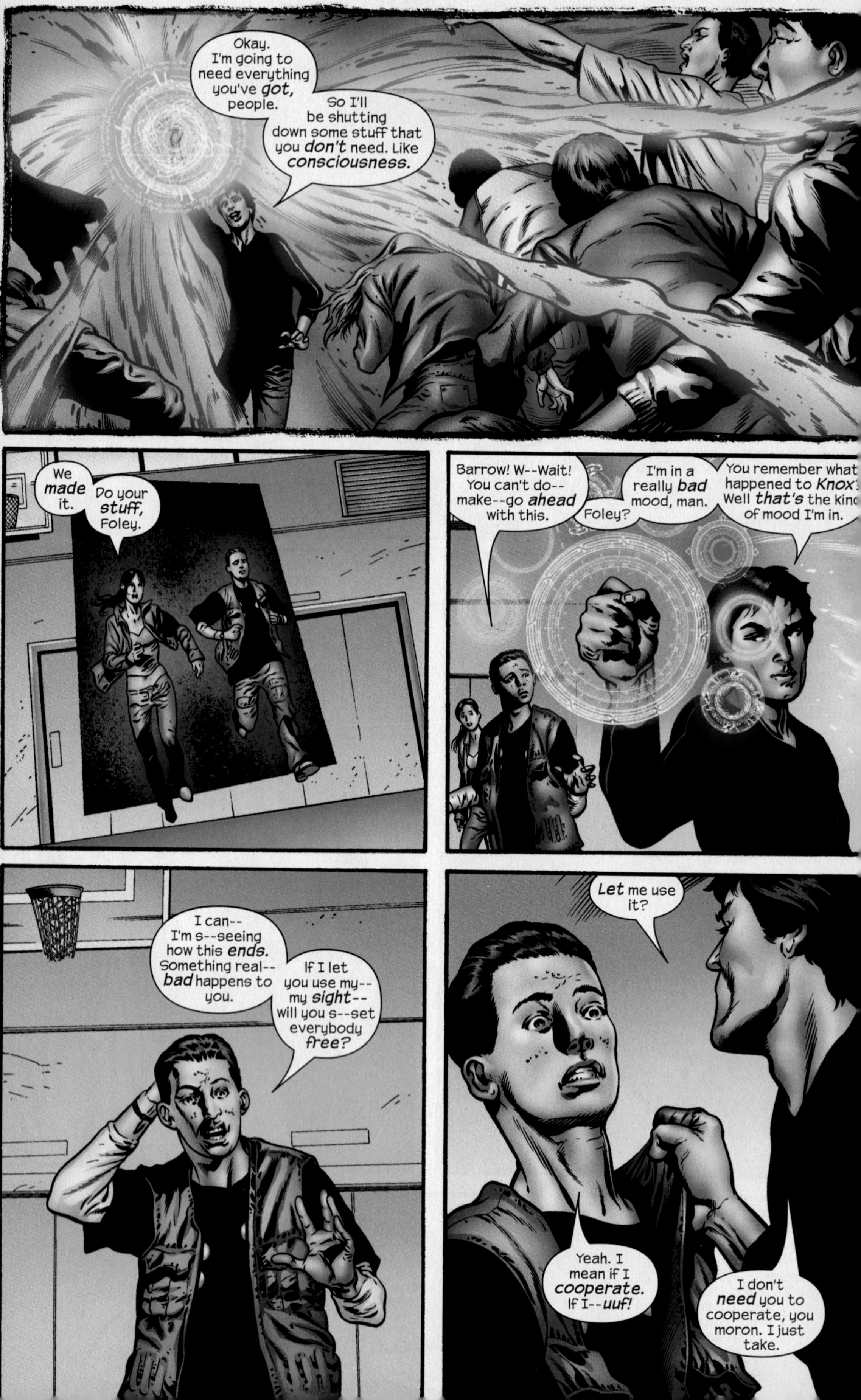

Okay. I'm going to need everything you've got, people.
So I'll be shutting down some stuff that you don't need. Like consciousness.
We made it.
Do your stuff, Foley.
Barrow! W--Wait! You can't do--make--go ahead with this.
Foley?
I'm in a really bad mood, man.
You remember what happened to Knox? Well that's the kind of mood I'm in.
I can--I'm s--seeing how this ends. Something real--bad happens to you.
If I let you use my--my sight--will you s--set everybody free?
Let me use it?
Yeah. I mean if I cooperate. If I--uuf!
I don't need you to cooperate, you moron. I just take.

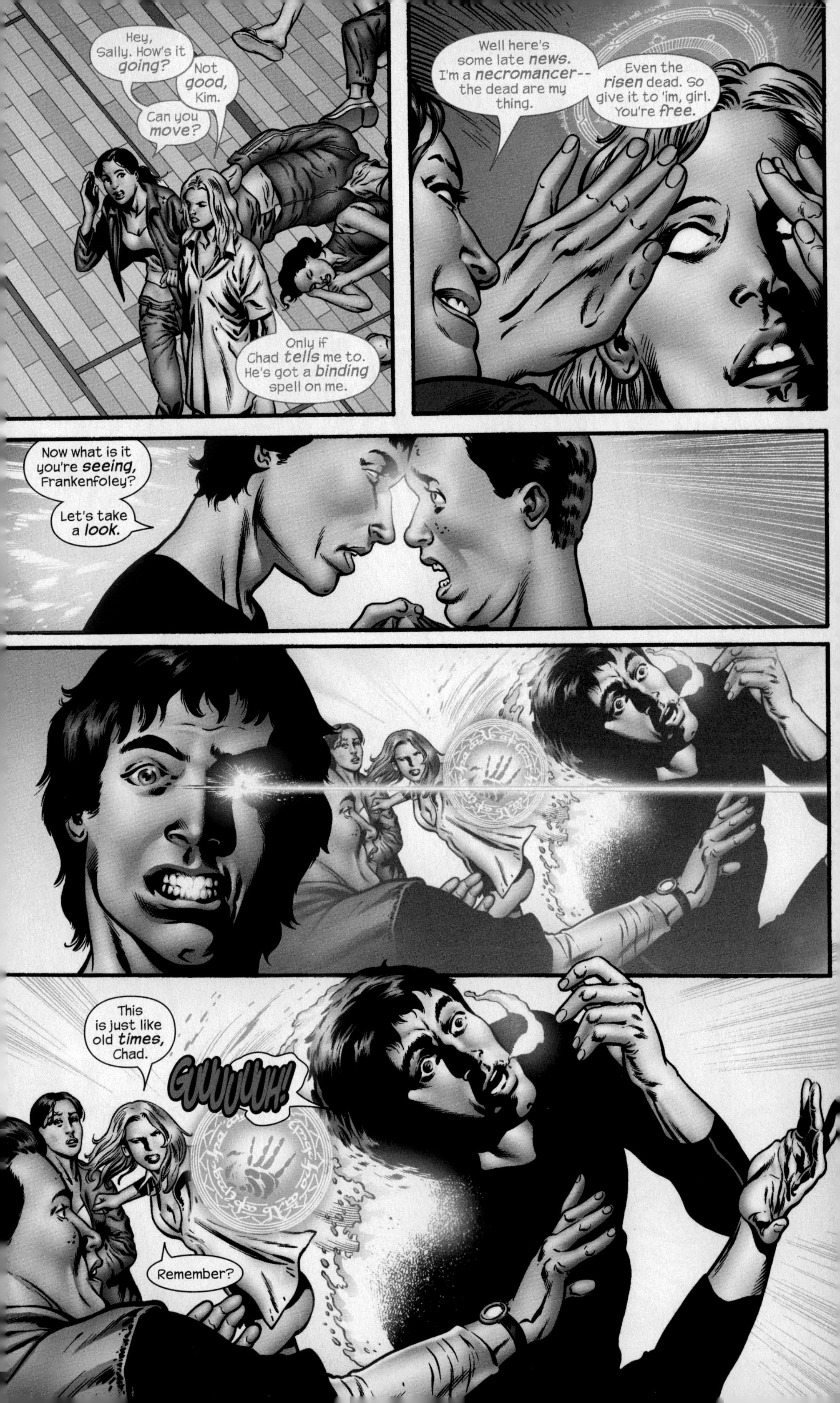
Hey, Sally. How's it going?
Not good, Kim.
Can you move?
Only if Chad tells me to. He's got a binding spell on me.
Well here's some late news. I'm a necromancer-- the dead are my thing.
Even the risen dead. So give it to 'im, girl. You're free.
Now what is it you're seeing, Frankenfoley?
Let's take a look.
This is just like old times, Chad.
GUUUUUH!
Remember?

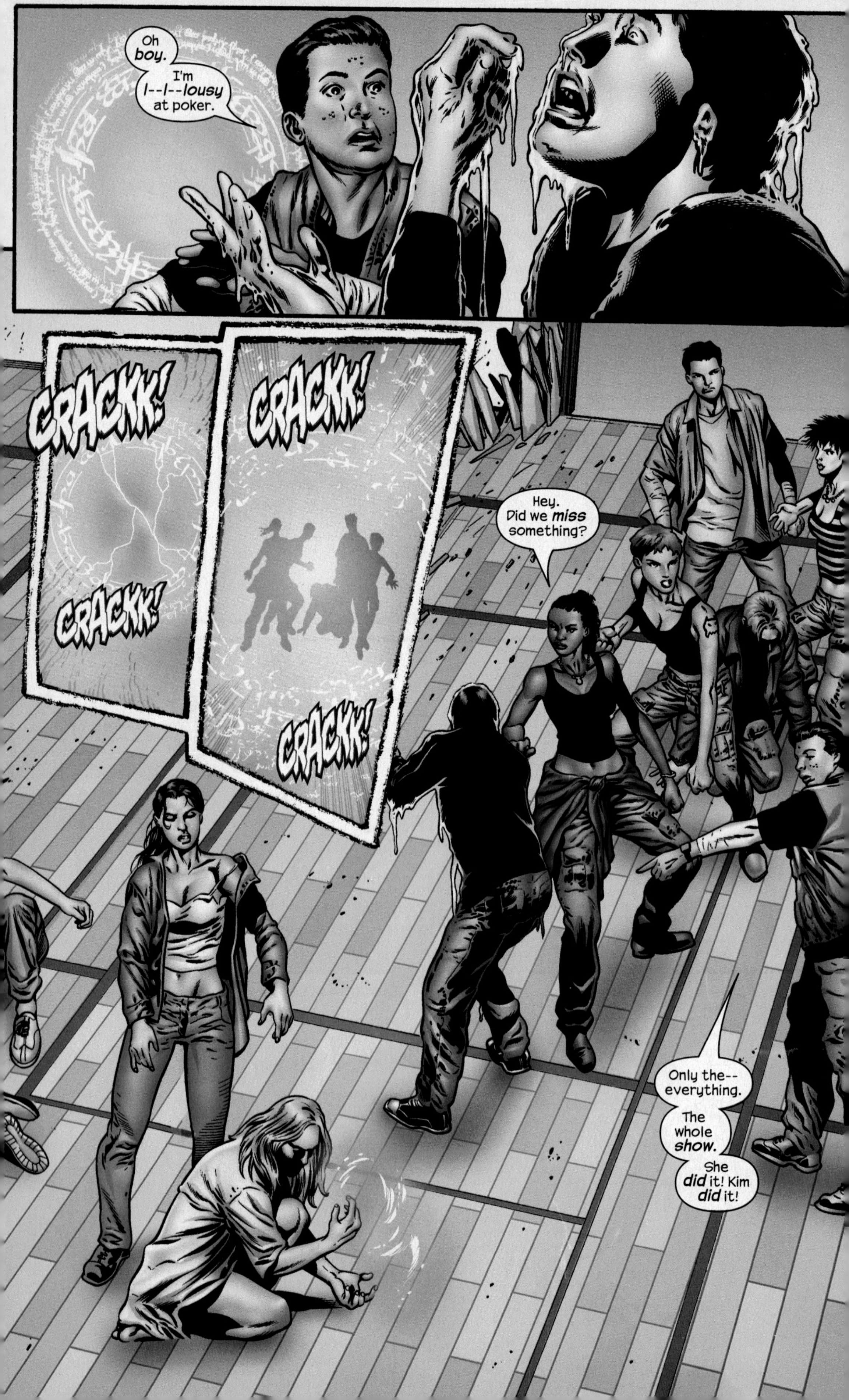

Oh boy.
I'm l--l--lousy at poker.
CRACKK!
CRACKK!
CRACKK!
CRACKK!
Hey. Did we miss something?
Only the-- everything.
The whole show.
She did it! Kim did it!

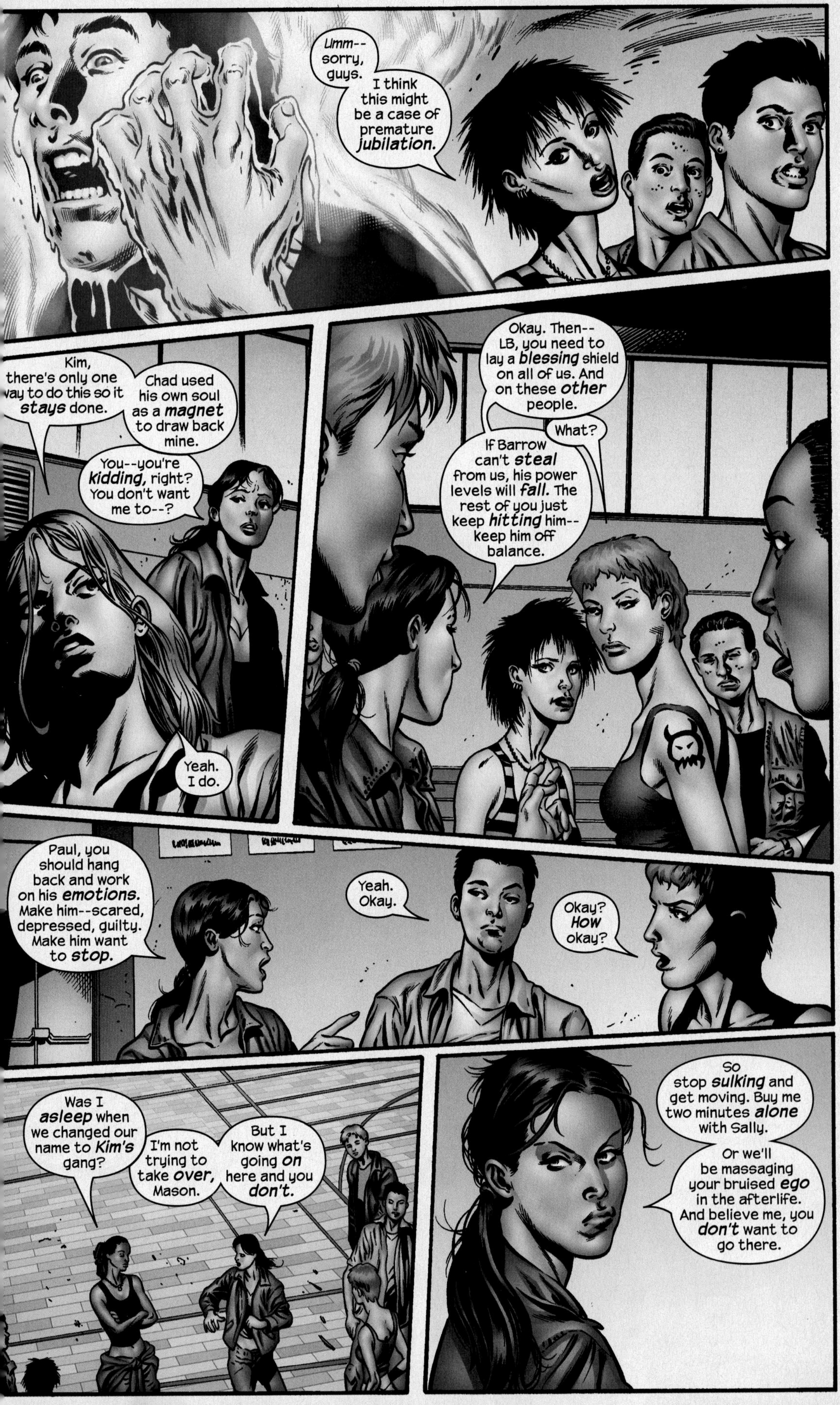

Umm--
sorry,
guys.
I think this might be a case of premature *jubilation.*
Kim, there's only one way to do this so it *stays* done.
Chad used his own soul as a *magnet* to draw back mine.
You--you're *kidding,* right? You don't want me to--?
Yeah. I do.
Okay. Then--
LB, you need to lay a *blessing* shield on all of us. And on these *other* people.
What?
If Barrow can't *steal* from us, his power levels will *fall.* The rest of you just keep *hitting* him--keep him off balance.
Paul, you should hang back and work on his *emotions.* Make him--scared, depressed, guilty. Make him want to *stop.*
Yeah. Okay.
Okay? *HOW* okay?
Was I *asleep* when we changed our name to *Kim's* gang?
I'm not trying to take *over,* Mason.
But I know what's going *on* here and you *don't.*
So stop *sulking* and get moving. Buy me two minutes *alone* with Sally.
Or we'll be massaging your bruised *ego* in the afterlife. And believe me, you *don't* want to go there.

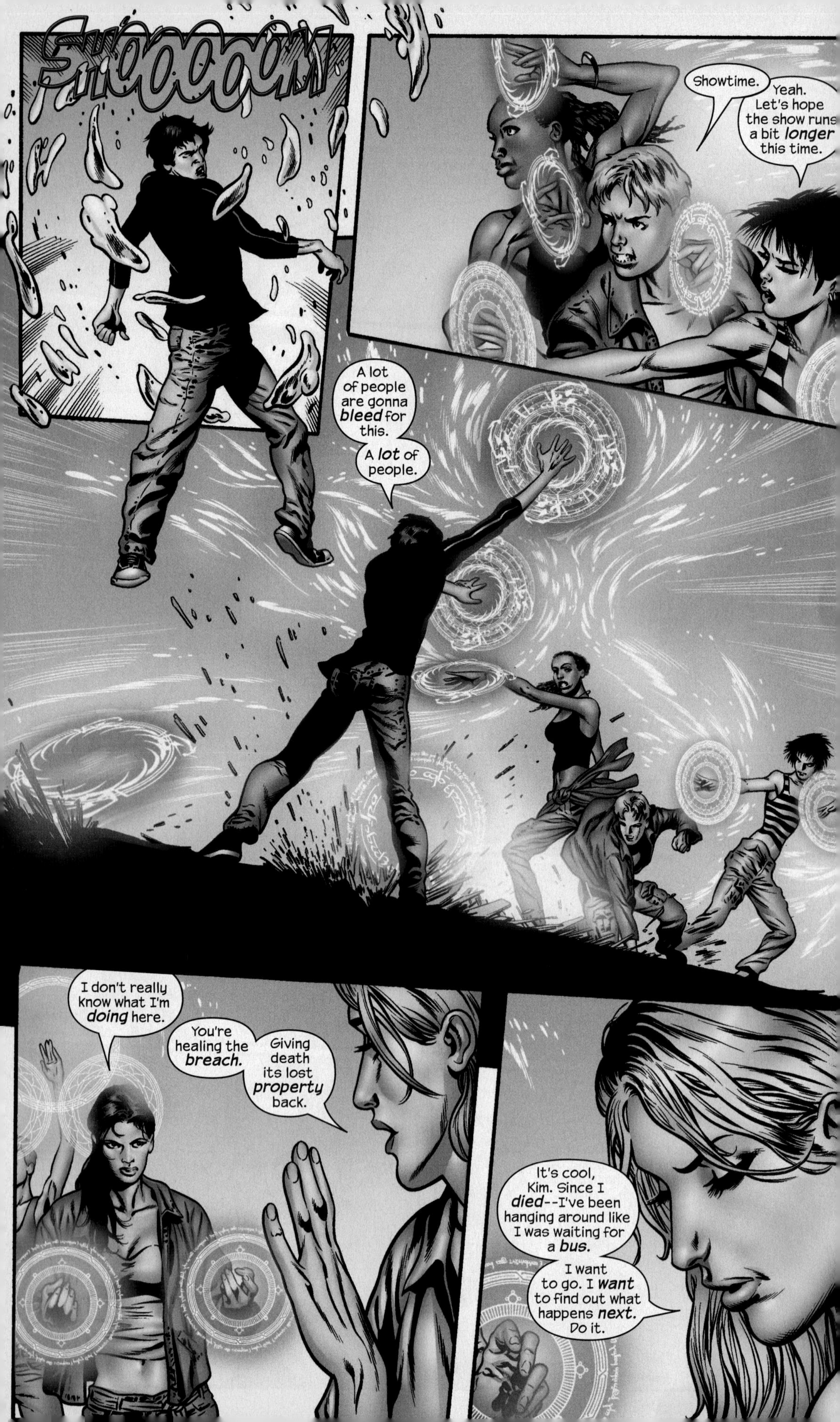
SHOOOOOOM
Showtime.
Yeah. Let's hope the show runs a bit *longer* this time.
A lot of people are gonna *bleed* for this.
A *lot* of people.
I don't really know what I'm *doing* here.
You're healing the *breach.*
Giving death its lost *property* back.
It's cool, Kim. Since I *died*--I've been hanging around like I was waiting for a *bus.*
I want to go. I *want* to find out what happens *next.* Do it.

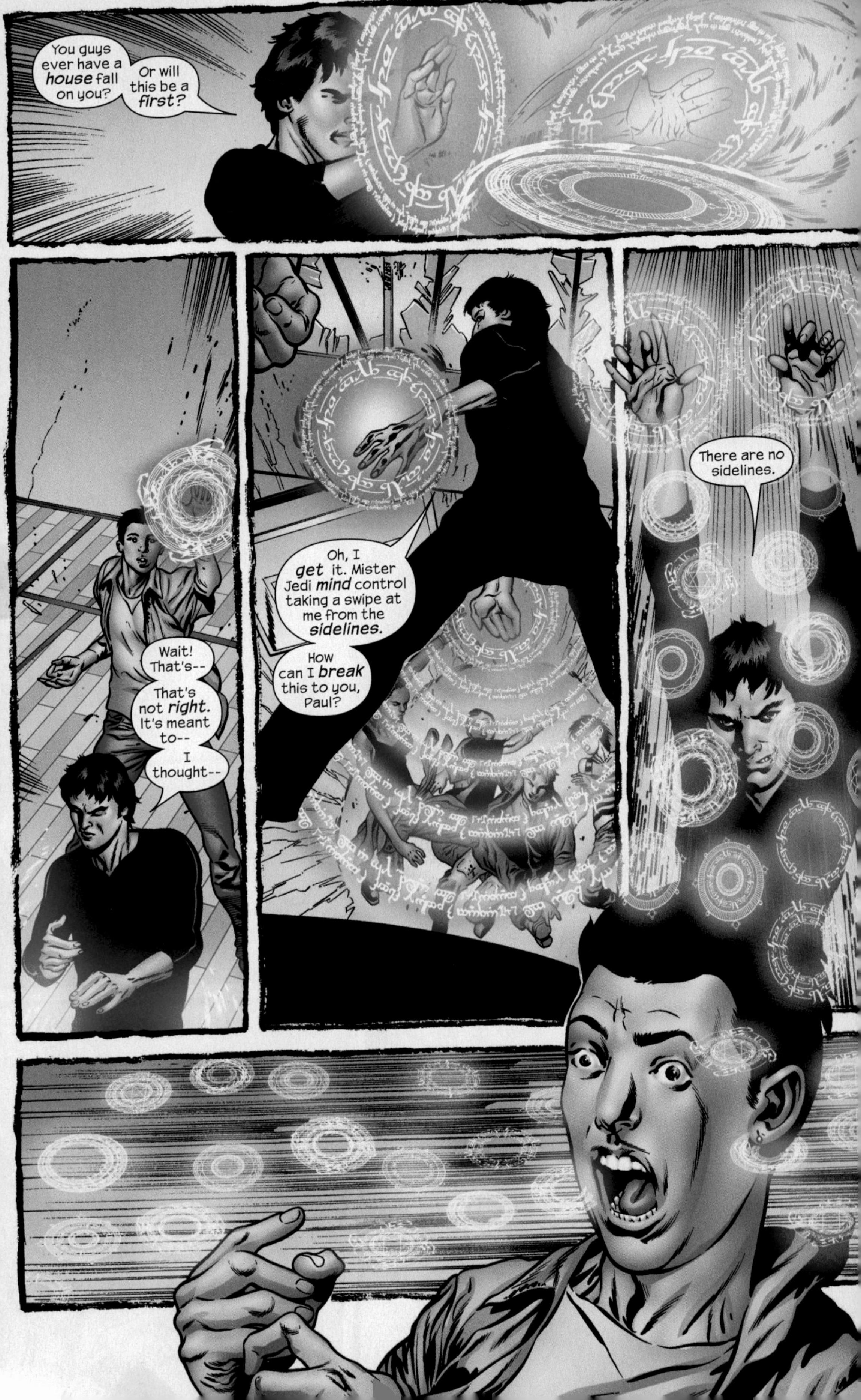
You guys ever have a house fall on you?
Or will this be a first?
Wait! That's--
That's not right. It's meant to--
I thought--
Oh, I get it. Mister Jedi mind control taking a swipe at me from the sidelines.
How can I break this to you, Paul?
There are no sidelines.

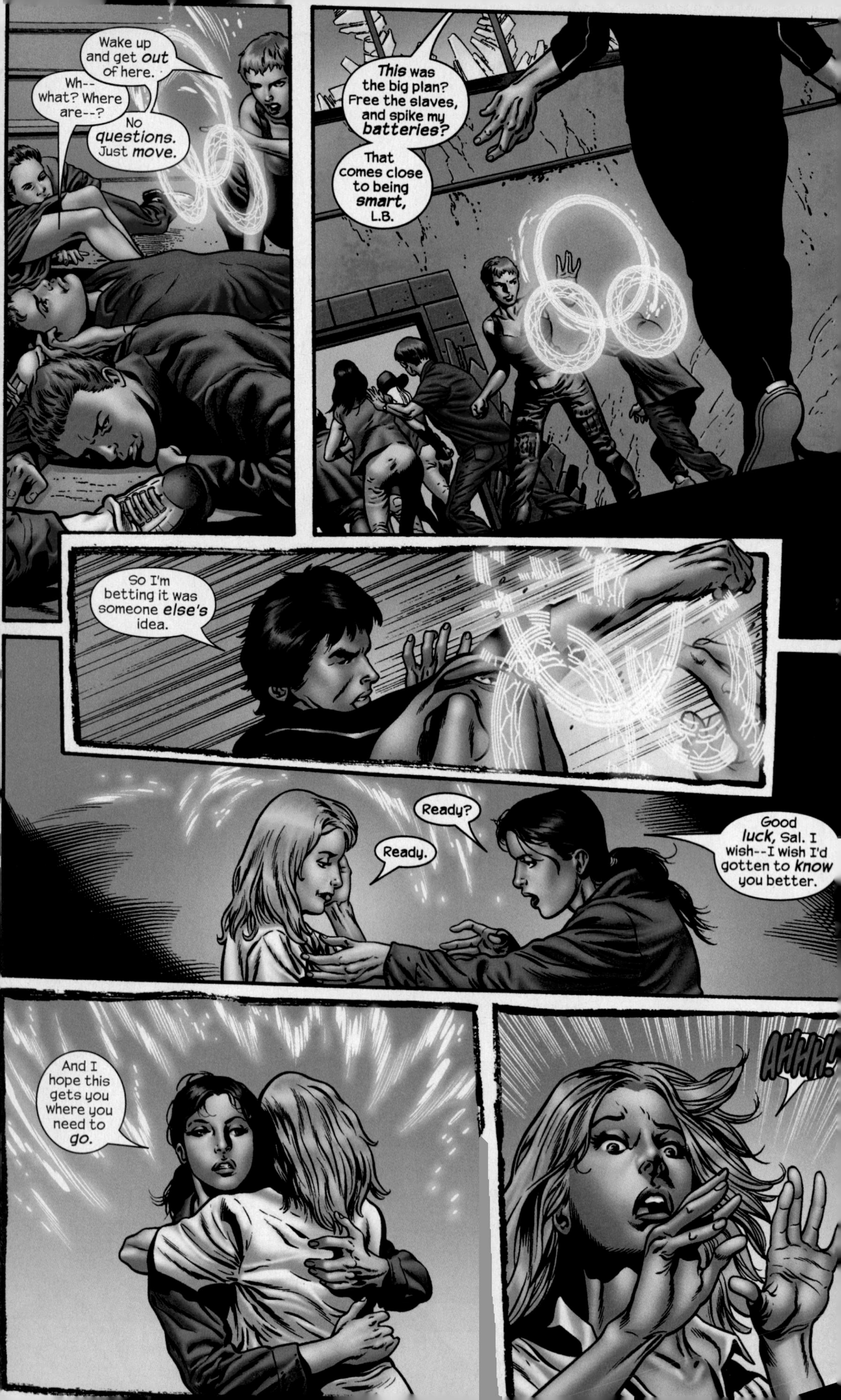

Wake up and get *out* of here.
Wh-- what? Where are--?
No *questions.* Just *move.*
This was the big plan? Free the slaves, and spike my *batteries?*
That comes close to being *smart,* L.B.
So I'm betting it was someone *else's* idea.
Ready?
Ready.
Good *luck,* Sal. I wish--I wish I'd gotten to *know* you better.
And I hope this gets you where you need to *go.*
AHHH!

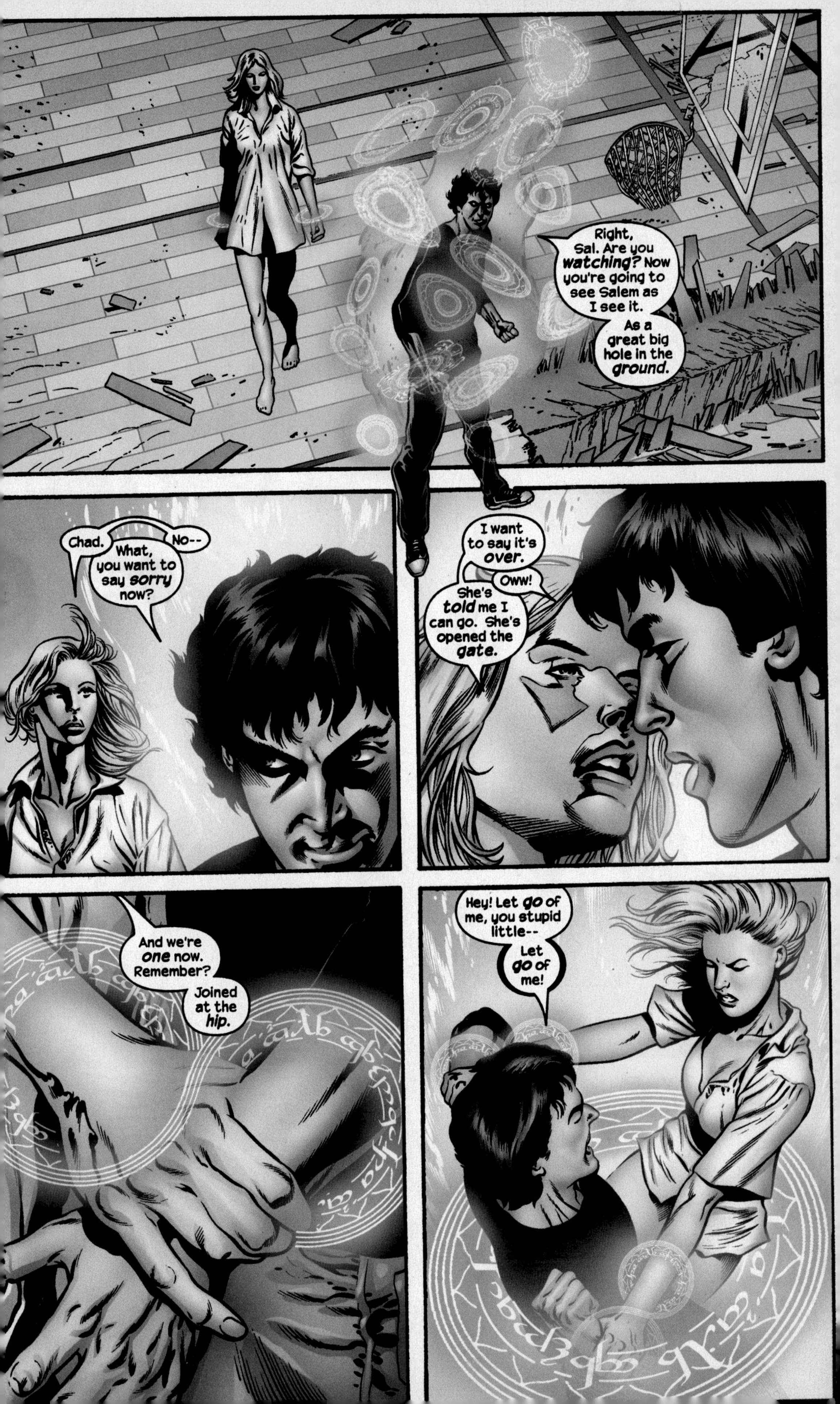
Right, Sal. Are you watching? Now you're going to see Salem as I see it.
As a great big hole in the ground.
Chad.
No--
What, you want to say sorry now?
I want to say it's over.
Oww!
She's told me I can go. She's opened the gate.
And we're one now. Remember?
Joined at the hip.
Hey! Let go of me, you stupid little--
Let go of me!

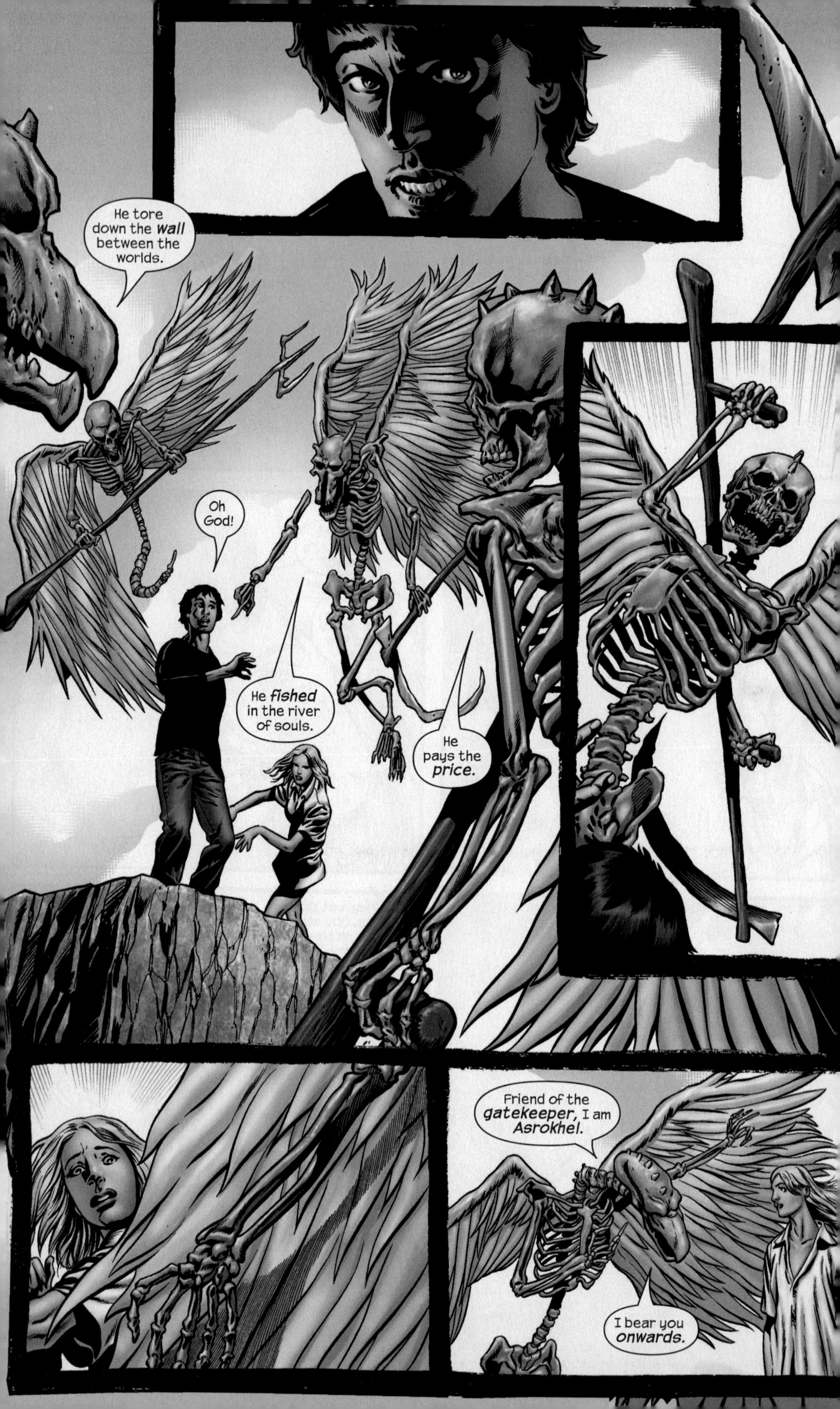
He tore down the *wall* between the worlds.
Oh God!
He *fished* in the river of souls.
He pays the *price.*
Friend of the *gatekeeper,* I am *Asrokhel.*
I bear you *onwards.*

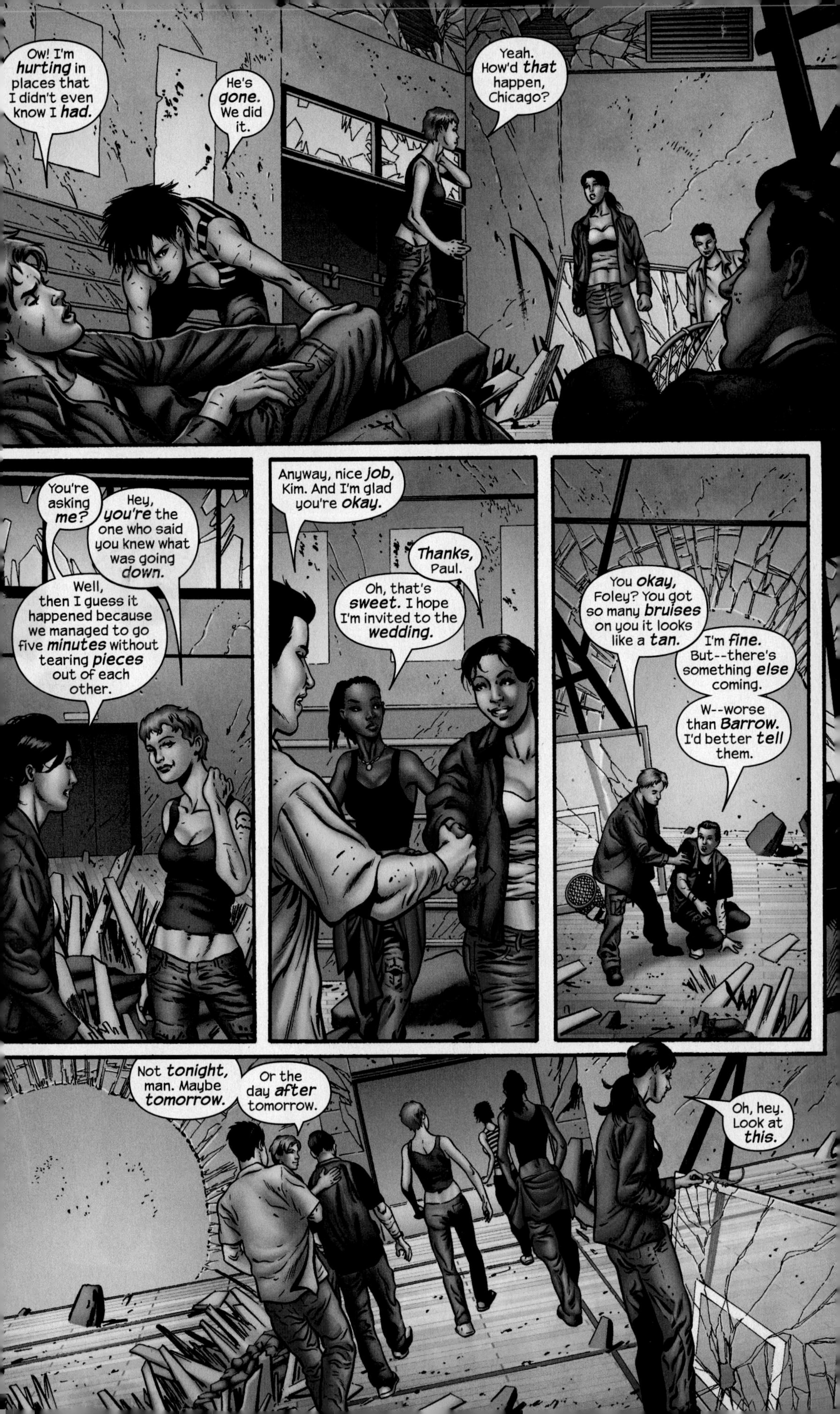
Ow! I'm hurting in places that I didn't even know I had.
He's gone. We did it.
Yeah. How'd that happen, Chicago?
You're asking me?
Hey, you're the one who said you knew what was going down.
Well, then I guess it happened because we managed to go five minutes without tearing pieces out of each other.
Anyway, nice job, Kim. And I'm glad you're okay.
Thanks, Paul.
Oh, that's sweet. I hope I'm invited to the wedding.
You okay, Foley? You got so many bruises on you it looks like a tan.
I'm fine. But--there's something else coming.
W--worse than Barrow. I'd better tell them.
Not tonight, man. Maybe tomorrow.
Or the day after tomorrow.
Oh, hey. Look at this.

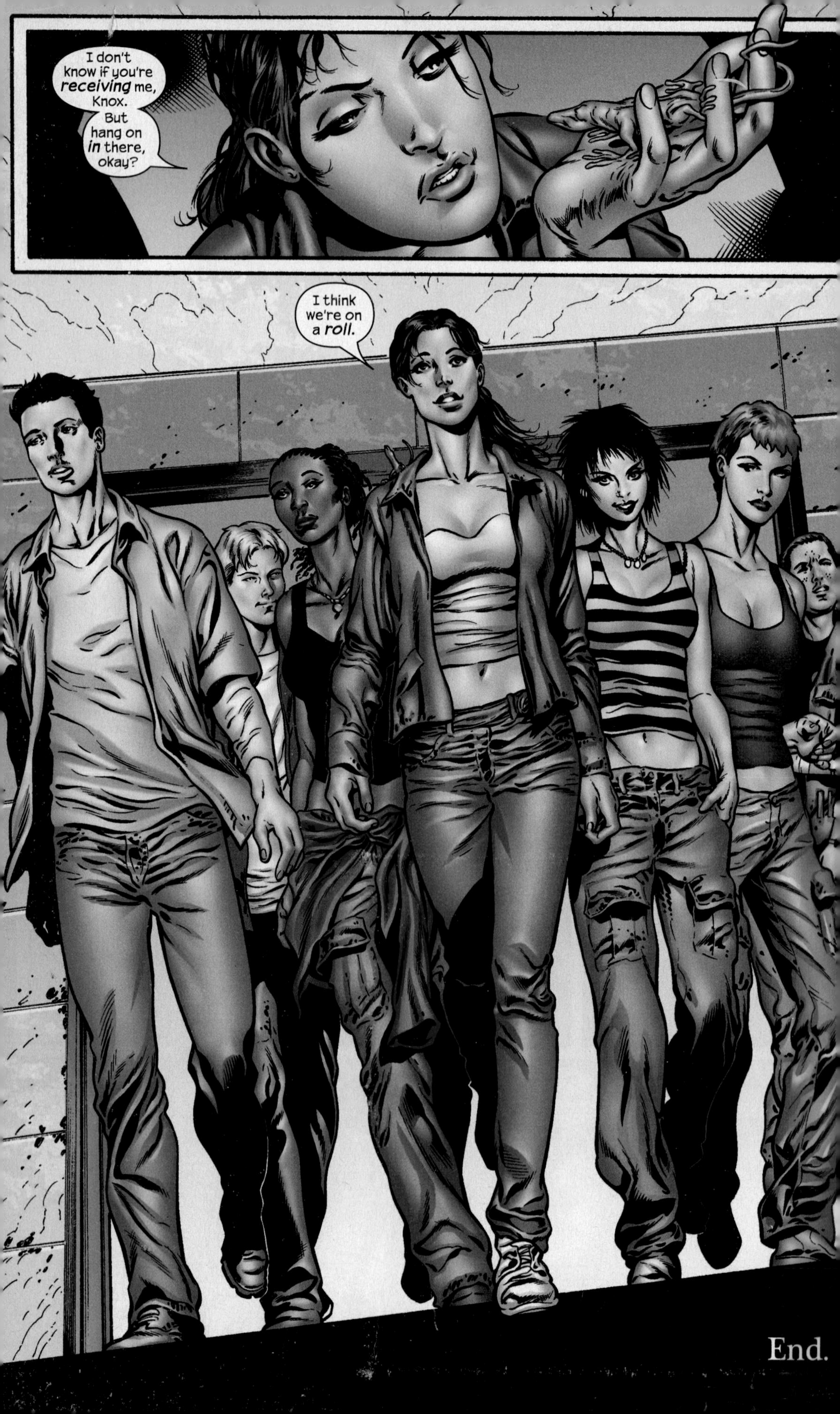
I don't know if you're receiving me, Knox.
But hang on in there, okay?
I think we're on a roll.
End.